# The Kids' World Almanac of Basketball

**BILL GUTMAN**

**Introduction by Willis Reed**

WORLD ALMANAC BOOKS
An Imprint of Funk & Wagnalls Corporation
A K-III Communications Company

# DEDICATION

## For Cathy

Library of Congress Catalog Card Number: 95-61362

ISBN: 0-88687-777-6 (hardcover)
ISBN: 0-88687-776-8 (softcover)

Printed in the United States of America

Design by Bill Smith Studio
Art Direction by Stevie Pettus-Famulari/Bill Smith Studio
Illustrations by Bernard Adnet
Cover Design by Brock Waldron/Bill Smith Studio

World Almanac® Books
An Imprint of Funk & Wagnalls Corporation
One International Boulevard
Mahwah, NJ 07495-0017

10   9   8   7   6   5   4   3   2   1

# Contents

# About the Author

Bill Gutman is the author of more than 125 books for children and adults. He began his writing career as a reporter on a daily newspaper in Greenwich, Connecticut, and later became the paper's sports editor.

His first book was a biography of former basketball great Pistol Pete Maravich, which was chosen as a *Sports Illustrated* Sports-Book-of-the-Month Club alternate selection. Since that time, Mr. Gutman has written biographies of many top sports stars, including Hank Aaron, Julius Erving, Pele, Bo Jackson, Michael Jordan, David Robinson, Magic Johnson, Shaquille O'Neal, Larry Johnson, and Hakeem Olajuwon.

He has also written a series of sports instructional books for children (*Go For It*), as well as several sports novels, three of which were highly recommended by the American Library Association. In addition, he has written histories of pro and college basketball and a history of major league baseball between 1941 and 1964.

Bill Gutman was born in New York City and grew up in Stamford, Connecticut. He received a B.A. from Washington College in Chestertown, Maryland, and did graduate work at the University of Bridgeport in Connecticut. Mr. Gutman presently lives in Dover Plains, New York, with his wife, Cathy, stepson, Allen, and a variety of pets.

# Introduction

## by Willis Reed

When basketball has occupied a major portion of your life, you can't help but welcome a book like this. *The Kids' World Almanac of Basketball* not only took me on a trip down memory lane to the days when I played in the NBA but also brought me back to the game's beginnings as well as right up to the pro and college game today. It's all here.

The thing that attracted me to basketball is still bringing kids to the sport today. You can play almost anywhere or you can practice alone. I was an only child growing up in Louisiana and spent a lot of time practicing by myself in the backyard. Later, when I was in the ninth grade, I had the key to the school gym and could again practice whenever I wanted.

I think I really started watching the NBA when Bill Russell joined the Celtics in 1956-1957. Russell became an instant idol, the guy I wanted to be like. Not only was he a great player who wanted to win every night, but he was left-handed like I was and also grew up in Louisiana. Little did I know that I would be banging heads with him some day.

During the time I played at Grambling State, from 1960 to 1964, there were all kinds of great players coming into the NBA. I began watching Oscar (Robertson) and Elg (Elgin Baylor), then Wilt (Chamberlain) and others. By that time, the game had become a tremendous challenge to me. I was lucky enough to be on an NAIA championship team at Grambling my freshman year, play four years, and graduate with my class.

Even if I never played in the NBA, basketball had already been a tremendous experience for me. I had two coaches who were very encouraging, Lendon Stone in high school and Fred Hobdy at Grambling. I played on the U.S. team that won a gold medal at the Pan American Games my junior year, then was an alternate on the 1964 Olympic team. At the trials I met people like Bill Bradley and Cazzie Russell.

The NBA proved the ultimate challenge. I played in an era of great centers. When I joined the Knicks for my rookie year of 1964-1965, it seemed I was up against a top center nearly every night. There was (Bill) Russell and Chamberlain for starters, then guys like Walt Bellamy, Nate

Thurmond, Jerry Lucas, and Zelmo Beaty. By the year we won our first championship, 1969-1970, Kareem (Abdul-Jabbar), Elvin Hayes, and Wes Unseld had joined the mix. And by the time we won our second title (1972-1973), Bob Lanier and Dave Cowens were in the league. One of the toughest things for me was playing against great talent every night. You always had to be ready to play or these guys would eat you up.

There are stories about many great players and their teams in the *Almanac*. In fact, you can follow the exploits of some of the top players right from college to the pros. You can even learn about the women's game, which is becoming more popular every year. And then there are all the little things—the stats, the wacky stories, the strange and unusual records, the most exciting games. It's a slam-dunk of basketball information, from start to finish.

I've always said that to enjoy and appreciate a sport at any level, you've got to have a sense of the history of that sport. You should know about the pioneers of the game, the people who made basketball successful long before guys like Shaq, Michael, the Admiral, Hakeem, the Mailman, and the other great players of today.

*The Kids' World Almanac of Basketball* gives you that, too. It's a book that basketball fans can enjoy for hours at a time, or just open to check a statistic on a favorite player or maybe to settle an argument with a friend. Either way, it's a book that will undoubtedly be opened again and again with something new and interesting jumping off the pages every time.

*Willis Reed was born on June 25, 1942, in Hico, Louisiana. He attended Grambling State, where he was part of a National Association of Intercollegiate Athletics (NAIA) national championship team in 1961. Willis was a second-round pick of the New York Knicks in the 1964 draft. The 6'10", 240-pound Reed became NBA Rookie of the Year in 1964-1965 and the league's Most Valuable Player in 1970 when he led the Knicks to their first ever NBA championship. Despite deteriorating knees, Reed was an important part of the Knicks' second title team in 1973, becoming finals MVP for the second time. He retired following the 1973-1974 season with more than 12,000 career points and an 18.7 points per game average. Since his retirement, Reed has coached the Knicks and the New Jersey Nets, and also at Creighton University. He was elected to the Basketball Hall of Fame in 1981 and is currently general manager of the New Jersey Nets.*

# A Brand-New Game

## CHAPTER 1

*B*asketball is unique among all the major sports for a very interesting reason. It didn't evolve or develop over a period of time. On the contrary, it is the only sport that was created or invented by request. The year was 1891 and the place was the International Training School of the Young Men's Christian Association (YMCA) in Springfield, Massachusetts. The school would later become Springfield College.

Dr. Luther Gulick was the head of the physical education department at the school. With winter coming, Dr. Gulick decided that the students were bored. They were no longer interested in the usual cold-weather activities: marching, gymnastics, and calisthenics.

Dr. Gulick decided to talk with James Naismith, a 30-year-old physical-education instructor at the school. Naismith had already talked about inventing a new game that could be played indoors during the cold weather. Dr. Gulick took Naismith up on his idea and asked him to create a brand-new sport.

# How Do You Invent a Sport?

*JAMES NAISMITH*

How do you invent a new sport, one that people will find stimulating, interesting, physically demanding, and fun? This was James Naismith's dilemma. First he thought about the games he knew. None of them seemed right for indoor play. Rugby was too rough, with too much hard tackling for a gymnasium floor. Soccer was too wide open. Kicking a ball around in a gym resulted in little more than a bunch of broken windows.

Then he tried lacrosse, but tempers flared and the students began smacking each other with their sticks. No, it would have to be a new game, one in which the players wouldn't need sticks or rackets, and one in which the ball wouldn't be flying everywhere.

Naismith decided he wanted a game played with a large round ball. But what should you do with it? Maybe throw the ball through some kind of goal, he thought. But what would be the purpose of this?

Finally, Naismith decided that goal should be up high. By throwing the ball up high, there would be less chance of injury. Feeling he was on the right track, Naismith began writing down rules for his new game. He also asked a janitor at the school if there were any kind of boxes that could be used for goals. What he got was a pair of peach baskets. He nailed them to a balcony at each end of the gym. Each basket was exactly 10 feet high. The object of the game, Naismith decided, would be to put the ball through the peach basket. And in December 1891, the game of basketball was officially born.

# The First Rules

In January 1892, the students at the International Training School returned from vacation. They found the first set of rules for the new game.

There was no mention of dribbling yet. But Naismith put the baskets 10 feet off the floor, and that's just where they are today. And players today still have but five seconds to put the ball in play. Otherwise, it was a very different game in the early days. But one thing was the same. When asked about the players, Naismith's description could easily be applied to today's great athletes.

"I had in mind the tall, agile, graceful, and expert athlete," he said, "one who could reach, jump, and act quickly and easily."

# The Earliest Games

The new sport was aptly named basketball because the object was to throw the ball into wooden peach baskets. The first games were played with nine players on a side. Within a year, the game was being played in smaller gyms with five players to a side. And it was also played with seven. It wasn't until 1897 that five on a side became the accepted way.

Also by 1897, the free throw line was added to the court, set 15 feet from the baskets. The first metal hoops replaced the peach basket as early as 1893, and by 1895 the first backboards began to appear. There were still places, however, where the game was played with a basket simply suspended on top of a vertical pole.

It also didn't take long for the dribble to begin appearing. It was the logical way to make the game flow more easily. That didn't mean players of great skills appeared overnight. The first games were painfully low scoring. Here's an example. A YMCA tournament was held in 1896 with the winner to be named "Champion of America." In the final game, two teams from Brooklyn, New York, battled it out for a full 30 minutes. When it ended, the East District defeated Brooklyn Central by the unlikely score of 4-0. Sounds more like a baseball game.

By the way, the early basketballs were made of leather. A rubber bladder was placed inside and inflated. The ball was then laced up. The balls often lost their shape and didn't give a true bounce.

# A Game for Everyone

When James Naismith created his new game, he envisioned it as a game for both men and women. Women began playing the game in Springfield as early as 1892. And that same year the sport began appearing at several women's colleges, including Smith and Vassar. Unfortunately, women would eventually be handicapped by a different set of rules. It would take nearly three-quarters of a century before women began playing and enjoying the game the same way as the men.

# The First College Teams

It was the students and teachers at Springfield who were there when Naismith introduced basketball who helped spread the game around the country. A man named Charles Bemies brought basketball to tiny Geneva College in Beaver Falls, Pennsylvania, in February 1892.

In 1894, the sport was introduced to the University of Chicago by Amos Alonzo Stagg, who is best remembered as a legendary college football coach. But he was also a basketball pioneer who insisted that basketball be played with only five players on a side.

There were also other schools beginning to form teams about the same time. The University of Iowa had started in 1893, Ohio State began in 1894, Temple University in Philadelphia started that same year, and Yale played the new sport the following year. That was about the time the college game really began.

The first official game between two colleges was in February 1895, when the Minnesota State School of Agriculture defeated Hamline University of St. Paul, Minnesota, by the score of 9-3. A month later, Temple was upset by Pennsylvania's Haverford College, 6-4. Nobody was drilling long-range jump shots back then.

It was, however, a game between Stagg's University of Chicago team and the University of Iowa in 1896 that was the first played with just five men to a side. That made for higher scores. In fact, when the two teams played a second time that year, the final score was 34-18. It was beginning to look as if the game were here to stay. But it would take more time before that game began to look like modern-day basketball.

# Play for Pay Begins

Not everyone who learned the new sport at the YMCA was a college student. Many of them were men who enjoyed basketball and wanted to keep playing. When they could no longer play at the Y, they had to look for other places to play. That sometimes meant renting places for their basketball games.

To get back the rent money, the players had to charge admission to the games. If they made more money than they had to pay for rent, they would split it up among themselves. That, in a sense, made them professionals.

It was as early as 1898 when a group of these professionals formed the first league. It was called the National Basketball League, but it was made up mostly of teams from the Philadelphia area, with a couple of New York teams joining in. William Scheffer was the man responsible for starting this first pro league.

The problem was that the league lasted only until 1903, when it disbanded. That was the beginning of nearly a half-century of professional leagues coming and going. College basketball would stabilize much more quickly than the professional game, though it wasn't long before great pioneer players came along in both.

# The NBA Is a Late Bloomer

Today, the National Basketball Association may be the most widely known and highly promoted professional sports league in the world. But considering the four so-called major sports—baseball, football, hockey, and basketball—the NBA was definitely a late bloomer.

In baseball, the National League was formed way back in 1876, the American League in 1901. The World Series as we know it began in 1903. The game soon became known as the National Pastime.

The National Football League got its start in 1920. Though it took many years for the league to really establish itself, it nevertheless operated continuously from that point on. The first season for the National Hockey League was 1917-1918. It would also take many years after that for the NHL to grow and prosper, but it too would operate continuously from that point.

The NBA didn't get its start until the 1946-1947 season. Until then, basketball as a professional sport didn't have the organization or fan support to keep a single major league in business. Taking the four major sports together, it has surely been basketball that has come the longest way in the shortest amount of time.

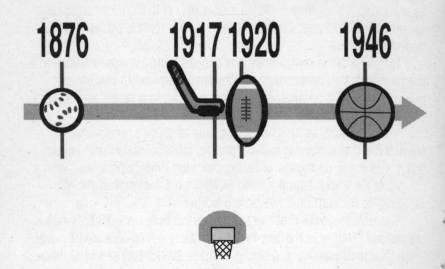

# Making the Game the Same

## CHAPTER 2

*T*he early rules of basketball didn't make for a fast-paced, exciting game, and the sport changed slowly. In fact, the college game saw the rules standardized much faster than the early pro game.

Using the college game as an example, here's how the rules of basketball evolved and changed. (The differences in the pro game will be covered later.) The college rules became standard more quickly because the early college game was much more organized than the pro game, especially after 1915 when the college, YMCA, and Amateur Athletic Union (AAU) rules were all made the same.

The game began with James Naismith's basic rules. Here's how they changed over the years to make the game what it is today. (All dates are the end dates for the season in which a rule changed.)

**1895** The free throw line was officially placed 15 feet from the basket. Before this, many gyms had the line 20 feet from the basket.

**1896** A field goal or basket was changed from counting as three points to two points. Free throws were changed from three points to one point.

**1897** Backboards were installed in most arenas.

**1901** A dribbler could not shoot the ball and could dribble it only one time, using both hands.

**1909** The dribbler was finally permitted to shoot. In addition, the dribble was defined as the "continuous passage of the ball," which made the double-dribble illegal.

**1911** Players were now disqualified after committing their fourth personal foul.

No coaching at all was allowed during the game, even during timeouts.

**1914** The bottom of the net was finally cut open so the ball could fall through.

**1915** The college, YMCA, and AAU rules became the same for the first time.

**1921** A player was allowed to reenter the game once. Before that, once a player left he could not return.

The backboards were moved 2 feet in from the wall of the court. Before that they were right on the wall and players could climb the padded wall to sink baskets.

**1922** Running, or "traveling," with the ball was changed from a foul to a violation. In other words, instead of the other team getting a free throw, the team in violation simply lost the ball.

**1924** The player who was fouled had to shoot his own free throws. Prior to that, there was usually one player who shot all his team's free throws.

**1929** The charging foul by a dribbler was called for the first time.

**1931** The "held ball" could be called when a closely guarded player withheld the ball from play for five seconds. The result was a jump ball.
    The ball was made smaller, with the maximum circumference reduced from 32 to 31 inches.

**1933** The ten-second center or midcourt line was introduced to cut down on stalling. That meant the team with the ball had to advance it over the center line within ten seconds of taking possession.

**1934** A player could now leave and reenter the game twice.

**1935** The ball was made smaller once again. The maximum circumference was reduced to between 29½ and 30¼ inches.

**1936** The three-second rule was introduced. No offensive player could remain in the free throw lane, with or without the ball, for more than three seconds.

**1938** The center jump after every basket scored was eliminated. That led to more continuous play.

**1940** The backboards were moved from 2 to 4 feet from the end line to permit more movement under the basket.

**1945** Defensive goaltending was banned. Big men could no longer swat the ball away once it started downward toward the basket.

Five personal fouls now disqualified a player. An extra foul was not permitted in overtime games.

Unlimited substitution of players was finally introduced.

**1949** Coaches were finally allowed to speak to players during a timeout.

**1957** The free throw lane was increased from 6 feet to 12 feet wide.

**1958** Offensive goaltending was banned. In other words, an offensive player could not tip a teammate's shot into the basket while the ball was directly above the rim of the basket.

There have been other changes over the years as well. For example, the 45-second clock was introduced in the 1985-1986 season, making a long, boring stall tactic impossible. (In fact, to make the game even livelier, the time was reduced to 35 seconds in 1993-1994.)

But the above changes were the ones that really brought basketball into the modern era. Anyone who now plays the game can see how the rule changes over the years made for a better, faster game.

It took until the 1930s for the pros to more or less standardize their rules and bring them closer into line with the above-mentioned college rules. The reason why the pros standardized their rules was simple. They wanted to get more college players to consider continuing with the sport and joining a pro team. With the old-time rules still being used by the pros, many college players turned their backs on the pro game. The standardization of rules for everyone helped the game at both ends.

# The Early Pro Game

## CHAPTER 3

F ans of professional basketball during the past
three decades have wit-
nessed a procession of
performers of incredible skill and
grace. In fact, longtime followers of
the NBA would be hard-pressed to
name all the great players they have
seen over the years.

Here is a random sampling: The ballhandling wizardry of Bob Cousy; the defensive and rebounding skill of Bill Russell; the strength and incredible scoring ability of Wilt Chamberlain; the variety of moves and point production of Elgin Baylor; the amazing all-around court excellence of Oscar Robertson and Jerry West; the sweeping sky hook of Kareem Abdul-Jabbar; the gravity-defying grace of Julius Erving; and the do-it-all leadership presence and clutch play of Magic Johnson and Larry Bird. Wow!

In today's pro game, players of any size can handle the ball, shoot the jumper, slam and jam, run like gazelles, and rebound high above the rim. The small men are incredibly quick and skilled, can leap high, and have the strength to go inside. The big men are amazing physical athletes. A 250-pound forward can have the grace of a much smaller man, yet be strong enough to play tight end on a pro football team.

But it wasn't always that way. In the early days of pro ball, both the game and the players were very different.

## You Call This a Basketball Court?

While the colleges provided gymnasiums and, in some cases, good outdoor courts for their early teams, the same wasn't true for the early pros. The players were like gypsies, picking up a game here and there, playing for various teams in different leagues. The better players were always in demand and might play for several teams at one time.

As for the gyms, well, there weren't very many. Games were played in some strange spaces. The only requirement was enough room to set up a couple of baskets and put down some lines to mark the court. The early pros often found themselves playing in dance halls, small high school gyms, or even basements.

One of the big attractions of the early game was a halftime dance. More people would pay their way in if there was additional entertainment besides the game. Players returning to the court following the halftime dance would often find the floor dusty and slippery from the action of the dancers and their street shoes.

It also wasn't unusual to play in a hall or basement that actually had pillars right in the middle of the court at several locations. Talk about a solid pick. The players learned to cut around the pillars to lose their defensive man.

Some courts back then had backboards, while others might just have a hoop at the end of the court supported by a long horizontal pipe. And if there was a backboard, it might be made of anything, even screening or wire.

So a pro ballplayer traveling to a game would have to be ready for anything. Oh yes, there were also rarely locker rooms or shower facilities, so the trip home might be a rather ripe one.

# Why They Are Known as Cagers

A popular slang term for basketball players over the years has been "cagers." Many people think the nickname somehow comes from the hoop and the net. Not so. The story is a little stranger than that and goes back to the early pro game.

Back in the first two decades of the century, a number of basketball courts were surrounded by either netting or a wire cage—which led to the name "cagers." The purpose was to keep the ball from going out-of-bounds. But these cage and net games brought up a number of interesting possibilities.

With the rather rigid cage, basketball games sometimes resembled hockey games, with players being slammed into the cage or running into the cage while chasing a loose ball. Players might finish the night with all kinds of bumps, cuts, and bruises. Players often wore hip pads, an aluminum cup, and elbow and knee guards. It was a rough game and the early pros had to be rough customers.

The net game was slightly different. The net was also anchored around the court, but it gave when you hit it, so players didn't get hurt as often. The net also kept the ball inbounds, and players often used the net to bounce off and get some added momentum. A man going after the ball in the corner might also fall victim to a clever player who would grab a piece of the net on each side and pull it together, trapping his opponent inside.

Players would also occasionally leap, grab the net next to the basket, and pull themselves up high in the air to grab a pass and put it in the hoop. In those days, there were next to no players tall enough or with enough leaping ability to slam dunk. So the net could be a great help.

# Basketball Nomads

Pro players in the early days often sold their services to several teams at once. They were paid strictly per game. The better players might get $25 a game, the average players just $10 a game. Most leagues were in action only on weekends. There wasn't enough money in the early days to make players full-time pros.

So the guys worked regular jobs during the week, then had to travel to their games on weekends. All the players weren't lucky enough to have cars, and there was no team bus to pick them up at all the different locations. Many had to get to games the best way they could. That often meant walking or taking a trolley or even a ferry boat. Sometimes it took a combination of methods of transportation.

It wasn't unusual on weekends for some pro players to have two games in one day, an afternoon and an evening game, often having to rush from one to the other. It wasn't so much the money that had the early pros hustling onto trolleys, taxi cabs, and ferry boats. It was the pure love of this new game that caught their fascination and their fancy. Most of them would have liked nothing better than to play basketball full-time and make a living from it. But that was still several decades away.

# The Game

What kind of a game did the early pros play? For openers, very few players were more than 6 feet tall. When a player like Horse Haggerty came along at 6'4" and 225 pounds, he was considered a giant. The center, or pivot man, was more often between 5'11" and 6'1".

The emphasis in the early days was on ball movement. In the very early days, the leather ball with the inflated bladder inside didn't have a true bounce, so there was very little dribbling. Instead, there were short, crisp passes with the players cutting and moving around the court very quickly. As Elmer Ripley, a great pioneer player, once said, "You moved the ball and you moved yourself."

In the early pro game, no one fouled out. Players could commit ten or 12 fouls and continue in the game. So the fouls were rough. Nat Holman, another early great, said basketball to many players then "meant chopping the opponent down." You were only thrown out of the game for fighting.

When games were played in dance halls, the players often wore special shoes with holes in the soles. They would then put Vaseline in the holes so the shoes would stick on the slippery floor.

The game was played with a man-to-man defense, no zones. Players were so skilled that a good team could beat a zone easily with rapid ball movement and accurate set shooting. So teams just didn't play zones. The two-handed set shot and the layup were the basic means of scoring. Later, some of the pivot men began developing a short hook shot.

Since there was a center jump after each basket, teams worked plays off the center jump. There was so much movement that every player on the team was involved in the offense. There were no differences between forward and guard. Only the center, or pivot man, had a set position.

The pivot man stayed around the foul line with his back to the basket. He rarely shot, just got the ball in the pivot and passed it to his teammates cutting off him. Scores were relatively low, with most teams scoring between 20 and 40 points a game.

That was basketball for its time, a fast and rough game. And the early pros were the very best players in the world, much as the pros are today. But it would be hard to see many of them playing in the NBA of today.

*THE ORIGINAL CELTICS IN 1920*

# Some Pioneer Pro Players

Here are just a few names from the distant past, players who contributed to the early game much in the same way the great players of later years contributed to their game. Remember, a great player is a great player in any era.

# Nat Holman

Born October 19, 1896, in New York City, Nat Holman was typical of a great basketball player. He had a fire burning inside him that willed him to win no matter what. He was also an accurate shooter and exceptional ballhandler. In addition, he was a very clever passer and a floor leader who instilled that will to win in all his teammates.

Holman played with a number of teams, making stops in Brooklyn, Syracuse, and Chicago. But his lasting fame came as a result of his play with the Original Celtics, the greatest barnstorming team of the era. A creative player, Holman helped the Celtics develop the pivot play and switching man-to-man defense.

He also coached City College of New York for 37 seasons. In 1950, Holman's CCNY

**NAT HOLMAN**

club became the only college team ever to win both the NCAA and NIT championships in the same year.

One of Holman's most vivid memories of the early days was a time the Celtics played a basketball game on a hockey rink in Providence, Rhode Island. The players banged each other into the boards, much as the hockey players did, showing once again just how different the early pro game was. Holman was elected to the Basketball Hall of Fame in 1964. He died on February 12, 1995.

# Barney Sedran

Barney Sedran stood 5'4" and weighed 115 pounds, yet he was one of the finest players of his time. Born in New York City on January 28, 1891, Sedran turned professional in 1912 after playing three years for CCNY. He started playing with Newburgh of the Hudson River League and then starred with Utica of the New York State League.

A professional for 14 years, Sedran is still remembered as one of the pro game's best early players, one who always seemed to play his best when his team went up against the Original Celtics. He was elected to the Hall of Fame in 1962. He died on January 14, 1969.

# Henry "Dutch" Dehnert

*HENRY "DUTCH" DEHNERT*

Another member of the Original Celtics, Dutch Dehnert was born in New York City on April 5, 1898. He was considered a "big" player in his day, standing 6'1" and weighing 210 pounds. He is the man credited with perfecting the pivot play, which the Celtics used in winning some 1,900 basketball games.

Dehnert had excellent speed for a big man, handled the ball beautifully in the pivot, and played a tough, rock-ribbed defense. He helped the Celtics capture a pair of American Basketball League titles in 1926 and 1927. And when the team temporarily disbanded the next year, Dehnert joined the Cleveland Rosenblums and led them to two ABL titles in 1929 and 1930.

Dehnert was elected to the Hall of Fame in 1968 and died on April 20, 1979.

# Charles "Tarzan" Cooper

Charles "Tarzan" Cooper was a huge center for his day, standing 6'4" and weighing 215 pounds. Born on August 30, 1907, in Newark, Delaware, Cooper was a great professional for 20 seasons.

His legend began in 1929 when he joined the New York Renaissance, the greatest of the all-black teams of that era. With Cooper playing in the middle for 11 years, the Rens won 1,303 times in 1,506 games, many of them as they barnstormed through the basketball world.

In 1932-1933, the Rens won an amazing 88 straight games. They also won the 1939 World Professional Tournament title. Tarzan was one of the strongest players of his time, an outstanding rebounder who keyed the Rens' fast break and could score well inside. He was

**CHARLES "TARZAN" COOPER**

inducted into the Hall of Fame in 1976 and died on December 19, 1980.

# Max Friedman

"Marty" Friedman was another early New York City-born player. He was born on July 12, 1889, and began a 17-year pro career in 1910. He was a real barnstorming pro, playing with many teams and many leagues. He took his game from Utica, New York, to Carbondale, Pennsylvania, and Cleveland, Ohio.

In 1921 he joined the New York Whirlwinds, one of the top teams of the day, playing alongside Barney Sedran and Nat Holman. A great defensive player, Friedman once led the Whirlwinds to a 40-27 victory over the Original Celtics before 11,000 fans.

Friedman was also instrumental in promoting his new sport on an international stage, organizing tournaments in France during World War I. He was elected to the Hall of Fame in 1971 and died on New Year's Day in 1986.

There were many other outstanding pioneer players, all of whom helped promote and spread a still young sport on the professional level. Because they never played in a single major league, like the NBA, their names and records are largely forgotten. Such was the lot of the barnstorming pro.

But basketball fans looking back at the infant days of the sport will find names such as Ed Wachter, Elmer Ripley, Bennie Borgmann, Al Heerdt, Johnny Beckman, Jack Inglis, Chief Muller, Andy Swells, Joe Lapchick, Davey Banks, Nat Hickey, and Chris Leonard. There are others as well. Some are in the Hall of Fame. Others are just names from a distant past, remembered by fewer and fewer people as the years roll by.

They were all pioneers.

# Today's

## CHAPTER 4

# NBA

## Teams

MAGIC

**D**uring the decade of the 1980s and into the 1990s, the National Basketball Association has become arguably the biggest attraction in professional sports. While the NBA has had a parade of great players since the 1950s, it was the arrival of Magic Johnson, Larry Bird, and Michael Jordan in the 1980s that really signaled the start of the basketball boom.

Let's look at some of the other reasons why basketball is so popular today and at the NBA teams that play the game.

Superstars Johnson, Bird, and Jordan, coupled with the marketing genius of Commissioner David Stern and his staff, quickly brought the NBA up on an equal par with Major League Baseball and the National Football League in visibility. Television coverage of basketball allows viewers to become even more intimately familiar with the players. Unlike the other major sports, basketball players don't wear any kind of headgear or face masks. Thus, they are easily recognizable and the emotional ups and downs of the game can be seen.

Also during the 1980s and 1990s, basketball was becoming more prominent on the world stage. Pro leagues were thriving in Italy, Spain, and Israel. The game was also played religiously in the former Soviet Union and former Eastern European bloc countries. Some people are even predicting that the court game will soon surpass soccer as the most popular sport in the world.

When the league started in 1946-1947, there were just 11 teams. A year later there were only eight. By 1949-1950, the league had grown to 17 teams. But a look at the standings saw teams from Rochester, Fort Wayne, Anderson, Tri-Cities, Sheboygan, and Waterloo nestled in among the New Yorks, Philadelphias, and Chicagos.

There were years of comings and goings of franchises, then moves from the smaller cities to larger ones. By 1960 the league was back down to eight teams. Ten years later, it was up to 14. The growth had started. By 1980 there were 22 teams, Magic Johnson and Larry Bird were rookie sensations, and the NBA was established big time for keeps.

# How the NBA Is Set Up

In 1994-1995, the National Basketball Association had 27 teams divided into two conferences and four divisions. The last expansion to that number occurred in 1989-1990. The first two Canadian franchises, in Toronto and Vancouver, began play in the fall of 1995 for the 1995-1996 season, bringing the total to 29 teams. The division setup as of 1995-1996 is shown on page 24.

Under the present setup, 16 teams make the playoffs, eight from each conference. The first round is a best-of-five series. The conference semifinals and finals, and the championship round, are all best-of-seven series. The first deciding playoff factor in each conference is record. So it is possible for just two teams from the Midwest Division

# National Basketball Association, 1995-1996

## EASTERN CONFERENCE

| Atlantic Division | Central Division |
|---|---|
| Boston Celtics | Atlanta Hawks |
| Miami Heat | Charlotte Hornets |
| New Jersey Nets | Chicago Bulls |
| New York Knicks | Cleveland Cavaliers |
| Orlando Magic | Detroit Pistons |
| Philadelphia 76ers | Indiana Pacers |
| Washington Bullets | Milwaukee Bucks |
| | Toronto Raptors |

## WESTERN CONFERENCE

| Midwest Division | Pacific Division |
|---|---|
| Dallas Mavericks | Golden State Warriors |
| Denver Nuggets | Los Angeles Clippers |
| Houston Rockets | Los Angeles Lakers |
| Minnesota Timberwolves | Phoenix Suns |
| San Antonio Spurs | Portland Trail Blazers |
| Utah Jazz | Sacramento Kings |
| Vancouver Grizzlies | Seattle SuperSonics |

to make the playoffs, while six teams from the Pacific Division get in. Thus, a third place team in one division can be left out, while a sixth place team in the other division (if it has a better record) can make it.

The NBA finals have become one of the most watched sporting events on television.

Here is a brief look at all 29 NBA teams in alphabetical order. Included are helpful facts, a brief history, and some of the top players who have graced each franchise in the past.

# Atlanta Hawks

**Mailing address:** One CNN Center, Suite 405, South Tower, Atlanta, Georgia 30303. **Telephone:** 404-827-3800. **Home court:** The Omni (16,510). **Team colors:** Red, white, and gold. **Regular season record through 1995:** W: 1,838. L: 1,794.

The franchise entered the NBA for the 1949-1950 season. They were known as the Tri-Cities Blackhawks because they had home courts in three different cities in Illinois. The team moved to Milwaukee in 1951-1952, where they changed their nickname to the Hawks, then to St. Louis in 1955-1956. In 1957-1958, the franchise won its only NBA championship ever. While still in St. Louis, they reached the final round on three other occasions. Then in 1968, the team was moved once again, this time to Atlanta.

Outstanding alumni: Bob Pettit, Cliff Hagan, Frank Selvy, Zelmo Beaty, Lenny Wilkens, Joe Caldwell, Lou Hudson, Pete Maravich, and Dominique Wilkins.

. . . . . . . . . . . . . . . . . . . . . . . . .

# Boston Celtics

**Mailing address:** 151 Merrimac Street, Boston, Massachusetts 02114. **Telephone:** 617-523-6050. **Home court:** Fleet Center (18,400). **Team colors:** Green and white. **Regular season record through 1995:** W: 2,389. L: 1,416.

The NBA's greatest and winningest franchise, the Boston Celtics entered the league in the inaugural season of 1946-1947 and have never let anyone forget who they are. From 1956-1957 to 1968-1969, the Celtics dominated their sport like no other team. During that time the Celtics won 11 NBA titles in 13 years, including an unprecedented eight in a row from 1958-1959 to 1965-1966. They have won five more since, for a total of 16 world championships, and have been runners-up three times. There have been so many great players passing through Boston that retired numbers abound atop the Boston court.

Outstanding alumni: Bob Cousy, Bill Sharman, Bill Russell, Tom Heinsohn, Frank Ramsey, John Havlicek, Sam Jones, K. C. Jones,

Satch Sanders, Jo Jo White, Dave Cowens, Paul Silas, Larry Bird, Cedric Maxwell, Robert Parish, Kevin McHale, Nate Archibald, Dennis Johnson, and Reggie Lewis.

• • • • • • • • • • • • • • • • • • • • • • • • • •

# Charlotte Hornets

**Mailing address:** One Hive Drive, Charlotte, North Carolina 28217. **Telephone:** 704-357-0252. **Home court:** Charlotte Coliseum (23,698). **Team colors:** Teal, purple, and white. **Regular season record through 1995:** W: 231. L: 343.

An expansion team born in 1988-1989, the Hornets have become one of the NBA's most popular franchises. Fans fill the huge Charlotte Coliseum at nearly every home game and have watched their team go through the growing pains of expansion. But with the addition of forward Larry Johnson in 1991-1992 and center Alonzo Mourning in 1992-1993, the team became a winner and playoff ballclub. With other fine players like Muggsy Bogues, Hersey Hawkins, and Dell Curry, the Hornets finished at 50-32 in 1994-1995 and came close to becoming one of the league's elite clubs.

Outstanding alumni: None (recent expansion).

• • • • • • • • • • • • • • • • • • • • • • • • • •

# Chicago Bulls

**Mailing address:** One Magnificent Mile, 980 North Michigan Avenue, Suite 1600, Chicago, Illinois 60611. **Telephone:** 312-455-4000. **Home court:** United Center (21,500). **Team colors:** Red, white, and black. **Regular season record through 1995:** W: 1,244. L: 1,133.

The Bulls are a franchise that has been in the NBA since 1966-1967. And while there were some very good Chicago teams in the early and middle 1970s, the team came of age in the late 1980s and early 1990s when the man considered the greatest player of all time joined them. His name, of course, is Michael Jordan and he led the Bulls to three straight NBA titles from 1990-1991 to 1992-1993. Jordan's unexpected retirement following the 1992-1993 season hurt the franchise, but they still kept up their winning tradition the following year. His comeback in March 1995 once again made the Bulls a title contender, though they were beaten in the Eastern Conference semifinals by the Orlando Magic.

Outstanding alumni: Guy Rodgers, Bob Boozer, Jerry Sloan, Bob Love, Chet Walker, Norm Van Lier, Tom Boerwinkle, Artis Gilmore, and Reggie Theus.

• • • • • • • • • • • • • • • • • • • • • • • • •

# Cleveland Cavaliers

**Mailing address:** Gund Arena, 1 Center Court, Cleveland, Ohio 44115. **Telephone:** 216-420-2000. **Home court:** Gund Arena (20,500). **Team colors:** Blue, black, and orange. **Regular season record through 1995:** W: 906. L: 1,144.

The Cavs, an NBA franchise since 1970-1971, began to put together some winning seasons by the mid-1970s. But it has been pretty much of a roller coaster ride since, with good years and bad years. And while the Cavaliers of the late 1980s and early 1990s have produced some fine teams, they have still not taken that final step to becoming one of the NBA's elite. The 1991-1992 team came the closest, going all the way to the Eastern Conference finals before losing in six games to the Bulls.

Outstanding alumni: Austin Carr, Lenny Wilkens, and World B. Free.

• • • • • • • • • • • • • • • • • • • • • • • •

# Dallas Mavericks

**Mailing address:** Reunion Arena, 777 Sports Street, Dallas, Texas 75207. **Telephone:** 214-748-1808. **Home court:** Reunion Arena (17,502). **Team colors:** Blue and green. **Regular season record through 1995:** W: 515. L: 715.

The Dallas Mavericks were an expansion team in 1980-1981, winning just 15 games in their maiden season. Yet by 1983-1984, the team had a winning record and was in the playoffs. In 1987-1988, the club won 53 games, then made it all the way to the Western Conference finals, where they lost to the Lakers in seven hard-fought games. In recent years, however, the team has fallen upon hard times, in 1992-1993 and 1993-

1994 winning a total of just 25 games. With a trio of young stars— Jim Jackson, Jamal Mashburn, and Jason Kidd— the Mavs were a much improved team in 1994-1995.

Outstanding alumni: Mark Aguirre, Sam Perkins, Rolando Blackman, and Derek Harper.

• • • • • • • • • • • • • • • • • • • • • • • •

# Denver Nuggets

**Mailing address:** McNichols Sports Arena, 1635 Clay Street, Denver, Colorado 80204. **Telephone:** 303-893-6700. **Home court:** McNichols Sports Arena (17,022). **Team colors:** Nuggets gold, Nuggets red, and Nuggets blue. **ABA regular season record through 1976:** W: 413. L: 331. **NBA regular season record through 1995:** W: 781. L: 777.

The Denver Nuggets were one of four American Basketball Association teams absorbed into the NBA when the ABA disbanded after the 1975-1976 season. One of the ABA's best, the Nuggets brought a solid team to the NBA and had a 50-32 record their first year in the older league. But there have been some ups and downs since. The Nuggets now have some fine young players and finally seem poised to give many teams problems.

Outstanding alumni: Spencer Haywood, Larry Jones, David Thompson, Dan Issel, Alex English, Kiki Vandeweghe, and Fat Lever.

• • • • • • • • • • • • • • • • • • • • • • • •

# Detroit Pistons

**Mailing address:** The Palace of Auburn Hills, Two Championship Drive, Auburn Hills, Michigan 48326. **Telephone:** 313-377-0100. **Home court:** The Palace of Auburn Hills (21,454). **Team colors:** Red, white, and blue. **Regular season record through 1995:** W: 1,737. L: 1,957.

Another venerable old franchise, the Pistons began in Fort Wayne, Indiana, in 1948-1949. The team moved to Detroit in 1957-1958, where they have been ever since. The franchise had many losing seasons in the early and middle years despite an array of fine individual stars. But the team finally reached the NBA finals in 1987-1988, then won the championship the next two years. That team aged quickly,

and in 1993-1994 the club was only 20-62. With star rookie Grant Hill, the Pistons improved to 28-54 in 1994-1995.

Outstanding alumni: Larry Foust, George Yardley, Mel Hutchins, Andy Philip, Gene Shue, Bailey Howell, Dave DeBusschere, Tom Van Arsdale, Dave Bing, Terry Dischinger, Bob Lanier, Kelly Tripucka, Isiah Thomas, and Bill Laimbeer.

# Golden State Warriors

**Mailing address:** Oakland Coliseum Arena, 7000 Coliseum Way, Oakland, California 94621. **Telephone:** 510-638-6300. **Home court:** Oakland Coliseum Arena (15,025). **Team colors:** Gold and blue. **Regular season record through 1995:** W: 1,842. L: 1,958.

Another original NBA franchise, but one that has traveled cross-country to relocate, the Warriors started out in Philadelphia in 1946-1947, moved to San Francisco in 1962-1963, then across the Bay to Oakland (and renamed Golden State) in 1971-1972. The Warriors have the distinction of winning the first ever NBA championship in 1947. The team won again in 1955-1956 and for a third time in 1974-1975. They have also made it to the finals on three other occasions. In recent years, the team has been hit hard by an injury jinx that has deprived it of some of its top players.

Outstanding alumni: Joe Fulks, Paul Arizin, Neil Johnston, Jack George, Tom Gola, Wilt Chamberlain, Guy Rodgers, Tom Meschery, Rick Barry, Nate Thurmond, Jeff Mullins, Cazzie Russell, and Robert Parish.

# Houston Rockets

**Mailing address:** The Summit, Ten Greenway Plaza, Houston, Texas 77046. **Telephone:** 713-627-0600. **Home court:** The Summit (16,279). **Team colors:** Red and gold. **Regular season record through 1995:** W: 1,120. L: 1,176.

The champs of 1993-1994 and again in 1994-1995, the Rockets gave the city of Houston its first title in any sport since the American Football League Oilers in the early 1960s. Up to then, however, it had been a somewhat frustrating journey. The franchise began as an expansion team in San Diego in 1967-1968, then moved to Houston in 1971-1972. There was a lot of losing in the early years, but the Rockets did make it to the NBA finals in 1981 and 1986. Remember the old expression, "If at first you don't succeed, try, try again"? That's what the Rockets did in 1994 and 1995, and boy, did they ever succeed.

Outstanding alumni: Elvin Hayes, Calvin Murphy, Rudy Tomjanovich, Mike Newlin, Moses Malone, and Ralph Sampson.

## Indiana Pacers

**Mailing address:** 300 E. Market Street, Indianapolis, Indiana 46204. **Telephone:** 317-263-2100. **Home court:** Market Square Arena (16,530). **Team colors:** Blue and yellow. **ABA regular season record through 1976:** W: 427. L: 317. **NBA regular season record through 1995:** W: 685. L: 873.

Another of the four ABA teams that entered the NBA in 1976-1977, the Pacers had better luck in their former league, winning three ABA titles and reaching the championship round on two other occasions. Once in the NBA, the Pacers struggled, producing just two winning seasons between 1977 and 1993. Then in 1993-1994, the franchise put its best club in years on the floor. Indiana went 45-37 in the regular season and then made it all the way to the Eastern Conference finals before losing to the Knicks in seven tough games. A year later they were Central Division champs at 52-30.

Outstanding alumni: Mel Daniels, Roger Brown, George McGinnis, Billy Knight, and Chuck Person.

## Los Angeles Clippers

**Mailing address:** L.A. Memorial Sports Arena, 3939 S. Figueroa Street, Los Angeles, California 90037. **Telephone:** 213-748-8000. **Home court:** L.A. Memorial Sports Arena (16,005). **Team colors:** Red, white, and blue. **Regular season record through 1995:** W: 749. L: 1,301.

An expansion franchise in 1970-1971, the team began play as the Buffalo (New York) Braves. From there, the team moved to San Diego in 1978-1979, where the nickname was changed to the Clippers. But they weren't through yet. In 1984-1985, they shuffled off to Los Angeles. Unfortunately, the team's best days were while they still resided in Buffalo. They had three winning seasons there, only two since. Needless to say, no NBA titles and many years out of the playoffs.

Outstanding alumni: Bob McAdoo, Randy Smith, Jim McMillian, Ernie DiGregorio, and World B. Free.

• • • • • • • • • • • • • • • • • • • • • • • • •

## Los Angeles Lakers

**Mailing address:** Great Western Forum, 3900 West Manchester Boulevard, P.O. Box 10, Inglewood, California 90306. **Telephone:** 310-419-3100. **Home court:** Great Western Forum (17,505). **Team colors:** Royal purple and gold. **Regular season record through 1995:** W: 2,239. L: 1,456.

The NBA's second most successful franchise behind the Celtics, the Lakers have had near-dynasty runs in two cities. The team joined the NBA in 1948-1949 as the Minneapolis Lakers, winning five championships in six years between 1948-1949 and 1953-1954. They also reached the finals in 1959. The Lakers moved to Los Angeles in 1960-1961. In the 1960s the team reached the finals six times and lost to Boston on each occasion. In the 1970s, there was another title in 1972, plus two more trips to the finals. Then in the 1980s, the team won another five championships in eight finals tries. And they reached the finals again in 1991. Talk about an exciting franchise. That's 11 championships in 24 final round appearances. Only the Celtics have done better.

Outstanding alumni: George Mikan, Slater Martin, Jim Pollard, Vern Mikkelsen, Clyde Lovellette, Larry Foust, Elgin Baylor, Jerry West, Rudy LaRusso, Frank Selvy, Gail Goodrich, Wilt Chamberlain, Happy Hairston, Jim McMillian, Kareem Abdul-Jabbar, Norm Nixon, Jamal Wilkes, Magic Johnson, Michael Cooper, Bob McAdoo, and James Worthy.

• • • • • • • • • • • • • • • • • • • • • • • •

# Miami Heat

**Mailing address:** Miami Arena, Miami, Florida 33136. **Telephone:** 305-577-4328. **Home court:** Miami Arena (15,200). **Team colors:** Red, yellow, black, and white. **Regular season record through 1995:** W: 205. L: 369.

A 1988-1989 expansion team, the Heat are just starting to make things hot for other NBA teams, having produced their first winning season ever in 1993-1994. Like with other recent expansion teams, losing becomes the norm the first few seasons until the team can begin picking up top draft choices and putting them together. If a few shrewd trades follow, the expansion team can become competitive and begin to challenge for the title.

Outstanding alumni: None (recent expansion).

# Milwaukee Bucks

**Mailing address:** Bradley Center, 1001 N. Fourth Street, Milwaukee, Wisconsin 53203. **Telephone:** 414-227-0500. **Home court:** Bradley Center (18,633). **Team colors:** Hunter green, purple, and silver. **Regular season record through 1995:** W: 1,246. L: 968.

An expansion team in 1968-1969, the Bucks made the leap from 27 to 56 victories their second year, and to an NBA championship in year three. They did it by drafting center Lew Alcindor (later known as Kareem Abdul-Jabbar), who was dominating right from his rookie year. When the team added another great veteran, Oscar Robertson, in 1970-1971, they won the title in record time for an expansion ballclub. In 1975, Abdul-Jabbar was traded to the Lakers and the Bucks had to rebuild. The franchise has generally been a winner, though in 1993-1994 the team finished at 20-62, the poorest record in franchise history. Young stars Glenn Robinson and Vin Baker led to an improved team in 1994-1995.

Outstanding alumni: Lew Alcindor/Kareem Abdul-Jabbar, Oscar Robertson, Bob Dandridge, Lucius Allen, Brian Winters, Junior Bridgeman, Marques Johnson, Sidney Moncrief, Bob Lanier, and Terry Cummings.

# Minnesota Timberwolves

**Mailing address:** Target Center, 600 First Avenue, Minneapolis, Minnesota 55403. **Telephone:** 612-673-1600. **Home court:** Target Center (19,006). **Team colors:** Royal blue, kelly green, and silver. **Regular season record through 1995:** W: 126. L: 366.

An expansion franchise that began play in 1989-1990, the Timberwolves are a team that hasn't been able to get off the ground. In fact, the ballclub won more games (22) its first year in the league than it did in the four seasons from 1991-1992 to 1994-1995 (15, 19, 20, 21). There were rumors the club would be moved out of Minnesota before the 1995-1996 season, but the NBA apparently wants to try keeping it there and playing in the large, modern Target Center. All the team needs now is ballplayers.

Outstanding alumni: None (recent expansion).

# New Jersey Nets

**Mailing address:** Meadowlands Arena, East Rutherford, New Jersey 07073. **Telephone:** 201-935-8888. **Home court:** Meadowlands Arena (20,029). **Team colors:** Red, white, and blue. **ABA regular season record through 1976:** W: 374. L: 370. **NBA regular season record through 1995:** W: 630. L: 928.

One of the four teams taken into the NBA when the ABA disbanded, the Nets have been an interesting franchise. They began as the New York Nets before moving to New Jersey in 1977-1978. Led by Julius Erving, the Nets were two-time ABA champs and reached the finals on one other occasion. In the NBA, they haven't fared as well. They also suffered a tragic loss when coming superstar Drazen Petrovic was killed in an auto accident in June 1993. Now, the team is again trying to build a steady winner, led by forward Derrick Coleman and guard Kenny Anderson.

Outstanding alumni: Rick Barry, John Roche, Lavern Tart, Julius Erving, John Williamson, Bernard King, Otis Birdsong, Buck Williams, and Drazen Petrovic.

# New York Knickerbockers

**Mailing address:** Madison Square Garden, Two Pennsylvania Plaza, New York, New York 10121. **Telephone:** 212-465-6000. **Home court:** Madison Square Garden (19,763). **Team colors:** Orange, white, and blue. **Regular season record through 1995:** W: 1,932. L: 1,869.

An original NBA franchise beginning in 1946-1947, the Knicks are considered one of the league's flagship teams. There have been a parade of fine players passing through Madison Square Garden, but the Knicks have won just a pair of NBA titles, in 1970 and 1973. In the eyes of many, the Knick ballclubs from the early 1970s were still the best New York teams ever, though the current club, which lost to the Rockets in a seven-game championship series in 1994, also represents one of the better New York teams.

Outstanding alumni: Harry Gallatin, Sweetwater Clifton, Dick McGuire, Carl Braun, Kenny Sears, Willie Naulls, Richie Guerin, Willis Reed, Dick Barnett, Dick Van Arsdale, Cazzie Russell, Walt Bellamy, Walt Frazier, Dave DeBusschere, Bill Bradley, Earl Monroe, Bob McAdoo, Ray Williams, Micheal Ray Richardson, and Bernard King.

• • • • • • • • • • • • • • • • • • • • • • • • • •

# Orlando Magic

**Mailing address:** Orlando Arena, One Magic Place, Orlando, Florida 32801. **Telephone:** 407-649-3200. **Home court:** Orlando Arena (15,291). **Team colors:** Electric blue, Quick silver, and Magic black. **Regular season record through 1995:** W: 218. L: 274.

The Magic are another example of a recent expansion team that has become a winner quickly because it drafted a franchise player— 7'1" center Shaquille O'Neal. Shaq joined the Magic in their fourth season, 1992-1993, and helped take them from a 21-61 team to a 41-41 ballclub. A year later the team added another blue-chip rookie, Anfernee Hardaway, and made the playoffs with a 50-32 mark. With several other very good players in tow, the Magic seem to be on their way, an example of an expansion team doing things right. In 1994-1995, they were Atlantic Division champs at 57-25 and made it all the way to the finals, where they were beaten by the Houston Rockets in four straight games.

Outstanding alumni: None (recent expansion).

• • • • • • • • • • • • • • • • • • • • • • •

## Philadelphia 76ers

**Mailing address:** Veterans Stadium, P.O. Box 25040, Philadelphia, Pennsylvania 19147. **Telephone:** 215-339-7600. **Home court:** The Spectrum (18,168). **Team colors:** Red, white, and blue. **Regular season record through 1995:** W: 2,017. L: 1,613.

The Philadelphia 76ers entered the league as the Syracuse Nationals in 1949-1950. Five years later they were NBA champions, and in 1963-1964 the team moved to Philadelphia (replacing the departed Warriors). The franchise won two more titles in Philly, in 1966-1967, when they were 68-13 in the regular season, and in 1982-1983, when they finished 65-17 and then took 12 of 13 playoff games en route to the championship. The team has also made its way into the final round on five other occasions. For basketball tradition, you can't beat Philadelphia.

Outstanding alumni: Dolph Schayes, Johnny Kerr, Larry Costello, Hal Greer, Chet Walker, Wilt Chamberlain, Billy Cunningham, Wally Jones, Archie Clark, George McGinnis, Julius Erving, World B. Free, Doug Collins, Darryl Dawkins, Bobby Jones, Maurice Cheeks, Moses Malone, and Charles Barkley.

• • • • • • • • • • • • • • • • • • • • • • •

## Phoenix Suns

**Mailing address:** 201 E. Jefferson, Phoenix, Arizona 85004. **Telephone:** 602-379-7900. **Home court:** America West Arena (19,023). **Team colors:** Purple, orange, and copper. **Regular season record through 1995:** W: 1,205. L: 1,009.

One of the NBA's best teams of the late 1980s and early 1990s, the Suns are still in quest of their first NBA title. They made it to the finals in 1993, only to lose to the Chicago Bulls. An expansion team that won just 16 games in its first season of 1968-1969, the

Suns had a winning record by year three and have been a very consistent franchise since that time, winning the Pacific Division title in 1994-1995. They are a perfect example of an expansion team that fit into the mainstream of the league very quickly.

Outstanding alumni: Gail Goodrich, Dick Van Arsdale, Connie Hawkins, Charlie Scott, Paul Westphal, Walter Davis, Alvan Adams, and Larry Nance.

• • • • • • • • • • • • • • • • • • • • • • •

## Portland Trail Blazers

**Mailing address:** One N. Center Court, Suite 200, Portland, Oregon 97227. **Telephone:** 503-234-9291. **Home court:** Rose Garden Arena (21,500). **Team colors:** Scarlet, black, and white. **Regular season record through 1995:** W: 1,085 L: 965.

 An expansion team in 1970-1971, the Portland Trail Blazers took seven years to develop a winning team. But since that time they have missed the playoffs on only one occasion. Better yet, that first winning season of 1976-1977 resulted in an NBA championship. The Blazers might have won more if center Bill Walton hadn't been injured so often in those years. Nevertheless, the club has produced winning teams in 16 of the last 19 seasons and made it to the NBA finals in both 1990 and 1992.

Outstanding alumni: Jeff Petrie, Sidney Wicks, Bill Walton, John Johnson, Lionel Hollins, Maurice Lucas, Jim Paxson, Mychal Thompson, Kiki Vandeweghe, and Clyde Drexler.

• • • • • • • • • • • • • • • • • • • • • • •

## Sacramento Kings

**Mailing address:** One Sports Parkway, Sacramento, California 95834. **Telephone:** 916-928-0000. **Home court:** ARCO Arena (17,317). **Team colors:** Red, white, and blue. **Regular season record through 1995:** W: 1,692. L: 2,003.

 The Kings are the NBA's most traveled team, first joining the league in 1948-1949 as the Rochester Royals and winning an NBA title in 1951. The club moved to Cincinnati in 1957 and were still called the

Royals, before moving to Kansas City-Omaha in 1972-1973 with the nickname changed to the Kings. In 1975-1976, they switched to Kansas City outright. Then in 1985-1986, they were again moved to Sacramento. Since 1966-1967, the team has made the playoffs just six times, and hasn't made it since 1985-1986. This old franchise deserves better.

Outstanding alumni: Bob Davies, Bobby Wanzer, Arnie Risen, Maurice Stokes, Jack Twyman, Clyde Lovellette, Oscar Robertson, Wayne Embry, Jerry Lucas, Adrian Smith, Happy Hairston, Tom Van Arsdale, Nate Archibald, Otis Birdsong, and Reggie Theus.

## San Antonio Spurs

**Mailing address:** Alamodome, 100 Montana Street, San Antonio, Texas 78203. **Telephone:** 210-554-7700. **Home court:** Alamodome (20,500). **Team colors:** Metallic silver, black, teal/fuschia/orange. **ABA regular season record through 1976:** W: 378. L: 366. **NBA regular season record through 1995:** W: 855. L: 703.

The Spurs are the fourth and last of the ABA teams that were absorbed into the NBA in 1976-1977. Unfortunately, the team has never reached the final round of the playoffs in either league. The franchise started as the ABA Dallas Chapparals, became the Texas Chapparals for one year, then the Spurs in 1972-1973. In the NBA, the team managed to reach the Eastern Conference finals in 1978-1979 and the Western Conference finals in 1982-1983. The current Spur team with league MVP David Robinson at center had the best record in the NBA in 1994-1995 at 62-20.

Outstanding alumni: Ron Boone, John Beasley, Donnie Freeman, George Gervin, Larry Kenon, Billy Paultz, James Silas, Mike Mitchell, Artis Gilmore, and Johnny Moore.

## Seattle SuperSonics

**Mailing address:** 190 Queen Anne Avenue N., Suite 200, Seattle, Washington 98109. **Telephone:** 206-281-5800. **Home court:** Seattle Center Coliseum (14,252). **Team colors:** Green and yellow. **Regular season record through 1995:** W: 1,189. L: 1,107.

Another expansion team from the NBA's growth spurt in the late 1960s, the Sonics began play in 1967-1968, having their first winning season in 1971-1972. In 1977-1978, the team surprised everyone by making it to the NBA finals, where they were beaten by the Bullets in seven games. A year later, the Sonics got their revenge, winning their only NBA title, over the Bullets in five. There have been some fine Seattle teams since then, but none better than the 1993-1994 team that had an NBA best 63-19 regular season record, but was then shocked in the first round of the playoffs by the Denver Nuggets.

Outstanding alumni: Bob Rule, Lenny Wilkens, Spencer Haywood, Fred Brown, Slick Watts, Gus Williams, Dennis Johnson, Jack Sikma, and Tom Chambers.

• • • • • • • • • • • • • • • • • • • • • •

## Toronto Raptors

**Mailing Address:** 150 York Street, Suite 1100, Toronto, Ontario, Canada M5H 3S5. **Telephone:** 416-214-2255. **Home court:** Toronto Skydome (temporary). **Team colors:** Raptor red, purple, and Naismith silver.

• • • • • • • • • • • • • • • • • • • • • •

## Utah Jazz

**Mailing address:** Delta Center, 301 West South Temple, Salt Lake City, Utah 84101. **Telephone:** 801-325-2500. **Home court:** Delta Center (19,911). **Team colors:** Purple, green, and gold. **Regular season record through 1995:** W: 862. L: 860.

An expansion team in 1974-1975, the Jazz started play in New Orleans. Victories came slowly. The team didn't have a winning season or make the playoffs until 1983-1984. By that time they were in Utah, having moved there in 1979-1980, keeping their nickname. Since that first winning season, the Jazz have stayed at .500 or better, but they have only reached the Western Conference finals once, in 1991-1992.

That step to the final plateau has been a huge one.

Outstanding alumni: Pete Maravich, Truck Robinson, Adrian Dantley, Darrell Griffith, and Mark Eaton.

• • • • • • • • • • • • • • • • • • • • • • • •

## Vancouver Grizzlies

**Mailing address:** 780 Beatty Street, Third Floor, Vancouver, British Columbia, Canada V6B 2M1. **Telephone:** 604-688-JUMP. **Home court:** General Motors Place (20,000). **Team colors:** Canadian red, Spirit turquoise, and B.C. (British Columbia) bronze.

• • • • • • • • • • • • • • • • • • • • • • •

## Washington Bullets

**Mailing address:** USAir Arena, Landover, Maryland 20785. **Telephone:** 301-773-2255. **Home court:** USAir Arena (18,756). **Team colors:** Red, white, and blue. **Regular season record through 1995:** W: 1,295. L: 1,482.

What's in a name, anyway? The franchise was started in Chicago in 1961-1962 and known as the Packers. A year later the name was changed to the Zephyrs. In 1963-1964, the team was moved to Baltimore and became the Bullets. Then in 1973-1974, they shuttled down the road to Washington. Got a scorecard? In between, there were some pretty good basketball teams, including the one that took the NBA title in 1977-1978. The team reached the finals on three other occasions, in 1971, 1975, and 1979. Since that time, the team has fallen on harder times and hasn't made the playoffs since 1987-1988.

Outstanding alumni: Walt Bellamy, Terry Dischinger, Gus Johnson, Bailey Howell, Kevin Loughery, Earl Monroe, Wes Unseld, Jack Marin, Phil Chenier, Elvin Hayes, Kevin Porter, Jeff Ruland, and Bernard King.

• • • • • • • • • • • • • • • • • • • • • • • •

While the NBA is bigger and better than ever, a far cry from the nine-team league that was still in existence as late as 1965-1966, there are some teams from the NBA's early days that are now but a distant memory. Many came from small midwestern cities that could never support a big-time team today. Here are some of the teams that once played in the NBA. It will be hard for today's fan to picture the Shaq or the Admiral playing under these banners.

Anderson Packers, Chicago Stags, Cleveland Rebels, Detroit Falcons, Indianapolis Jets, Indianapolis Olympians, Pittsburgh Ironmen, Providence Steamrollers, St. Louis Bombers, Sheboygan Redskins, Toronto Huskies, Tri-Cities Blackhawks, and Waterloo Hawks.

# Great NBA Moments

## CHAPTER 5

**B**asketball has always been a sport that naturally lends itself to great moments. The combination of individual skills within the team concept has produced a treasure trove of amazing accomplishments over the years. In many cases, it's the big name players who produce the big moments. Unlike some other sports, it seems to be more difficult for the journeyman player to take over a game and make it all happen.

Records in basketball don't go back as far as they do in football, baseball, and hockey, but the great moments in the game are no less amazing. Here are just some of the more exciting, breathtaking moments that have occurred during nearly a half-century of NBA play.

# Wilt Hits the Century Mark

As a rookie with the Philadelphia Warriors in 1959-1960, Wilt Chamberlain took the basketball world by storm. The 7'1", 275-pound giant was from day one the strongest man in the NBA, and he was playing in an era when only one other center, the Celtics' 6'10" Bill Russell, could possibly stay with him on defense.

In his rookie year, Chamberlain smashed the existing season scoring record by averaging an amazing 37.6 points a game. He took more shots, made more shots, took more free throws, and gathered in more rebounds than any other player in the league.

But that still didn't prepare anyone for what Wilt would do a few years later on the night of March 2, 1962. That night, Wilt and the Warriors traveled to Hershey, Pennsylvania, to meet the New York Knicks on a neutral court. The big guy came out on fire against the Knicks, scoring 13 of his team's first 19 points.

When the first quarter ended, the Warriors had a 42-26 lead, and Wilt already had 23 points—a good night's work for most players. At the half, Philly had a 79-68 lead, and Wilt had reached 41 points. It looked as if he had a shot at 80. In the third quarter the big guy kept shooting, and when the period ended he was up to 69 points—just four short of his own record for a regulation game.

Now his teammates were conscious of getting him the ball. With 10:10 left, Wilt got his 75th point, a new record. With a little more than five minutes left, he took an alley-oop pass from Al Attles and jammed home two more. He now had 89. The Knicks were trying everything to stop him.

Then he was over 90 and still going. A fadeaway jumper gave him 96 points. Another resounding dunk gave him 98 with 1:19 remaining. He missed his next shot, but then the Knicks missed one as well. Philly came downcourt again. Joe Ruklick had the ball and lobbed a high pass above the rim. Wilt timed his jump, grabbed the ball in both hands, and jammed it hard through the hoop. He had scored his 100th point of the game.

It was incredible. Philly won the game, 169-147, as Wilt connected on 36 field goals in 63 attempts and—not normally a good free throw shooter—hit 28 of his 32 foul shots.

Wilt Chamberlain is still the only NBA player ever to score 100 points in a game. It's a record that may, indeed, never be broken and a great moment that may never be seen again.

# More Wilt

By scoring 100 points in a single game, Wilt Chamberlain performed an incredible basketball achievement. But what he did over the 80 games of the 1961-1962 season may have been even more amazing. Over that span, he scored 50 points or more in 46 of the Warriors' games. Most players don't score 50 points in a game ever in their basketball lives.

That wasn't all. The whole season was a great moment for him. In 80 games, Wilt became the first and only player ever to score more than 4,000 points in a season. He finished with 4,029 points for an almost unbelievable average of 50.4 points a game—for an entire season!

# Magic Moments Start Early

When Earvin "Magic" Johnson joined the Los Angeles Lakers in 1979-1980, fans couldn't wait to see him in action. After all, there had never been a 6'9" rookie who played point guard. Magic had led Michigan State to an NCAA title that spring in just his sophomore season. Now he was in the NBA, joining a fine Laker team led by center Kareem Abdul-Jabbar.

As it turned out, Magic was the real goods. He was an all-star his first season, averaging 18 points a game, and passing, rebounding, and playing defense brilliantly. The Lakers won the Pacific Division with a 60-22 record. Then they marched to the final round of the playoffs where they met Julius Erving and the Philadelphia 76ers.

After five games, it looked like the Lakers were taking command with a 3-2 lead. But Abdul-Jabbar had sprained his ankle and couldn't play in game six. Laker fans wondered who would take his place. That's when coach Paul Westhead walked up to Magic Johnson and said, "You're the starting center tomorrow night!"

It was no joke. The Lakers came out for game six with their point guard and sometime forward playing center. The Sixers must have felt they could exploit the talented rookie. But it was the Lakers who took the early lead as Magic Johnson was everywhere. He was moving high and low, passing, rebounding, and starting and finishing the fast break.

The game was close all the way, but in the final minutes Magic once again excelled. He scored nine points down the stretch as the Lakers won the game and the championship, 123-107.

Fans who watched the game in person and on television knew immediately that they had seen a truly great moment. Playing center for the first and only time in his pro career, Magic Johnson scored 42 points, grabbed 15 rebounds, and had seven assists, three steals, and a blocked shot. It was as if he were Bill Russell/Wilt Chamberlain/Kareem Abdul-Jabbar all wrapped into one. An incredible performance.

# It's Cooz in OT

The 1952-1953 season was Bob Cousy's third with the Boston Celtics. That year, the Celtics finished third in the Eastern Division with a 46-25 record. Cousy had produced an oustanding year, finishing third in scoring and leading the league in assists by a wide margin.

In the first round of the playoffs, the Celtics went up against the Syracuse Nationals in a best-of-three series. Boston won the first game, 87-81, at Syracuse, then returned to Boston Garden for a game that would become a classic. For four quarters, it was close. Then Cooz sank a free throw in the closing seconds, tying the score at 77-77 and sending the game into overtime.

In the first overtime, he again had to hit a free throw to tie things at 86-all. Double-overtime. In the second OT, Cousy was on the spot again. This time he had to hit a clutch one-hander to tie the score at 90 and send it into a third overtime.

With 18 seconds left in the third extra session, Syracuse had a 99-94 lead. It looked like the game was over. But then Cooz drove the lane, was knocked down, and somehow made the shot. He added a free throw to cut the lead to two. Seconds later, the Celts stole the ball and gave it to Cousy. He raced downcourt as the seconds ticked off. Just before the buzzer he launched a running, one-handed, 25-foot shot. As the buzzer sounded, the ball swished through the net. It was now 99-99. Cousy's heroics had sent the game into yet another overtime, the fourth.

This time it was all Cooz. After Syracuse took a 104-99 lead, the 6'1" guard brought the Celts back. He hit a foul shot, then a pair of field goals to tie things once more. In the closing minutes, the Celts forged ahead and Cousy controlled the ball with his dribbling. When he was fouled, he connected on his free throws.

When it ended, the Celtics had a 111-105 victory, and Bob Cousy had scored a then playoff record 50 points. Of those, 25 had come in the four five-minute overtimes. Most of them were clutch. In addition, he had hit a remarkable 30 of 32 shots from the foul line. Cooz, of course, would go on to become one of the greatest ever. But back in 1952-1953, he produced one of the greatest moments ever in NBA history.

# Where's Willis?

One of the most courageous and inspiring moments in basketball occurred in the 1969-1970 playoffs, during the final round between the New York Knicks and Los Angeles Lakers. That year the Knicks had reeled off a memorable 18-game winning streak and cruised to the Eastern Division title. The Lakers had their trio of all-time greats: Wilt Chamberlain, Jerry West, and Elgin Baylor.

For the first four games, it went according to script, with the two evenly matched teams splitting the four contests. Knick center Willis Reed was one of the few men in the league with the physical strength to match Wilt. But Willis was playing on tender knees, and at the 3:56 mark of the third quarter of the fifth game, with the Lakers leading 25-15, he took a nasty fall while trying to drive past Wilt. He left the game and did not return.

In his absence, the Knicks switched to a 1-3-1 offense, designed to take Chamberlain away from the hoop, and played their usual trapping, gambling defense. They caught the Lakers midway through the final period and won, 107-100. But Reed was definitely out of game six with a badly torn muscle in his right thigh. If there was a seventh game, maybe. No promises.

The Lakers adjusted and won game six in L.A. easily, 135-113. So it was back to Madison Square Garden, where a packed house came out for the final game. And as the two teams warmed up, everyone was asking the same question: Where's Willis? The Knick captain was nowhere to be seen.

Finally, just minutes before the opening tap, Reed appeared and the Garden erupted in a frenzy. Everyone in the building, including the Lakers, watched the Knick captain take some warm-up shots. As soon as the game began, it was obvious that Reed was dragging his right leg. But as the Knicks got the ball he trailed the play, took a pass, and hit a jumper from behind the key. The Garden went wild again.

Minutes later, Reed hit yet another 20-footer. On defense, he used his strength and bulk to contain the immobile Chamberlain. With Reed providing the inspiration, the Knicks spurted to a 17-8 lead. Guard Walt Frazier was playing a sensational game, and the Knicks led by a score of 69-42 at the half. Early in the third period it was 79-54, and the weary, limping Reed left the game for good. He had scored just four points, those two early jump shots.

From there, the Knicks cruised to the title, winning 113-99. They had done it with their star center virtually playing on one leg. Yet his courage in coming out and going against the 275-pound Chamberlain inspired all the Knicks. It was a great moment, and they prevailed.

# Michael, Michael, and More Michael

In the third game of the 1985-1986 season, Michael Jordan broke his left foot. It happened when he hit the floor after one of his patented slam dunks. It was the start of Michael's second season in the NBA, following a Rookie of the Year campaign in which he averaged 28.2 points a game and looked to be the league's next great superstar.

But the break sidelined him nearly the entire season. He finally returned to play the last 15 games in just a part-time role. Despite a 30-52 record, the Chicago Bulls made the playoffs, and Michael was given the go-ahead to play full-time. In the first round, the Bulls had to go up against the tough Boston Celtics.

Despite the long layoff, Michael was about to create the first of many great moments in a memorable career. In the opener against Larry Bird and company, Michael was nearly unstoppable. He challenged Bird, Kevin McHale, and Robert Parish inside, and went around defensive whiz Dennis Johnson as if he wasn't there. When it ended, Boston had a 134-104 win, but Michael Jordan had 49 points.

If that wasn't enough, he came back in the second game and did even better. When he hit two free throws at the end of regulation, it tied the game at 116-116 and gave him 54 points on the night.

The game would go into double-overtime, with the Celtics finally winning, 135-131. When it ended, however, Michael had played 53 minutes and hit 22 of 41 shots from the floor and 19 of 21 from the foul line. That gave him 63 points on the night, the most points ever scored in a NBA playoff game. Not only had Michael proved he was over his injury, but he showed everyone that he was as good as anyone who had ever played the game.

# Jumpin' Joe Ahead of His Time

His name was Joe Fulks and he's just a distant memory to all but a few old-time and dedicated fans. He was 6'5" and weighed 190

pounds. The Kentucky-born Fulks joined the Philadelphia Warriors for the NBA's first official season of 1946-1947. In an era when most players still took two-handed set shots or an occasional running one-hander, Fulks was taking turnaround jump shots, switching hands in the air, and doing things in what was considered a very unconventional manner.

He wasn't a perfect player. His defense was weak and despite his jumping ability, he wasn't fast. Yet he was the NBA's first scoring champ, averaging 23.2 points that first year, almost seven points better than the next best scorer. But by 1948-1949 the league had a new scoring champ, big George Mikan of the Minneapolis Lakers. In fact, early in the season Mikan had set a league record with 48 points in a game.

On February 10, 1949, Fulks and the Warriors hosted the Indianapolis Jets on a cold and snowy night. With only some 1,500 fans braving the elements, Jumpin' Joe Fulks was about to give the NBA one of its first great moments.

Early in the game it was apparent that Fulks was hot. The Warriors kept getting the ball to him and he was taking those crazy shots of his. But they kept going in. By halftime the Warriors had a 49-38 lead, and Fulks had 30 points, hitting 13 of his 25 attempts.

In the second half, all eyes were on Fulks, and every player on the Indianapolis team took a try at stopping him. None could. Late in the third period Fulks had 47 points. He then grabbed an offensive rebound, whirled, and hit a short, one-hand jumper. He had broken Mikan's record.

Now everyone screamed for Fulks to go higher. Though he was exhausted from a recent stomach ailment, he kept shooting and scoring. With four minutes left he drained a long set shot for his 59th point. His next hoop came on a fast break layup. That made him the first player to crack the 60-point mark with 61. And with less than a minute to go, Fulks took the ball into the corner, then swished a twisting, jumping two-hander, another crazy shot, for his 63rd point of the night.

It was an incredible performance in an era when that wasn't supposed to happen. Fulks set records for points in a half (33), shots attempted (56), and field goals scored (27). All those records have since been broken, but at the time, they were looked upon as almost superhuman. And that's how Joe Fulks must have felt on a snowy night in Philadelphia way back in 1949.

# The Ultimate Winner

If the ultimate great moment comes when a team clinches the championship, then Bill Russell was basketball's ultimate producer of great moments. Russell was the key to the great Boston Celtic dynasty of the 1950s and 1960s. But he started winning even earlier than that.

During his final two seasons at the University of San Francisco, the 6'10" center led the Dons to a pair of NCAA championships. His teams lost just one game during those two years, early in his junior season. He left behind a 51-game winning streak.

The Celtics drafted Russell in the first round, but he first stopped to play for the 1956 United States Olympic basketball team. When he finally joined the Celtics 24 games into the season, he transformed them immediately. Russell was first and foremost a team player, a guy who excelled on the defensive end. He was a wonderful shot blocker and rebounder, an expert at kicking the ball out to start the Celtics' fast break. And, most important of all, he hated to lose—even a single game.

Boston won the championship that year, then lost it to St. Louis the following season when Russell had to sit out with an ankle injury. Then the team set a record for all major sports by winning eight championships in a row. Bill Russell played for 13 seasons and in that time the Celtics won 11 NBA titles, each one an incredible great moment for the players and fans.

Boston's great guard, Bob Cousy, who played on six of the Russell-led title teams, was the other Celtic who had the same obsessive passion for winning. It was Russell and Cousy who set the tone for what would be known as Celtic pride. Add Russell's two NCAA titles to his Celtic totals, and that's 13 championships in 15 years of basketball. How close to perfect can you get?

# The
# NBA

## CHAPTER 6

# Champions

The NBA championship series has always been a best-of-seven contest. Only the preliminary rounds have changed. Early rounds used to be a best-of-three series, and now they are a best-of-five. And, of course, the more teams in the league, the more that make the playoffs. In the early days, six teams were in the playoffs. In 1994-1995, 16 of the league's 27 teams won a playoff berth.

Here is a brief recap of the championship series beginning in 1946-1947: the teams, their coaches, their regular season records, the finals results, the finals MVP (begun in 1969), and a few highlights from each season and the playoffs.

 **1946-1947**

Philadelphia Warriors (35-25, Eddie Gottlieb) defeated Chicago Stags (39-22, Harold Olsen), 4 games to 1

Eddie Gottlieb's Warriors made quick work of the Stags behind the shooting of Joe Fulks, the league's scoring champion.

• • • • • • • • • • • • • • • • • • • • • • • •

**1947-1948**

Baltimore Bullets (28-20, Buddy Jeannette) defeated Philadelphia Warriors (27-21, Eddie Gottlieb), 4 games to 2

The Bullets, a team without a real star, prevailed over Fulks and the Warriors in six games. Howie Dallmar of the Warriors led the league in assists with just 2.5 per game.

• • • • • • • • • • • • • • • • • • • • • • • •

**1948-1949**

Minneapolis Lakers (44-16, John Kundla) defeated Washington Capitols (38-22, Red Auerbach), 4 games to 2

The Lakers had entered the league from the defunct National Basketball League and started the NBA's first dynasty. George Mikan led the league in scoring with a 28.3 average, then averaged 30.3 points in ten playoff games.

• • • • • • • • • • • • • • • • • • • • • • • •

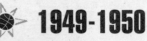 **1949-1950**

Minneapolis Lakers (51-17, John Kundla) defeated Syracuse Nationals (51-13, Al Cervi), 4 games to 2

The league was getting competitive as more top players began coming in. The Nats were led by Dolph Schayes and scrappy player/coach Al Cervi, but they were no match for Minneapolis's Mikan, Jim Pollard, Vern Mikkelsen, and Arnie Ferrin in the finals. This time the 6'10" Mikan averaged 31.3 points in 12 playoff games.

• • • • • • • • • • • • • • • • • • • • • • • •

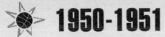

# 1950-1951

Rochester Royals (41-27, Les Harrison) defeated New York Knickerbockers (36-30, Joe Lapchick), 4 games to 3

It was a year in which neither division winner (Philadelphia and Minneapolis) made the finals. Rochester was led by ballhandling whiz Bobby Davies, big Arnie Risen, and Bobby Wanzer. The Knicks got outstanding play from Vince Boryla, Harry "The Horse" Gallatin, and Max Zaslofsky but lost the seventh game, 79-75.

· · · · · · · · · · · · · · · · · · · · · · · · · · · · ·

# 1951-1952

Minneapolis Lakers (40-26, John Kundla) defeated New York Knickerbockers (37-29, Joe Lapchick), 4 games to 3

The Lakers reclaimed league supremacy. In the playoffs, Mikan again dominated underneath, averaging 15.9 rebounds in 13 games. The Lakers won the deciding game, 82-65.

· · · · · · · · · · · · · · · · · · · · · · · · · · · · ·

# 1952-1953

Minneapolis Lakers (48-22, John Kundla) defeated New York Knickerbockers (47-23, Joe Lapchick), 4 games to 1

This time the Lakers made it look easier, winning four straight after the Knicks took the opener. Mikan was second in scoring to Philly's Neil Johnston, but he was still the league's best rebounder at 14.4. The Knicks had a fine backcourt with Carl Braun and Dick McGuire, but the Minneapolis front line of Mikan, Pollard, and Mikkelsen was too strong.

· · · · · · · · · · · · · · · · · · · · · · · · · · · · ·

# 1953-1954

Minneapolis Lakers (46-26, John Kundla) defeated Syracuse Nationals (42-30, Al Cervi), 4 games to 3

On paper, the Lakers had the league's best team, but the playoffs were a struggle. Mikan brought them through in seven games, as they won the finale at Minneapolis, 87-80. It was the Lakers' fifth title in six years, but the NBA's first superteam and dynasty was about to lose its prime mover. Just after the season, Mikan announced his retirement. He made a brief comeback two years later, but he wasn't the same player. And the Lakers weren't the same team.

## 1954-1955

Syracuse Nationals (43-29, Al Cervi) defeated Fort Wayne Pistons (43-29, Charles Eckman), 4 games to 3

The seventh game was a 92-91 squeaker. Dolph Schayes and Paul Seymour led the Nats, while the Pistons featured big Larry Foust, George Yardley, and Mel Hutchins.

## 1955-1956

Philadelphia Warriors (45-27, George Senesky) defeated Fort Wayne Pistons (37-35, Charles Eckman), 4 games to 1

Bob Pettit of St. Louis was the new league scoring king, but Paul Arizin and Neil Johnston of Philly were right behind and were one-two in field goal percentage. Philadelphia guard Jack George was second to Boston's Bob Cousy in assists, and Philadelphia rookie Tom Gola was fourth. No doubt the Warriors had the best team in the league. But everything was about to change.

## 1956-1957

Boston Celtics (44-28, Red Auerbach) defeated St. Louis Hawks (34-38, Alex Hannum), 4 games to 3

This was the year Bill Russell joined the Celtics. From his first day, he made them the best team in the league. He had help, of course, from Cousy, Bill Sharman, Tom Heinsohn, Frank Ramsey, and Jim Loscutoff. The 34-38 Hawks carried the Celts to seven games. The deciding contest at Boston was a classic, going into double overtime. The Celtics prevailed, 125-123, but only after Bob Pettit, playing with a cast on his broken left wrist, missed a short shot at the buzzer.

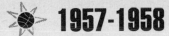

# 1957-1958

St. Louis Hawks (41-31, Alex Hannum) defeated Boston Celtics (49-23, Red Auerbach), 4 games to 2

It looked like the Celtics all the way until Bill Russell hurt his ankle and couldn't play in the final two games of the championship series. Even without Russell, it took a magnificent 50-point performance by the 6'9" Pettit for the Hawks to win the championship, 110-109.

• • • • • • • • • • • • • • • • • • • • • • • • • • •

# 1958-1959

Boston Celtics (52-20, Red Auerbach) defeated Minneapolis Lakers (33-39, John Kundla), 4 games to 0

Though the Hawks were division champs at 49-23, the sub-.500 Lakers upset them in the division semifinals, behind a sensational rookie forward named Elgin Baylor. The Celtics also had to struggle in the semis against Syracuse. But against the Lakers, the Celtics had things their way. It was the first time ever a final series was decided by a four-game sweep.

• • • • • • • • • • • • • • • • • • • • • • • • • • •

# 1959-1960

Boston Celtics (59-16, Red Auerbach) defeated St. Louis Hawks (46-29, Ed Macauley), 4 games to 3

Playoff basketball was beginning to get a reputation as a special kind of game, played on a higher level than the regular season. In the seventh game of the finals, Boston's superiority finally prevailed as the Celts won, 122-103. Russell and the Celts had faced and beaten a new challenge this year—a 7'1" rookie named Wilt Chamberlain, who had joined Philadelphia.

• • • • • • • • • • • • • • • • • • • • • • • • • • •

# 1960-1961

Boston Celtics (57-22, Red Auerbach) defeated St. Louis Hawks (51-28, Paul Seymour), 4 games to 1

This time around the Celtics showed their strength, beating the Hawks handily. It was a year in which another pair of outstanding rookies came in, Oscar Robertson with Cincinnati and Jerry West with the Lakers (who had moved to Los Angeles).

## 1961-1962

Boston Celtics (60-20, Red Auerbach) defeated Los Angeles Lakers (54-26, Fred Schaus), 4 games to 3

This was the beginning of an incredible rivalry that would carry over through the 1980s. The Lakers had superstars Baylor and West, while the Celtics had the usual cast of characters. The Lakers battled to a 3-2 lead with Baylor setting a playoff record of 61 points in one game. Boston was forced to win game six in L.A., 119-105, then the deciding contest in Boston, 110-107, in overtime.

## 1962-1963

Boston Celtics (58-22, Red Auerbach) defeated Los Angeles Lakers (53-27, Fred Schaus), 4 games to 2

This time it was easier, though the Celts had a tough time with the pesky Cincinnati Royals in the semifinals. The Lakers put up a fight but still couldn't get over the wall known as Russell and the Celtics. Boston clinched this one in the sixth game at Los Angeles.

## 1963-1964

Boston Celtics (59-21, Red Auerbach) defeated San Francisco Warriors (48-32, Alex Hannum), 4 games to 1

This one was supposed to be closer because it was Russell vs. Chamberlain. Wilt and the Warriors had moved from Philly to San Francisco the year before. But it followed a familiar pattern. Wilt would win the battle (better stats) but Russell the war. It was the first year the Celtics played without the great Bob Cousy (who had retired), but a second-year pro named John Havlicek from Ohio State would prove a superstar in his own right. Plus Sam Jones and K. C. Jones (no relation) now formed a great Boston backcourt.

## 1964-1965

Boston Celtics (62-18, Red Auerbach) defeated Los Angeles Lakers (49-31, Fred Schaus), 4 games to 1

Boston won the first game, 142-110, and the last, 129-96, to pretty much show how things were in 1964-1965. It's more amazing how the Celtics dominated the era when you look at the names on the other rosters: Chamberlain, West, Robertson, Baylor, Bellamy, Reed, Lucas, Beaty, Thurmond, Rodgers, Wilkens. The Celts had now won an unprecedented seven straight championships. Despite losing, the Lakers' Jerry West averaged an amazing 40.6 points in 11 playoff games.

## 1965-1966

Boston Celtics (55-25, Red Auerbach) defeated Los Angeles Lakers (45-35, Fred Schaus), 4 games to 3

What did the Lakers have to do to win? Boston had a 3-1 lead when the Lakers came back to win the fifth game at Boston and sixth at L.A. Then came the deciding contest at Boston Garden, and the Lakers ... almost did it. But the Celtic magic prevailed as they took their eighth straight title with a 95-93 victory.

## 1966-1967

Philadelphia 76ers (68-13, Alex Hannum) defeated San Francisco Warriors (44-37, Bill Sharman), 4 games to 2

At long last another team won an NBA title. Wilt was back in Philly, joined by the likes of Hal Greer, Chet Walker, Billy Cunningham, Wally Jones, and Luke Jackson. It was a great team that set a regular season mark and then rolled through the playoffs. San Francisco had league scoring champ Rick Barry, who scored 55 points in one of the title games. But the victory was especially sweet for Chamberlain, since many had said he couldn't lead a team to the championship.

 ## 1967-1968

Boston Celtics (54-28, Bill Russell) defeated Los Angeles Lakers (52-30, Bill van Breda Kolff), 4 games to 2

Now the Celtics were growing to legendary proportions. Russell was a young coach but an aging player. The team finished eight games behind Philly in the regular season. But when they met in the division finals, they rallied from a 3-1 deficit to win the series in seven games. Then they did their usual number on the Lakers, winning game six, 124-109, to capture a tenth title in 12 years.

 ## 1968-1969

Boston Celtics (48-34, Bill Russell) defeated Los Angeles Lakers (55-27, Bill van Breda Kolff), 4 games to 3

This was the most amazing win of all. The Celts were fourth in the East during the regular season, but then they whipped Philly in five games and the Knicks in six to win the division. Next came the Lakers, a team that now had Wilt Chamberlain in the middle to go with Baylor and West. It came down to a seventh game in Los Angeles, and the Celtic magic worked one more time. Boston won it, 108-106, for their 11th title in 13 years. And right after it ended, Bill Russell and Sam Jones retired. The Celtic dynasty was over.

Finals MVP: Jerry West, Los Angeles

 ## 1969-1970

New York Knickerbockers (60-22, Red Holzman) defeated Los Angeles Lakers (46-36, Joe Mullaney), 4 games to 3

These Knicks played an incredible team game emphasizing ball movement and defense. They won their division by four games over the fast-closing Milwaukee Bucks and star rookie Lew Alcindor (who later became Kareem Abdul-Jabbar). Knick center Willis Reed played the seventh game of the final with a badly torn thigh muscle. L.A. had now suffered seven straight losses in the finals the team reached since moving from Minneapolis.

Finals MVP: Willis Reed, New York

# 1970-1971

Milwaukee Bucks (66-16, Larry Costello) defeated Baltimore Bullets (42-40, Gene Shue), 4 games to 0

The Milwaukee Bucks left no doubt as to the best team of 1970-1971, having added veteran Oscar Robertson to a club already featuring young Lew Alcindor (Kareem Abdul-Jabbar). Alcindor led the league in scoring; Robertson was third in assists. The playoffs were easy. The Bucks defeated the Warriors in five games, 4-1; beat the Lakers in five games, 4-1; and then swept the Bullets.

Finals MVP: Lew Alcindor, Milwaukee

# 1971-1972

Los Angeles Lakers (69-13, Bill Sharman) defeated New York Knickerbockers (48-34, Red Holzman), 4 games to 1

At long last, the Lakers put it all together. First they set a new regular season record with a 69-13 mark. Then in the playoffs, Chamberlain, West, and company topped Chicago, 4-0, beat the 63-19 Bucks, 4-2, and easily erased the Knicks, 4-1. The Lakers had been five-time champs in Minneapolis, but this was their first win in eight finals tries in L.A. It was a long time coming and it was worth it.

Finals MVP: Wilt Chamberlain, Los Angeles

# 1972-1973

New York Knickerbockers (57-25, Red Holzman) defeated Los Angeles Lakers (60-22, Bill Sharman), 4 games to 1

The Knicks had just the fourth best record in the league, and star center Willis Reed was playing on knees so fragile that he wasn't the same force in the middle. Yet in the conference finals, the Knicks topped the 68-14 Celtics (with an injured and subpar John Havlicek), winning the seventh game, 94-78, at Boston. Surprisingly, the Lakers fell in five as Reed turned back the clock and played very well. Following the season, Wilt Chamberlain retired.

Finals MVP: Willis Reed, New York

# 1973-1974

Boston Celtics (56-26, Tom Heinsohn) defeated Milwaukee Bucks (59-23, Larry Costello), 4 games to 3

Boston won the title they felt they should have won the year before. Havlicek was still there, joined by Dave Cowens, Jo Jo White, and Paul Silas. The Celtics cruised into the finals, then had a real struggle against Abdul-Jabbar and the Bucks. As usual, Boston won the seventh game, this time at Milwaukee, 102-77.

Finals MVP: John Havlicek, Boston

# 1974-1975

Golden State Warriors (48-34, Al Attles) defeated Washington Bullets (60-22, K. C. Jones), 4 games to 0

A real shocker. The Bullets couldn't win a game in the finals. Golden State had high-scoring Rick Barry and a team of role players behind him. The Bullets had Elvin Hayes, Wes Unseld, Phil Chenier, Mike Riordan, and Kevin Porter. Go figure. The league was full of new stars—Elvin Hayes, Wes Unseld, Bob Lanier, Bob McAdoo, Spencer Haywood, Pete Maravich, Sidney Wicks, Nate Archibald, Calvin Murphy—and it still had Abdul-Jabbar. But the Warriors won the title.

Finals MVP: Rick Barry, Golden State

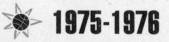

# 1975-1976

Boston Celtics (54-28, Tom Heinsohn) defeated Phoenix Suns (42-40, John MacLeod), 4 games to 2

It took the Phoenix Suns just seven years to go from expansion to the NBA finals. Paul Westphal and Alvan Adams led this surprising team to playoff wins over Seattle and 59-23 Golden State before they came up short against the Celtics. Game five, however, was a classic, a triple-overtime thriller that the Celtics won, 128-126.

Finals MVP: Jo Jo White, Boston

# 1976-1977

Portland Trail Blazers (49-33, Jack Ramsay) defeated Philadelphia 76ers (50-32, Gene Shue), 4 games to 2

With four ABA teams joining the league, the NBA was up to 22 teams and many more great players. Yet the final series was a big surprise. A young Portland team, with center Bill Walton healthy, faced the 76ers with stars Julius Erving, George McGinnis, Doug Collins, and Lloyd Free (later known as World B. Free). When the Sixers won the first two, it looked like it was over. But suddenly Portland stormed back and won the next four to take their first championship. More teams, more upsets, more interest.

Finals MVP: Bill Walton, Portland

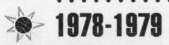

# 1977-1978

Washington Bullets (44-38, Dick Motta) defeated Seattle SuperSonics (47-35, Lenny Wilkens), 4 games to 3

An odd series in that neither finalist was a division winner. The Bullets and Sonics battled for seven games until the Bullets won, 105-99. It was beginning to look like a balanced league with many teams in the hunt.

Finals MVP: Wes Unseld, Washington

# 1978-1979

Seattle SuperSonics (52-30, Lenny Wilkens) defeated Washington Bullets (54-28, Dick Motta), 4 games to 1

The Celtics were last in their division, the Lakers third, and the Knicks fourth. The Sonics were far from a super team, but they had solid, efficient players who meshed very well and a strong back-court of Gus Williams, Dennis Johnson, and "Downtown" Freddie Brown. Washington had Elvin Hayes and Wes Unseld but had to battle just to reach the final. So the roles reversed from the year before, Seattle winning easily.

Finals MVP: Dennis Johnson, Seattle

# 1979-1980

Los Angeles Lakers (60-22, Paul Westhead) defeated Philadelphia 76ers (59-23, Billy Cunningham), 4 games to 2

The Celtics went from last to first with rookie Larry Bird in the lineup, while the Lakers added Magic Johnson to a cast that already included Kareem Abdul-Jabbar. But the Celts were upset by Julius Erving and the Sixers in the conference finals. Then Magic and the Lakers went to work, winning the final game at Philly, 123-107. This was the game in which Johnson played center for an injured Abdul-Jabbar and scored 42 points with 15 rebounds and seven assists.

Finals MVP: Magic Johnson, Los Angeles

# 1980-1981

Boston Celtics (62-20, Bill Fitch) defeated Houston Rockets (40-42, Del Harris), 4 games to 2

Another title for the Celtics. Larry Bird, Kevin McHale, Nate Archibald, Robert Parish, Cedric Maxwell—a very solid team. The Rockets had Moses Malone, Calvin Murphy, and Rudy Tomjanovich, but they were no match for the Celts.

Finals MVP: Cedric Maxwell, Boston

# 1981-1982

Los Angeles Lakers (57-25, Pat Riley) defeated Philadelphia 76ers (58-24, Billy Cunningham), 4 games to 2

The solid Sixers upset the 63-19 Celtics in the conference finals, delaying the anticipated finals matchup between Magic Johnson and Larry Bird. In the finals, Julius Erving and company couldn't handle the Magic Man and Kareem.

Finals MVP: Magic Johnson, Los Angeles

# 1982-1983

Philadelphia 76ers (65-17, Billy Cunningham) defeated Los Angeles Lakers (58-24, Pat Riley), 4 games to 0

Philadelphia acquired center Moses Malone and became the best team in the league. The Sixers swept New York, lost just once in the conference finals to Milwaukee, and then swept the Lakers. Los Angeles lost Bob McAdoo and rookie James Worthy to injury and just couldn't keep up with the powerful Sixers.

Finals MVP: Moses Malone, Philadelphia

# 1983-1984

Boston Celtics (62-20, K. C. Jones) defeated Los Angeles Lakers (54-28, Pat Riley), 4 games to 3

This was the one everyone wanted: Magic against Bird, the Lakers against the Celtics, the old rivalry revisited. Two of the games went into overtime, each won by the Celtics. Each team won one game on the other's home court. It finally came down to a seventh at Boston, and the Celtics prevailed, 111-102. Bird averaged 27.5 points in 23 playoff games, while Magic set a record with 21 assists in a single game in the finals.

Finals MVP: Larry Bird, Boston

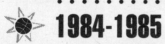
# 1984-1985

Los Angeles Lakers (62-20, Pat Riley) defeated Boston Celtics (63-19, K. C. Jones), 4 games to 2

These were clearly the two best teams in the league. In addition, the team rivalry and the individual rivalry (Magic vs. Bird) were helping to attract new legions of fans to the NBA. Boston buried the Lakers in the opener, 148-114, but after that Abdul-Jabbar and L.A. took over, winning four of the next five. At age 38, the big guy proved he could still dominate a game.

Finals MVP: Kareem Abdul-Jabbar, Los Angeles

# 1985-1986

Boston Celtics (67-15, K. C. Jones) defeated Houston Rockets (51-31, Bill Fitch), 4 games to 2

It was a Celtic year all the way, with a great regular season record and a relatively easy march to yet another title. Houston had the Twin Towers, 7'4" Ralph Sampson and 7'0" Hakeem Olajuwon. But Boston's experience and defensive strength was too much for Houston.

Finals MVP: Larry Bird, Boston

# 1986-1987

Los Angeles Lakers (65-17, Pat Riley) defeated Boston Celtics (59-23, K. C. Jones), 4 games to 2

This time it was the Lakers' year. Abdul-Jabbar was 40 by playoff time and still a marvel. And Magic, James Worthy, Byron Scott, Michael Cooper, and Mychal Thompson all had outstanding seasons. Boston had the same cast of characters, but Kevin McHale was playing with a broken bone in his foot and the rest of the Celtics couldn't run with the Lakers. Incidentally, during the regular season a third-year pro with the Chicago Bulls, Michael Jordan, won the scoring title with an amazing 37.1 average.

Finals MVP: Magic Johnson, Los Angeles

# 1987-1988

Los Angeles Lakers (62-20, Pat Riley) defeated Detroit Pistons (54-28, Chuck Daly), 4 games to 3

The Pistons were the new kids on the block, a solid team that played a very physical defense, which helped lower scores and set the stage for what other teams would do in the early 1990s. Center Bill Laimbeer and forwards Rick Mahorn and Dennis Rodman were the resident bad boys, while guards Isiah Thomas, Joe Dumars, and Vinnie Johnson could fill the hoop. The Lakers had to win the sixth game, 103-102, and the seventh, 108-105, to win their fifth title of the decade.

Finals MVP: James Worthy, Los Angeles

 # 1988-1989

Detroit Pistons (63-19, Chuck Daly) defeated Los Angeles Lakers (57-25, Pat Riley), 4 games to 0

This was a year that officially marked the changing of the guard in the NBA. Boston was third in its division as Larry Bird missed nearly the entire season with injury. L.A. won its division, but Kareem was in his final season at age 42. Hamstring injuries to Magic and Byron Scott finished L.A. against Detroit, which won four straight to capture the crown.

Finals MVP: Joe Dumars, Detroit

# 1989-1990

Detroit Pistons (59-23, Chuck Daly) defeated Portland Trail Blazers (59-23, Rick Adelman), 4 games to 1

The Portland Trail Blazers found they couldn't mix it up with the bad boys from Detroit. The Pistons made it two straight with their usual brand of basketball mayhem and talent. They were a team that kept coming at you and wore you down. Clyde Drexler led the Blazers.

Finals MVP: Isiah Thomas, Detroit

# 1990-1991

Chicago Bulls (61-21, Phil Jackson) defeated Los Angeles Lakers (58-24, Mike Dunleavy), 4 games to 1

The post-Kareem Lakers were still formidable because of the continued brilliance of Magic Johnson. But the Bulls had had the best basketball player on the planet for several years and now had surrounded Michael Jordan with additional talent. Chicago swept the aging Pistons in the conference finals, and then, after losing the first game to L.A., won four straight for their first NBA crown. Jordan had won his fifth straight scoring title in the regular season and averaged 31.1 points in the playoffs.

Finals MVP: Michael Jordan, Chicago

# 1991-1992

Chicago Bulls (67-15, Phil Jackson) defeated Portland Trail Blazers (57-25, Rick Adelman), 4 games to 2

This was the year the Bulls established themselves as basketball's best team, putting together a brilliant regular season and moving easily through the playoffs with the exception of a seven-game battle with the Knicks in the conference semifinals. Jordan averaged 34.5 points in 22 playoff games. One other note: Prior to the season, Magic Johnson retired because he had HIV, the virus that causes AIDS.

Finals MVP: Michael Jordan, Chicago

# 1992-1993

Chicago Bulls (57-25, Phil Jackson) defeated Phoenix Suns (62-20, Paul Westphal), 4 games to 2

This season brought about a new term: three-peat. Could the Bulls become the first team since the Celtics in the 1960s to win three straight titles? Both the Knicks and Suns had better records in the regular season, but the Bulls still had Michael Jordan. Chicago topped the Knicks in six in the conference finals, then did the same thing to the Charles Barkley-led Suns. Jordan put together games of 31, 42, 44, 55, 41, and 33 points to set a finals record with a 41.0 average. Then months after the season, Jordan shocked the basketball world by announcing his retirement.

Finals MVP: Michael Jordan, Chicago

# 1993-1994

Houston Rockets (58-24, Rudy Tomjanovich) defeated New York Knickerbockers (57-25, Pat Riley), 4 games to 3

The city of Houston rejoiced when the Rockets brought it the first championship of any kind in more than three decades. With Magic, Bird, and now Jordan gone, Houston center Hakeem Olajuwon was nearly unanimously acclaimed the best player in the NBA, at least for 1993-1994. New York played a physical, pounding defensive game that kept scores down and brought criticism from many who said the game was getting boring.

Finals MVP: Hakeem Olajuwon, Houston

# 1994-1995

Houston Rockets (47-35, Rudy Tomjanovich) defeated Orlando Magic (57-25, Brian Hill), 4 games to 0

The Houston Rockets not only made it two straight NBA titles, but they did it in a most unlikely way. After a mediocre regular season, the Rockets started the playoffs from the sixth-seeded position, never had the home court advantage, and had to win "must" road games on several occasions. A controversial midseason trade brought veteran Clyde Drexler to Houston, reuniting him with former college teammate Hakeem Olajuwon. The two were instrumental in a great comeback against Phoenix in the semifinals, rallying the team from a 3-1 deficit. The Rockets then defeated the San Antonio Spurs (an NBA best 62-20) in six games in the Western Conference finals before sweeping the young Orlando Magic in four. Along the way the team set a playoff record with nine road wins. In addition to Olajuwon and Drexler, Robert Horry, Sam Cassell, Kenny Smith, and Mario Elie all raised the level of their games in the playoffs. It was a title to remember.

Finals MVP: Hakeem Olajuwon, Houston

There they are, 49 NBA champions. Not surprisingly, the Boston Celtics have the most titles, 16, while the Lakers are next with 11. That's 27 titles between just two franchises, more than half of the total. The Lakers have been to the most finals. Besides winning 11 times, they've been beaten in the final round on 13 occasions. Boston, while winning 16, has lost just three times.

Other multiple winners include the Chicago Bulls (three), the Philadelphia/Golden State Warriors (three), the Syracuse Nationals/Philadelphia 76ers (three), the Detroit Pistons (two), the New York Knicks (two), and the Houston Rockets (two). Seven other teams have won just once. So with the exception of the Celtics and Lakers, the NBA title has always been hard to come by.

# Some Unusual Pro Basketball Moments

CHAPTER 7

**P**rofessional basketball has come a long way since its humble beginnings in basements and dance halls. As in any sport, there have been many strange, interesting, and unusual moments and zany characters along the way. Many come from the early days of the game, but some have also been part of the modern-day version of hoops. Players are players, and that means pro ball has always abounded with individuals, many of whom march to the tune of their own drummer.

Here are just some of the things that make basketball more than just passing, shooting, and rebounding.

# Where Are the Jet Planes?

Nat Holman, one of the greatest players from the early days of the game, remembered the travel conditions of the early pros. Sometimes barnstorming teams would play two games in one day. One time he and the Original Celtics took a train overnight from New York to Michigan for an afternoon game just outside Detroit. The team was already tired because there weren't enough berths on the train and some of the players were up all night.

After the game, the seven players piled into one car, put their baggage on top, and began a 125-mile drive to their night game in Battle Creek, Michigan. Just outside of town it began snowing, and soon they were driving through a terrible blizzard. They got to the arena in time to see the fans leaving. Because the promoter didn't want to return the money, the team had to stay and play the next night.

Holman also remembered taking a train out of New York City to play in Bridgeport, Connecticut. There was just one train back to New York at night, and so the players always kept one eye on the clock and one on the game. They didn't want to get stuck overnight.

"We would play our game, throw our sweaters on, and carry the rest of our clothes as we ran for the train," Holman said. "Someone got ice cream and sandwiches for the trip back. It was really a trying situation, very tiring."

# Dollars and Cents

In today's NBA, the million-dollar contract is the norm, a starting point for negotiations. How many millions? How many years? But it wasn't always that way. There was a time when a pro basketball player was embarrassed to admit how *little* he made.

Matt Guokas, Sr.—whose son Matt, Jr., has been an NBA player and coach and a commentator—recalled playing back in the 1930s. Guokas played for the Brooklyn Visitations of the old American League. There were no long-term contracts. Rather, the players were paid on a per game basis.

"You were almost embarrassed to tell anyone what you were making," Guokas once admitted. "If you went home with $30 or $35 in your pocket, it was a big deal. Most of the leagues played weekends, so I had a job in a ball-bearing factory in Philadelphia and even coached a high school team while playing pro ball.

"But none of us who played then looked down on basketball as an inferior or minor league sport. It was our game and we played it."

You just didn't get rich.

# Officiating Can Be Dangerous to Your Health

Sid Borgia was a recognizable figure on NBA courts in the 1950s and 1960s. He didn't have a good jump shot, couldn't shoot a hook, and couldn't make a behind-the-back pass. But Sid Borgia could control a basketball game with his whistle. He was a referee who took his job as seriously as Bob Cousy or Wilt Chamberlain took theirs.

Only Borgia's job was sometimes more dangerous. In the early days of the league, rivalries were intense and fans got as emotional as the players. Borgia remembered how the fans in Syracuse hated the Boston Celtics, and whenever the Celts were in town, the fans came out with a vengeance.

On this particular night, the Nats were on their game and leading the Celtics by about 20 with just three minutes left. Borgia was standing at center court when a fan suddenly hollered, "Hey, Borgia, if you had any guts you'd call a technical foul on [Boston Coach Red] Auerbach!"

Never one to back down, Borgia said, "Any time you want to try my guts, let me know." He figured that would be the end of it. But the fan didn't want it that way.

"What about right now?" the fan shouted. And with that, he ran out on the court and grabbed Borgia. The ref had to defend himself and began throwing punches, knocking a couple of teeth out of the heckler's mouth. And that *still* wasn't the end of it.

After he left town, Borgia learned the fan had pressed charges and there was a warrant out for his arrest. But basketball had to come first. All parties agreed to let the matter go until after the play-offs. Then a number of fans testified in the ref's behalf and the charges were finally dropped.

"With all the fans who always seemed to be against me when I reffed," Borgia said, "I was really surprised how many were willing to go out of their way to testify for me."

And who said everyone hates the refs?

# The 24-Second Rule

Anyone who watches NBA basketball knows about the 24-second rule. Whenever the ball changes possession, the team getting possession has 24 seconds to put up a shot. If they don't, it's a violation and the ball goes back to the other team.

The NBA has had the 24-second rule since the 1954-1955 season—a long time. The reason was simple. League officials wanted to eliminate stalling, speed the game up, and allow for more scoring. They figured that would stimulate fan interest. But there was one game some four years earlier that is always pointed to as the real reason for the beginning of the 24-second rule.

It was played November 22, 1950, at Minneapolis. George Mikan and the powerful Lakers were hosting the Fort Wayne Pistons. The Fort Wayne coach, Murray Mendenhall, decided there was only one way to win in Minneapolis: Hold the ball. For much of the game, he ordered his players to just stand there with the ball, make a pass once in a while, and hold it again.

The Lakers didn't challenge and the game was played at a snail's pace. The fans seemed to be falling asleep, when they weren't booing. Finally, with just a few seconds left, the Lakers held a one-point lead. But that one-point lead was by the unlikely score of 18-17.

Fort Wayne had the ball and gave it to their big center, Larry Foust. Foust got the ball behind the foul line and saw Mikan standing there, hands in the air like a goalpost. He shot a one-hander between Mikan's arms and it went into the hoop as the buzzer sounded.

As Foust said, "It was a stinking ball game, a rotten ball game." It was also, at 19-18, the lowest-scoring game in NBA history. Several years later, when teams began stalling again, the league finally decided to do something about it. Hence, the 24-second rule. It's been there ever since.

# What's a Tri-Cities?

Bob Cousy and the Boston Celtics—to basketball fans everywhere, the two nearly always go together. Cousy, of course, is the Hall of Fame former star guard of the Celts, who helped establish the winning tradition and Celtic pride, which meant you gave 100 percent every single game.

But had it not been for a strange twist of fate, Bob Cousy might never have played in Boston, and never been united with Bill Russell. And who knows how many of those Celtics championships never would have happened.

Cooz was an All-American at Holy Cross in Massachusetts during the 1949-1950 season. When it came time for the NBA draft that year, Boston's Red Auerbach passed the Cooz by, picking 6'11" Charlie Share of Bowling Green. Cousy waited, then learned he had been drafted by Tri-Cities. That's when he asked the classic question: "What's a Tri-Cities?"

He didn't even know where the franchise was located. The answer was Moline, Illinois, though the team played home games at two other Illinois cities as well. Hence, Tri-Cities. But before the new season started, Tri-Cities traded Cooz to the Chicago Stags. Then the Stags franchise folded. Their players had to be divided up among the other teams in the league.

When there were just three players left, Commissioner Maurice Podoloff decided to settle the issue in a logical way—put the names

of the three players in a hat and let the
Knicks, Warriors, and Celtics each
draw a name.

The Knicks drew first and picked
Max Zaslofsky, an all-star. They were
overjoyed. Next came Philly. They drew
the paper with veteran guard Andy
Phillip's name on it. A good choice for
them. Auerbach looked disgusted. The
two players he wanted were gone. He
was "stuck" with Cousy.

Well, the player Auerbach was
stuck with was later described by team owner Walter Brown as having
saved the franchise. Bob Cousy might have asked what a Tri-Cities
was, but he sure knew what a basketball was and what to do with it.

# When the Game Was Getting Foul

The NBA was just trying to find its legs in the late 1940s and early
1950s. Franchises were coming and going, and all teams were trying
to find an edge, any way to win basketball games. One result of this
was a game that was getting rougher and rougher, with fouls being
called more and more often. Fouling became a technique for winning—and for dull basketball.

There was no 24-second clock then, so the team with the lead
would begin stalling. The defensive team would then foul a player. If
the shot was made, the team leading the game wouldn't want to allow
a field goal. Then they would be trading their one-point foul shot for a
two-point field goal. So they would foul the other team immediately.

This system of trading fouls led to a game where the two teams
were walking from one foul line to the other. The sound of the ref's whistle was heard more than the sound of the ball going through the hoop.

Still another technique was for a team to send out a little-used
substitute and have him provoke the other team's star into a fight.
That way, both players would be ejected, but one team would lose a
star, the other a lowly sub. A perfect example was the 1953 four-
overtime game between Boston and Syracuse. It was a game in
which Boston's Bob Cousy scored 50 points.

But the game had something else. Some 107 fouls were called

and 130 foul shots taken. Of Cousy's 50 points, 30 came as a result of the 32 free throws he was awarded. Also, 11 players fouled out. Early in the game, Celtic reserve Bob Brannum provoked a fight with Syracuse star Dolph Schayes. Both were ejected, and Schayes couldn't compete in a big game.

It was like that in the regular season as well. In other words, the NBA was becoming foul. To speed up the game and eliminate excessive fouling, in 1954-1955 the league limited a team to six fouls a quarter. Beyond that, bonus free throws were awarded. The constant foul trading stopped.

## Taking the Game Too Seriously

Over the years there have been all kinds of basketball coaches. But perhaps no coach became so caught up in the game of basketball as Joe Lapchick. Lapchick's court roots went way back. He was a star center for the Original Celtics and later a successful college coach at St. John's and pro coach with the New York Knicks.

Lapchick's excitability came out in many ways. But when game

and coach got too intense, something else would happen. Lapchick would pass out, literally faint. While coach at St. John's, he once fainted when the team was behind in a big game, only to awaken to find they had a ten-point lead. Lapchick was able to joke about that. "When I fainted, we were behind," he quipped. "When I woke up, we were ahead. That dealt coaching one heck of a blow."

Coaching the Knicks in 1952, Lapchick became more and more upset as he watched the Fort Wayne Pistons slowly chip away at what had been a big Knick lead. When the Pistons won in the final seconds, Lapchick staggered off the court and passed out in the locker room. He had to spend three days in the hospital recovering from that one.

Another time Lapchick fainted after having cut a likable player from the Knick team. He felt so bad that his nerves caused him to pass out. On another occasion, after watching his Knicks blow a 12-point lead in the last five minutes, the coach began sobbing on the bench and later didn't remember doing it.

In those days, smoking was allowed on the bench, and Lapchick would often smoke an entire pack of cigarettes during a game. A fine coach, yes, but perhaps one who should have found a less taxing profession.

# Blowing More Smoke

Joe Lapchick smoked cigarettes on the bench to settle his nerves. But Boston's Red Auerbach smoked for a different reason. Auerbach, of course, coached basketball's greatest dynasty, the Boston Celtics of the 1950s and 1960s. He was on the bench when the Celts won eight NBA titles in a row and nine in ten years.

Auerbach was a coach who looked for every single edge, even if it meant rubbing his opposing coaches the wrong way. A lifelong cigar smoker, Auerbach always brought a big stogie to the games. Whenever he felt his team had the game in hand, whether it be midway through the third quarter or in the final minutes, he would fire up the stogie and puff away contentedly as the opposing team and coaches burned in their own way.

Whenever Red lit up at the Boston Garden, the fans would go crazy. They loved the tradition and their coach. And maybe the Celtics played just a little harder, trying to get a big enough lead to allow their coach the luxury of an early smoke.

There was one game in the mid-1960s when the Celtics went up against archrival Los Angeles at the Boston Garden. The Celtics came out on absolute fire. Bill Russell was blocking shot after shot, getting rebounds, and starting the fast break. At the other end, the Celts were finishing the break or simply hitting their shots. Before the first quarter ended, they were up by more than 20 points, and what did Auerbach do? He fired up a victory cigar, maybe the earliest on record. The fans went nuts and the players didn't dare lose that lead.

Red Auerbach would have fit in perfectly with the in-your-face basketball of today.

# Madison Square Garden It Wasn't

When the NBA began in 1946-1947, it was at first called the Basketball Association of America (BAA). At that time, there was also a rival league, the National Basketball League (NBL). The NBL may have had better players and better teams in the mid-1940s. Included in the NBL were the Syracuse Nationals, the Rochester Royals, and the Minneapolis Lakers with George Mikan. But what the NBL didn't have was big arenas. That was the advantage the BAA and later the NBA had. Some of the places the NBL players had to perform in were ridiculous.

For instance, there was the Edgerton Park Arena in Rochester, New York. The Rochester Royals had an outstanding team then, but the arena was so small that the backboards were attached to the walls at both ends of the arena. Players driving to the hoop had three choices: stop on a dime, run into the wall, or run right through the doors into the night.

The Royals would have attendants at each end of the court. Their job was to open the doors whenever a player drove to the hoop. And you never knew what would happen when players went out those doors.

During the winter they would often plow into snowdrifts and come back into the game with snow all over their shoes and legs. Sometimes a fan would arrive late and would just be ready to come in the door when a player would barrel through at full speed. There were some unexpected collisions that way too.

After a while, most guys learned to veer into the wall without getting hurt. They just didn't like the option of the open doors. You never knew what was waiting outside in the cold.

# From Pizza to MVP

Anyone who has seen the Phoenix Suns' Charles Barkley play knows he is seeing the real goods. Sir Charles is one of the NBA's best and one of its more ferocious competitors. Following the 1992-1993 season, this great veteran and future Hall of Famer was deservedly named the league's Most Valuable Player. At 6'6", 255 pounds, Barkley combines power and finesse as perhaps no other player ever has.

But it wasn't always that way. During his first couple of years at Auburn University, Sir Charles didn't take the game quite as seriously, practicing and playing hard only when he felt like it. His most serious business then was apparently eating pizza. And he showed it, his weight going as high as 305 pounds.

At the Auburn campus he quickly acquired a variety of nicknames, not all of them flattering. During various periods, Barkley was called Tons of Fun, Food World, the Goodtime Blimp, the Bread Truck, the Crisco Kid, Fat Boy, the Leaning Tower of Pizza, and the Round Mound of Rebound. The last one followed him to the NBA for a couple of years.

So predictable was Charles in those years that a pizza delivery outlet near his apartment expected a call every night. The order was always the same. All Barkley would say was, "This is Charles," and the people at the pizza joint would answer, "We'll be right there." Minutes later, two large pizzas would arrive and Barkley would have his nightly snack.

Luckily, Charles finally decided it was better for his wallet to snack on opposing forwards, most of whom he has been devouring ever since.

# Backboard Busters

For some reason the fans love it. But they shouldn't. After all, it can delay the game for up to an hour. And the potential is always there for a serious injury. We're talking about backboard busting, something that only a few select players have been able to accomplish.

The first of the big backboard busters was Darryl Dawkins, the 6'11", 265-pound center for the Philadelphia 76ers. The man who called himself Chocolate Thunder turned the trick twice within 22 days in 1979. The first occurred in a game against the Kings at Kansas City on November 13. Dawkins went up for a two-handed jam and the entire board seemed to explode, the glass shattering and covering several players and the court.

The fun-loving Dawkins was quite pleased with himself and begin giving his dunks special names. But none did backboard damage until December 5, when the Sixers were hosting San Antonio at the Spectrum. Again Dawkins went straight up with a two-handed jam, and this time he ripped the hoop right off the backboard.

"I didn't mean to do it," Dawkins said. "It was the power, the Chocolate Thunder. I could feel it surging through my body, fighting to get out. I had no control."

## Shaq Attaq

Shortly after Darryl Dawkins's destruction, the NBA ordered that all backboards be equipped with collapsible rims that would give if players hung on them. That seemed to solve the problem—that is, until Shaquille O'Neal came along. Shaquille is a 7'1", 300-pound center who joined the Orlando Magic from LSU in 1992. Shaq was a fine player already, a power center and the top rookie in the league. Everyone said he was capable of extraordinary things, but no one thought he would equal Darryl Dawkins's achievement.

Shaq was already known for his monster jams when the Magic traveled to Phoenix in early February 1993 to play the Suns. Early in the game, he got the ball underneath, went up, and slammed it home. He hung on the rim for a split second, then let go. As he did, the backboard and rim began following him. The bar holding the backboard had given way, and the entire setup sagged slowly to the floor.

"I've hit them harder than that before, a lot harder than that," said Shaq. "I was a little surprised, but when it started coming down, I ran the other way."

Then, in the second-to-last game of the year, Shaq did it again. The Magic were playing the New Jersey Nets at the Meadowlands

Arena. Midway through the first period, Shaq went up again and slammed the ball home. When he looked up, everything was coming down on him. The backboard had come loose from its top supports and was swinging downward. Then the 24-second clock, sitting on top of the backboard, also came down and almost clocked Shaq on top of the head. Shaq just shrugged his shoulder as if to say, "Oh, well."

What next? The collapsible rims couldn't hold the Shaq. Maybe the league will have to go to cast-iron backboards. They just may hold up.

# NBA Superstars of the Past

## CHAPTER 8

Pro basketball has had great players since the early days of the century. But it wasn't really until the start of the modern NBA in 1946 that basketball's superstars had a chance to shine on the same stage as baseball and football's best. It's true that the game has changed over the years, but most truly great players could undoubtedly adjust to any era. Bob Cousy, a 6'1" guard who played from 1950-1951 to 1962-1963, and Bill Russell, who began to play with the Boston Celtics in 1956, would both be amazing players today.

Let's take a brief look back at some of the greats of the NBA and see just how they played the game of basketball.

# Kareem Abdul-Jabbar

7'2", 267-pound center. Born Lew Alcindor, April 16, 1947, New York City. A star the first time he put on a basketball uniform and still a star the last time he took it off, Abdul-Jabbar went from Power Memorial High in New York City across the country to UCLA, where he led the Bruins to three straight national championships. Drafted by the Milwaukee Bucks in 1969, he led them to an NBA title the very next year. Kareem was traded to the Lakers in 1975 and helped his new team to five more NBA titles. Known for his famous sky hook, this six-time Most Valuable Player was in the NBA for a record 20 years and retired with 38,387 points (a 24.6 average), the most in NBA history. Elected to the Hall of Fame in 1995.

# Nate Archibald

"Tiny" 6'1", 160-pound guard. Born September 2, 1948, New York City. The only NBA player ever to have led the league in both scoring and assists in the same year, Archibald did it in 1972-1973, when he averaged 34.0 points and had 910 assists for the Kansas City-Omaha Kings. A cat-quick point guard, Tiny could shoot the lefty jumper or penetrate through much bigger men in the middle as he went to the hoop. Traded to the Celtics in 1978-1979, Tiny finally tasted an NBA title with the 1980-1981 team. He retired following the 1983-1984 season. Elected to the Hall of Fame in 1990.

# Rick Barry

6'7", 220-pound forward. Born March 28, 1944, Elizabeth, New Jersey. One of the great scorers in NBA history, Barry joined the San Francisco Warriors in 1965-1966 after an outstanding career at Miami. As a senior he averaged 37.4 points a game, and in his second year with San Francisco he led the NBA in scoring with a 35.6 average. Barry then jumped to the American Basketball Association, averaged 30.5 points for four years, then rejoined the Warriors. He helped them win an NBA title in 1974-1975 and retired after the 1979-1980 season. The last NBA player to shoot his free throws underhanded, Barry's 90.0 percent career average is second best all-time as of 1995, behind the still active Mark Price. Elected to the Hall of Fame in 1986.

## Elgin Baylor

6'5", 225-pound forward. Born September 16, 1934, Washington, D.C. The first of the do-it-all forwards, Baylor could handle the ball, rebound, and score with the best of them. He could take the ball coast to coast, had a variety of great moves, and played a lot bigger than 6'5". He averaged 31.3 points at the University of Seattle and 27.4 points in 14 NBA seasons, all with the Lakers. The Elg was Rookie of

the Year in 1958-1959 and a ten-time All-NBA first team choice. He still holds the NBA regulation game playoff scoring record of 61 points. Elected to the Hall of Fame in 1976.

## Walt Bellamy

"Big Bells" 6'11", 245-pound center. Born July 24, 1939, New Bern, North Carolina. Bellamy had one of the great rookie years in NBA history when he broke in with the Chicago Packers in 1961-1962 and averaged 31.6 points a game and while grabbing 1,500 rebounds. It looked as if he would take his place alongside Bill Russell and Wilt Chamberlain as one of the great centers of his era, but his numbers and his stature declined in the latter part of his career as he traveled to three other teams. He still averaged 20.1 points for his 14-year career, scored 20,941 points, and is seventh on the all-time rebounding list with 14,241. Elected to the Hall of Fame in 1993.

# Larry Bird

6'9", 220-pound forward. Born December 7, 1956, West Baden, Indiana. Pure and simply one of the greatest players ever to walk onto a basketball court. After nearly leading tiny Indiana State to the NCAA title in 1978-1979 (they lost to Magic Johnson and Michigan State in the finals), Bird joined the Boston Celtics without missing a beat. He was Rookie of the Year, a three-time Most Valuable Player, and a member of three championship teams. Though he didn't have blazing speed or great jumping ability, Bird compensated with incredible court vision and a total instinct for the

game and the way it should be played. He averaged 24.3 points in a career that ended with a back injury in 1991-1992. He was a winner who made all those around him better.

# Wilt Chamberlain

**"The Big Dipper"** or **"Wilt the Stilt"** 7'1", 275-pound center. Born August 21, 1936, Philadelphia, Pennsylvania. The one and only, an offensive force whose likes will never be seen again. Perhaps the strongest man ever to play in the NBA, Wilt once scored 100 points in a game and averaged 50.4 points for an entire season. Late in his career, Wilt blended his talents to those of his team and didn't worry as much about scoring. In fact, he once led the league in assists to show everyone the kind of passer he was.

He still averaged 30.1 points for his career, second only to Michael Jordan, and his 31,419 points are second to Kareem Abdul-Jabbar. As for rebounds, Wilt's 23,924 lead everyone. A four-time MVP, Wilt played on two championship teams and was elected to the Hall of Fame in 1978.

## Bob Cousy

"Cooz" 6'1", 175-pound guard. Born August 9, 1928, New York City. One of the game's flashiest players, Cousy was probably a man ahead of his time, a point guard who could easily fit into the game of the 1990s and excel. Cooz had a burning desire to win and helped the Celtics to six of their NBA titles. Possessor of great court vision, he delivered the ball to teammates in every way conceivable. Play with Cooz and you always had to be ready for the blind pass. He could score too, using a quick one-handed set shot and running one-hander, as well as the drive. He once scored 50 points in a playoff game and was elected to the Hall of Fame in 1970.

## Dave Cowens

6'9", 230-pound center. Born October 25, 1948, Newport, Kentucky. A first-round draft choice of the Boston Celtics in 1970, Cowens surprised everyone by becoming a full-fledged NBA center and a major force. He made up for his lack of size with hustle and desire. In fact, he played the game with a kind of controlled fury and never gave less than 100 percent. He helped the Celtics to a pair of NBA titles in 1974 and 1976, scored more than 13,000 points, and grabbed more than 10,000 rebounds. He retired in 1980, became restless, and returned to play 43 games for Milwaukee in 1982-1983, then retired for good. Elected to the Hall of Fame in 1990.

# Julius Erving

**"Dr. J"** or **"Doc"** 6'7", 210-pound forward. Born February 22, 1950, Roosevelt, New York. One of the true all-time greats and the most high-flying, acrobatic player the NBA had seen before Michael Jordan, Erving left the University of Massachusetts after his junior year and joined the young ABA in 1971-1972. A year later, he won the first of three ABA scoring titles, and when the league folded, he was sold by the New Jersey Nets to the Philadelphia 76ers. Julius went on to become a five-time all-NBA first team selection and the league's Most Valuable Player in 1980-1981. He helped the Sixers to an NBA title in 1983 and retired after the 1986-1987 season with 30,026 combined points. Dr. J will always be remembered for his high-flying, gravity-defying drives to the hoop. Elected to the Hall of Fame in 1993.

## Walt Frazier

**"Clyde"** 6'4", 205-pound guard. Born March 29, 1945, Atlanta, Georgia. A great clutch player and riverboat gambler on defense, Frazier keyed the great New York Knickerbocker teams that won NBA titles in 1970 and 1973. Smooth both on and off the court, Clyde was a four-time All-NBA first team selection and seven-time member of the All-Defensive Team. He averaged 18.9 points per game in a career that spanned 13 seasons from 1967-1968 to 1979-1980. Offensively, he had the ability to hit the jumper and penetrate underneath, and he was always a threat to pass to an open teammate. On defense, he was a ballhawk who loved to go for the steal. Elected to the Hall of Fame in 1986.

## Joe Fulks

**"Jumpin' Joe"** 6'5", 190-pound forward. Born October 26, 1921, Birmingham, Kentucky.

Died March 21, 1976. Perhaps the first great jump shooter in NBA annals, Fulks was a high-scoring forward who began play with the Philadelphia Warriors in the NBA's first season of 1946-1947. He led the league in scoring that year, repeating the next season, then averaged a career best 26.0 points a game in 1948-1949. Definitely a player for his time, Jumpin' Joe helped the Warriors win the first ever NBA title and retired after the 1953-1954 season. Elected to the Hall of Fame in 1977.

## George Gervin

**"The Iceman"** 6'7", 185-pound guard. Born April 27, 1952, Detroit, Michigan. A four-time NBA scoring champion, Gervin didn't always get the recogni-tion he deserved during his playing days. Maybe it was because he was an ABA player who came into the NBA when his team, the San Antonio Spurs, joined the league in 1976-1977. Ice could shoot the long jumper as well as go to the hoop. With his height and lanky build, he was tough to stop either way. A five-time All-NBA first team selection, the Iceman still holds a record by having scored 33 points in a single quarter. His combined ABA/NBA totals are 26,595 points and a 25.1 average. He retired after the 1985-1986 season.

## John Havlicek

**"Hondo"** 6'5", 205-pound guard/forward. Born April 8, 1940, Martins Ferry, Ohio. Another true all-time great, Hondo began as one of the Boston Celtics' fabled sixth men who came off the bench to ignite the team. He grew into a full-time starter and mainstay who helped the Celts win eight NBA titles. A fine player on Ohio State's 1960 NCAA title team, Hondo was a tireless per-former in both the collegiate and professional ranks, known for his stamina, toughness, and clutch play. He played for 16 seasons, retiring after the 1977-1978 season when he still averaged 16.1 at age 38. He averaged 20.8 points for his career, winding up with 26,395 total points, sixth on the NBA's all-time list. Elected to the Hall of Fame in 1983.

# Elvin Hayes

**"The Big E"** 6'9", 235-pound forward. Born November 17, 1945, Rayville, Louisiana. A sensational scorer and rebounder in both college and the NBA, Hayes had four great seasons at the University of Houston, averaging 25.1 points as a freshman and 36.8 as a senior. As a rookie with San Diego in 1968-1969, Hayes didn't miss a beat and was the NBA's leading scorer with a 28.4 average, grabbing 1,406 rebounds. A year later, he won

the first of two rebounding titles. The Big E's only NBA title came in 1978 as a member of the Washington Bullets. He was an All-NBA first teamer three times and retired after the 1983-1984 season with 27,313 points, fourth on the NBA's all-time list. Elected to the Hall of Fame in 1989.

# Dan Issel

6'9", 240-pound center. Born October 25, 1948, Batavia, Illinois. An unsung superstar who battled taller centers his entire career and scored against all of them, Issel was an All-American at Kentucky who averaged 25.8 points for four years, 33.9 as a senior. He then joined the Kentucky Colonels of the ABA, won the scoring title as a rookie in 1970-1971, and was finally traded to Denver in 1975-1976. He then came into the NBA with the Nuggets and played until 1985, completing a great 15-year career. His combined ABA/NBA stats show 27,482 points and a 22.6 average. Issel resigned as coach of the Denver Nuggets during the 1994-1995 season. Elected to the Hall of Fame in 1993.

## Magic Johnson

6'9", 225-pound guard. Born August 14, 1959, Lansing, Michigan. One of the greatest ever and among a trio of players—the other two are Larry Bird and Michael Jordan—credited with helping the NBA become hugely popular in in the 1980s. The Magic Man broke new ground immediately. Never before had there been a 6'9" point guard, a big player who could handle the ball as well as smaller men. But then again, Magic could do it all. He's second in the NBA all-time in assists, retired with a 19.7 career scoring average, was a nine-time All-NBA first teamer and a three-time Most Valuable Player, won an NCAA title as a sophomore at Michigan State in 1979, and won an NBA crown, the first of five, the next year. His great moments are too numerous to mention. Great court vision, a student of the game, an artist—that describes Magic. He retired after the 1990-1991 season.

## Bob Lanier

**"The Big Cat"** 6'11", 265-pound center. Born September 30, 1948, Buffalo, New York. Another outstanding center just a notch below the top guys, big

Bob was a great scorer and court presence for the Detroit Pistons and Milwaukee Bucks. A first team All-American at St. Bonaventure in 1970, Lanier averaged 27.6 points in four years of action for the Bonnies. He came into his own his second year with the Pistons, averaging 25.7 points and grabbing 1,132 rebounds. Though he averaged 20.1 points for his career, a series of never-ending injuries caused him to average just 68.5 games a year and maybe prevented him from becoming one of the elite centers. Elected to the Hall of Fame in 1992.

# Jerry Lucas

"Luke" 6'8", 235-pound center/forward. Born March 30, 1940, Middletown, Ohio. A player with wonderful timing, a sense for the game, and especially a sense for the ball, Luke was one of the best rebounders ever for his size, averaging 15.6 rebounds a game over an 11-year NBA career. He entered the NBA following a brilliant career at Ohio State in which he and John Havlicek led the Buckeyes to one NCAA title and two more appearances in the finals. He was twice college basketball's Player of the

Year. In 1964 he was the NBA Rookie of the Year, averaging 17.7 points and 17.4 rebounds. A three-time All-NBA first team selection, Luke finally was part of an NBA title team with the 1972-1973 Knicks. Elected to the Hall of Fame in 1979.

# Pete Maravich

"Pistol Pete" 6'5", 200-pound guard. Born June 22, 1947, Aliquippa, Pennsylvania. Died January 5, 1988. The Pistol is still college basketball's all-time scoring champion, having averaged an amazing 44.2 points in three years of play at Louisiana State. In the NBA, beginning with Atlanta in 1970-1971, he was also a superstar, a ballhandling wizard who could make the play for others or for himself. Offensively, he had few equals. As a basketball entertainer, he was a top drawing card. Fans came to see him play because they could never predict what he would do with the basketball. He also led the league in scoring with a 31.1 average as a member of the New Orleans Jazz in 1976-1977. Pistol Pete retired after the 1979-1980 season with a 24.2 scoring average. Elected to the Hall of Fame in 1986.

# Kevin McHale

6'10", 225-pound forward. Born December 19, 1957, Hibbing, Minnesota. Though he retired recently, after the 1992-1993 season, McHale is already considered an all-time great. A lanky power forward, he used his long arms to advantage on both offense and defense. When he first joined the Boston Celtics in 1980-1981, he came off the bench, winning the NBA Sixth Man Award in both 1984 and 1985. He was a first team All-NBA choice in 1987 when he averaged a career high 26.1 points. In addition, he was a three-time pick for the All-Defensive team and was part of three Celtic title teams. Offensively, he was extremely tough to stop in close because of those long arms.

# George Mikan

6'10", 245-pound center. Born June 18, 1924, Joliet, Illinois. Mikan was the first truly dominant center in pro basketball, and while he doesn't appear that big by today's standards, he was a giant in his time. Not especially mobile, big George operated under the hoop, scoring and rebounding, and leading the Minneapolis Lakers to five NBA titles. He was also a four-time scoring champion and five-time All-NBA first team selection. Before the Lakers came into the NBA, Mikan did the same thing in the competitive NBL, winning a pair of league crowns and a pair of scoring titles in two years. He retired at the age of 29 in 1954, made a brief comeback two years later, then retired for good. Elected to the Hall of Fame in 1959.

# Earl Monroe

"The Pearl" 6'3", 190-pound guard. Born November 21, 1944, Philadelphia, Pennsylvania. The man of a thousand moves, Earl the Pearl excited the fans every time he touched the basketball. From the time he averaged 41.5 points a game as a senior at

Winston-Salem State, he knew how to put the ball in the hoop. The Pearl was NBA Rookie of the Year with the Baltimore Bullets in 1967-1968 and was All-NBA first team the next year. Traded to the Knicks early in the 1971-1972 season, the Pearl played with the New Yorkers' title team in 1973, then finished his career in 1980 after thrilling Madison Square Garden fans. Bad knees cut his effectiveness in his later years, but he still averaged 18.8 points for his career. Elected to the Hall of Fame in 1989.

## Bob Pettit

6'9", 215-pound forward. Born December 12, 1932, Baton Rouge, Louisiana. A great player for his time or any time, Pettit used every ounce of talent in his body to become the best player he could be. An All-American at LSU, he joined the Milwaukee Hawks in 1954-1955. A year later the team moved to St. Louis and Pettit led the NBA in both scoring and rebounding. He helped the Hawks to an NBA title in 1958 and then led the league in scoring once more in 1958-1959. A ferocious competitor, he played with a number of injuries, including a cast on his broken left wrist. There's little doubt he would still be a star in today's game. Pettit retired in 1965 after just 11 years, finishing with 20,880 points (a 26.4 average) and 12,849 rebounds (a 16.2 average, third best ever). Elected to the Hall of Fame in 1970.

## Willis Reed

6'10", 240-pound center. Born June 25, 1942, Hico, Louisiana. A tough, determined player and a true leader, Reed was the heart and soul of the fine Knick teams of the late 1960s and early 1970s. Always battling injuries, as well as bigger centers, he led the Knicks to NBA crowns in 1970 and 1973. He was the NBA Rookie of the Year in 1965 but played just ten seasons because of recurring knee injuries. Had he not been hurt, his numbers would have been

better, but no one had a bigger heart. Reed was the NBA's Most Valuable Player in 1970 and a first team all-star that year. He was the finals MVP twice and was elected to the Hall of Fame in 1981.

## Oscar Robertson

**"The Big O"** 6'5", 220-pound guard. Born November 24, 1938, Charlotte, Tennessee. Before there was a Michael Jordan, it was Oscar Robertson who usually got the most votes as the best all-around basketball player ever. Some still pick the Big O, a guy who could do it all. After a three-time All-American career at the University of Cincinnati, where he averaged 33.8 points, Robertson joined the Royals, averaged 30.5 points, led the league with 690 assists, and grabbed 716 rebounds. He

never missed a beat. He led the league in scoring average once and in assists six times. A nine-time All-NBA first team selection, the Big O finally tasted a championship with the Milwaukee Bucks in 1971. He was the league's MVP in 1964 and the all-time leader in assists until Magic Johnson eased past him. Robertson played until 1973-1974, scoring 26,710 points, fifth on the NBA's all-time list. Elected to the Hall of Fame in 1979.

## Bill Russell

**"Russ"** 6'10", 220-pound center. Born February 12, 1934, Monroe, Louisiana. In 1980 the Professional Basketball Writers Association of America declared Bill Russell the Greatest Player in the History of the NBA. Defensively he had no peer. An incredible rebounder and shot blocker with the vision to start the fast break, Russell led the Celtics to 11 NBA titles in 13 years, beginning with his rookie season of 1956-1957—an incredible achievement. He was a five-time MVP and is the second all-time rebounder in NBA history with 21,620. Only archrival Wilt Chamberlain had more. But Russell's greatest legacy is the most important one: winning. Even his college team, the University of San Francisco, won two straight NCAA titles and 55 straight games while he was there. He retired a champion after the 1968-1969 season and was elected to the Hall of Fame in 1974.

## Dolph Schayes

6'8", 220-pound forward. Born May 19, 1928, New York City. One of the NBA's great forwards from the era of the 1950s, Schayes was one of those players who seemed to get better with age. He helped the Syracuse Nationals to an NBA title in 1955. Though 6'8" and capable of taking the ball to the hoop, he also loved to come outside and shoot a long, arcing two-handed set shot, a blast from basketball's past. All told, he was an all-NBA first teamer six times and still good

enough to average 23.6 points a game in 1960-1961 at the age of 33. He retired after the 1963-1964 season, averaging 18.2 points for his career. Elected to the Hall of Fame in 1972.

## Isiah Thomas

6'1", 182-pound guard. Born April 30, 1961, Chicago, Illinois. Another so-called small man who proved you don't have to be tall to be a superstar, Thomas fit that bill from the time he led Indiana to the NCAA title as a sophomore in 1981. Drafted number one by the Detroit Pistons, he starred in the Motor City for 13 seasons. He was an All-NBA first teamer for three straight years (1984-1986) and led the NBA with 13.9 assists per game in 1984-1985. A point guard who could direct traffic, pop the jumper, go to the hoop, and play rugged defense,

Thomas was an integral part of two Pistons' title teams in 1989 and 1990. He retired after the 1993-1994 season with more than 18,500 points.

## Nate Thurmond

6'1", 235-pound center. Born July 25,1941, Akron, Ohio. Had Thurmond not played in the same era as Bill Russell and Wilt Chamberlain, he might have been *the* dominant center in the game. As it was, he played the two giants as well as anyone, holding his own on the boards and on defense in general. In 1965 he set a record by grabbing 18 rebounds in a single quarter and he averaged more than 20 rebounds a year several times in his 14-year career. Bad knees reduced him to part-time status his final years, but he still averaged 15 points a game and grabbed 14,464 rebounds, sixth best on the all-time list. Elected to the Hall of Fame in 1984.

## Bill Walton

6'11", 235-pound center. Born November 5, 1952, La Mesa, California. When people mention the big redheaded center, they often talk about what might have been. Continuing, persistent, and chronic foot problems shortened an NBA career that appeared on the brink of brilliance. One of the greatest college centers ever, Walton led UCLA to 88 straight victories and a pair of NCAA titles. He was a three-time All-American drafted first by the Portland Trail Blazers in 1974. Then the injuries started. But in his third year he led the Blazers to the NBA crown. A great defensive player and rebounder, Walton missed three entire seasons to injury but came back to help the Celtics win a title in 1986. He was still good enough to be elected to the Hall of Fame in 1993.

## Jerry West

6'3", 185-pound guard. Born May 28, 1938, Cheylan, West Virginia. An all-time NBA superstar, West was one of the greatest clutch players ever. As good as he was in the regular season, he was even better in the playoffs. Until Magic Johnson and Michael Jordan came along, West was usually linked with Bob Cousy and Oscar Robertson as the three best guards ever. A ten-time All-NBA first team selection, West helped the L.A. Lakers to the 1972 championship after the frustration of losing to the Celtics in the finals all throughout the 1960s. In 1964-1965, he averaged 40.6 points in 11 playoff games and finished his career in 1974 with 25,192 points, ninth on the NBA's all-time list. Later a coach and currently general manager of the Lakers, West was elected to the Hall of Fame in 1979.

# NBA Superstars of the Present

## CHAPTER 9

I t's never been easy to really define a true superstar. Any player who puts together one or two great seasons becomes a superstar in the eyes of many. But true superstars excel year after year. They obviously have pure talent. But they must have much more than that as well. A superstar on the court is first and foremost a team player, but one who has the ability to take over a game, at least for a short time, if necessary. He is also a player who makes those around him better.

In the NBA today, superstars don't have to be players who have been in the league eight to ten years. They may have played only two or three years but have already exhibited the qualities that put them on the brink of joining the elite few.

Let's take a glimpse at the very best and most charismatic players in the NBA today.

# Charles Barkley

"**Sir Charles**" 6'6", 255-pound forward. Born February 20, 1963, Leeds, Alabama. One of the most charismatic players of his era and a true superstar, Sir Charles is a do-it-all player who can go coast to coast with the dribble, hit the three, go inside on offense, and rebound with the best of them. Barkley played eight seasons with the 76ers before going to the Suns in 1992-1993. He led Phoenix to the NBA finals that year and was the league's Most Valuable Player. A member of the 1992 Olympic Dream Team, he has averaged more than 20 points a game every year after his rookie season of 1984-1985.

# Derrick Coleman

"**D.C.**" 6'10", 258-pound forward. Born June 21, 1967, Mobile, Alabama. A player with superstar talent, the only question with Coleman is whether he wants it badly enough. There's no doubt that the man they call D.C. is one of the very best, a player who can score, rebound, and also take control of a game. An All-American at Syracuse, D.C. was the first pick overall in the 1990 NBA draft, then became NBA Rookie of the Year. With the Nets in 1993-1994, he averaged 20.2 points and 11.3 rebounds a game, ninth best in the league.

# Clyde Drexler

"**Clyde the Glide**" 6'7", 222-pound forward. Born November 7, 1963, Wichita, Kansas. One of the smoothest forwards in the NBA, Drexler was the heart and soul of a very good Trail Blazer team for a decade. A member of the "Phi Slamma Jamma" Houston Cougars team while in college, Drexler was a first-round draft choice in 1983. He led the Blazers into the NBA final round twice and has been a 20-point scorer his entire career. The Glide had a brilliant season in 1991-1992, averaging 25.0 points a game and becoming an All-NBA first team selection. He was also a member of the 1992 Olympic Dream Team.

Drexler was traded to the Houston Rockets midway through the 1994-1995 season and helped the team win a second straight NBA title.

## Joe Dumars

6'3", 195-pound guard. Born May 24, 1963, Shreveport, Louisiana. Quiet, unassuming, not flashy—but oh, what a player. Dumars may be one of the NBA's best-kept superstar secrets. Only his peers know just how good he is. Early in his career he played second fiddle in Detroit to Isiah Thomas but then fit in beautifully alongside Isiah at shooting guard. He went from a 9.4 scorer as a rookie in 1985-1986 to a 23.5 scorer in 1992-1993. A great defensive player as well, he is a four-time member of the NBA All-Defensive Team and helped the Pistons to a pair of NBA titles in 1989 and 1990.

## Patrick Ewing

7'0", 240-pound center. Born August 5, 1962, Kingston, Jamaica. The key to the powerful New York Knick teams of the 1990s, Ewing is an outstanding scorer and shot blocker. He has averaged more than 20 points a game every year since joining the Knicks as the NBA's number one draft choice in 1985. At Georgetown University, he led the Hoyas to a national championship and two other appearances in the final game. He was a member of the gold medal-winning Olympic team in 1984 and the Dream Team in 1992 and was an All-NBA first team choice in 1990 when he averaged 28.6 points a game.

# Anfernee Hardaway

**"Penny"** 6'7", 200-pound guard. Born July 18, 1972, Memphis, Tennessee. It's not easy to call such a young player a superstar, but Hardaway appears to have all the goods and the desire. A 6'7" point guard, he proved in his rookie year with Orlando, in 1993-1994, that he could do it all. He was second on the team behind Shaquille O'Neal in scoring with a 16.0 average, led the Magic with 544 assists, finished third in rebounds with 439, led in steals with 190, and was second in blocks with 51. In 1994-1995, when he made the All-NBA first team, he averaged 20.9 points and 7.2 assists as Orlando topped the Atlantic Division and made it all the way to the NBA finals.

# Kevin Johnson

**"K.J."** 6'1", 190-pound guard. Born March 4, 1966, Sacramento, California. The do-everything guard of the Suns, Johnson had perhaps his finest season in 1993-1994. But he has been an acknowledged star for several years, making the All-NBA second team three times from 1989-1991. It was difficult for any guard to make the first team in those years with Magic and Michael around, but K.J. was close behind. He has been a top assist man as well as a fine scorer. His leaping ability lets him dunk like a much taller man. The NBA's Most Improved Player in 1989, he raised his scoring average from 9.2 to 20.4. He's been at that high level ever since.

# Larry Johnson

**"L.J."** 6'7", 250-pound forward. Born March 14, 1969, Tyler, Texas. A prototype power forward, Johnson is agile enough to handle the ball and shoot from the outside. But underneath he can bang with much bigger men. A former college basketball Player of the Year at UNLV, he led the Rebels to a national title, then became the NBA's top draft choice—by Charlotte—in 1991. He was Rookie of the Year and followed that with an All-NBA second team performance the next year. He not only averaged 22.1 in 1992-1993 but led the NBA in minutes played. A bad back hampered him in 1993-1994, but he recovered to play at an all-star level again in 1994-1995.

# Michael Jordan

**"Air Jordan"** or **"His Airness"** 6'6", 198-pound guard. Born February 17, 1963, Brooklyn, New York. The man considered by most as the greatest all-around basketball player ever to lace up a pair of sneakers, Jordan's legend began his freshman year at North Carolina and continued to the Chicago Bulls, where he was Rookie of the Year and a 28.2 per game scorer in 1984-1985. Beginning in 1986-1987, he won seven straight NBA scoring titles, led the league in steals three times, was the league's MVP on a trio of occasions, was a first team all-star seven times, was Defensive Player of the Year, and led his team to three straight NBA titles in 1991, 1992, and 1993. In between, there were spectacular, gravity-defying, incredible drives and hoops nearly every game. His 32.2 career scoring average is the best ever. He retired unexpectedly following the 1992-1993 season, played minor league baseball in 1994, then rejoined the Bulls in March 1995 for the final 17 games of the season and the playoffs. He expects to continue playing in 1995-1996.

# Karl Malone

"**The Mailman**" 6'9", 256-pound forward. Born July 24, 1963, Summerfield, Louisiana. Big, strong, talented, and tough, Malone is called "the Mailman" because he delivers the goods. He's been doing it for the Utah Jazz since 1985-1986, when he was a first-round pick out of Louisiana Tech. A six-time All-NBA first team selection, Malone has been a model of consistency. His scoring averages since his third year of 1987-1988 read 27.7, 29.1, 31.0, 29.0, 28.0, 27.0, 25.2, and 26.7. In addition, he has missed just four games in ten years. Malone was also a member of the 1992 Olympic Dream Team.

## Moses Malone

6'10", 255-pound center. Born March 23, 1955, Petersburg, Virginia. Like old man river, Moses Malone keeps rolling along. He was one of the youngest players in pro basketball when he joined the old Utah Stars of the ABA at the age of 19 in 1974. Now, with San Antonio, he's the oldest. Though limited to 55 games by injury in 1993-1994, Moses tried it again in 1994-1995. It's been a great career. He's been a three-time Most Valuable Player, a four-time All-NBA first team selection, a five-time rebounding champ, and a member of the 1983 NBA champion 76ers. His total of 27,409 points in the NBA through 1995 is third on the all-time NBA list, while his 16,212 rebounds are fifth best. He is also third in games played, second in free throws attempted, and first in free throws made. That's how good he's been.

## Reggie Miller

6'7", 185-pound guard. Born August 24, 1965, Riverside, California. Though he averaged more than 20 points a game for four straight years, from 1989-1990 through 1992-1993, Miller probably achieved more notoriety from the 1993-1994 season, when he wound up with a 19.9 average. The lanky backcourt-man of the Indiana Pacers is

now considered the best long-range shooting guard in the NBA, a prime-time player who loves a challenge and won't back down from anybody. He proved it to a national television audience in the Eastern Conference finals in 1994 when he scored 25 fourth-quarter points to cap a 39-point effort in a win over the New York Knicks.

## Alonzo Mourning

"Zo" 6'10", 240-pound center. Born February 8, 1970, Chesapeake, Virginia. In a few short years, Mourning has proved he can hold his own against any center in the NBA. Some said he was too small to go against the O'Neals, Robinsons, Motumbos, Olajuwons, and Ewings, but this ferocious competitor out of Georgetown averaged 21.0 points as a rookie, 21.5 his

second season, and 21.3 his third season of 1994-1995. Zo and Larry Johnson give the Hornets arguably the best young superstar combination in the NBA. There are even those who feel Zo has the most all-around game of any pro center this side of Hakeem Olajuwon. His best days still lay ahead because he wants to be better every single game.

## Hakeem Olajuwon

"Hakeem the Dream" 7'0", 255-pound center. Born January 21, 1963, Lagos, Nigeria. The NBA's best player in 1993-1994, Olajuwon was all-everything— the league's Most Valuable Player and Defensive Player of the Year and the player who led the Houston Rockets to the NBA championship. Amazingly, Olajuwon never picked up a basketball until he was 15 years old, and now he's widely considered the best all-around center in the league. A star at the University of Houston, he joined the Rockets in 1984-1985 without missing a beat, averaging 20.6 points as a rookie. He has led the league in rebounding and blocked shots twice, and has been an All-NBA first team selection five times and member of the All-Defensive team five times. He averaged 27.3 points per game in 1993-1994 and topped it with a 27.8 average in 1994-1995. He then led the Rockets to a second straight NBA title, becoming finals MVP once more.

# Shaquille O'Neal

**"The Shaq"** 7'1", 300-pound center. Born March 6, 1972, Newark, New Jersey. In the spotlight since becoming the NBA's top draft choice in 1992, O'Neal may now be one of the most highly visible active players in the world. Not only has he played at an all-star level, but he has made numerous commercials, cut a rap CD, and been featured in a major motion picture. Undoubtedly the strongest player in the league, Shaq is a power center who was Rookie of the Year in 1992-1993, when he averaged 23.4 points, grabbed 1,122 rebounds, and had 286 blocks. In 1993-1994, he scored at a 29.3 clip (second best by a scant margin), had 1,072 rebounds, and led the Magic into the playoffs for the first time. In 1994-1995, he led the league in scoring with a second straight 29.3 season, as the Magic won their division and went all the way to the NBA finals. Yes, sir, the Shaq Attaq is here to stay.

# Scottie Pippen

6'7", 225-pound forward. Born September 25, 1965, Hamburg, Arkansas. Pippen spent the first six years of his career playing in the biggest shadow ever cast in sports, that of the great Michael Jordan. But even with Jordan leading the Bulls to three straight NBA titles, Pippen's stock rose each year until he was considered a superstar in

gritty point guard who led the Cavaliers in scoring (17.3) and assists (559) in 1993-1994. In 1992-1993, Price was an All-NBA first team selection as he averaged 18.2 points and added 602 assists. A very steady player and one of the best three-point shooters in the league, he would receive even more ink if the Cavs had taken an NBA title.

his cwn right. Some were even saying he was the second best all-around player in the league behind Jordan, and in 1994-1995 he was an All-NBA first team selection. In addition, he's been a three-time All-Defensive team choice and is good enough to play four positions on the basketball court: point guard, shooting guard, small forward, and power forward. And then there's those three NBA titles. He also led the league in steals in 1994-1995. Pippen was also a member of the 1992 Olympic Dream Team.

## Mark Price

6'0", 178-pound guard. Born February 15, 1964, Bartlesville, Oklahoma. As of 1995, Price was the NBA's all-time leading free thrower, having made 1,883 of 2,078 for a 90.6 percent success rate. But Price does more than that. He's a

## David Robinson

"The Admiral" 7'1", 235-pound center. Born August 6, 1965, Key West, Florida. Whenever there is a debate about the best NBA center of the 1990s, Robinson always gets a lot of votes. The Admiral had his best season in 1993-1994, leading the NBA in scoring with a 29.8 average and clinching the title in the last game with an incredible 71-point effort. An All-American at Navy in 1986-1987, Robinson served two years in the Naval Reserve before joining the Spurs. Despite the layoff, he was Rookie of the Year in 1990. He's also been the NBA Defensive Player of the Year, a three-time All-NBA first team choice, and a three-time member of the All-Defensive team. His competition for these honors includes Hakeem Olajuwon, Shaquille O'Neal, and Patrick Ewing. Robinson is probably the fastest and quickest of the big centers, a player who can run with anyone. He led the Spurs to an NBA best record of 62-20 in 1994-1995 and for his efforts was named the league's Most Valuable Player.

## Dennis Rodman

**"The Worm"** 6'8", 210-pound forward. Born May 13, 1961, Trenton, New Jersey. "The Worm" is a strange nickname for one of the most unique and unpredictable players in the NBA. It's hard to guess what Rodman will say or do next. But he is a winner, playing a big part in the Detroit Pistons' championship teams of 1989 and 1990. By the sheer force of his will and determination, he has made himself into the very best rebounder in the NBA, taking four straight titles from

1991-1992 through 1994-1995. He had 1,530 rebounds in 1991-1992 for an average of 18.7 a game. Those numbers hadn't been seen in years, not since the days of Russell and Chamberlain. Traded to the Spurs before the 1993-1994 season, Rodman had 1,379 boards in 79 games and helped make David Robinson the league scoring champ. He averaged a league best 16.8 caroms in 1994-1995 and was named to the All-Defensive team.

## Latrell Sprewell

6'5", 190-pound guard. Born September 8, 1970, Milwaukee, Wisconsin. Maybe we're jumping the gun on this one, but Sprewell surprised everyone in 1993-1994, making the All-NBA first team in just his second season in the league. Injuries to Tim

Hardaway, Chris Mullin, and Sarunas Marciulionis gave Sprewell a chance to take over the Warrior backcourt. He averaged 21.0 points in 82 games and was third on the team with 401 rebounds. A year earlier he was on the All Rookie Team after averaging 15.4 points a game, and in 1994-1995 he averaged 20.6 points. A fine shooter from both inside and out, Sprewell could be at the beginning of an outstanding career.

## John Stockton

6'1", 175-pound guard. Born March 26, 1962, Spokane, Washington. Stockton became the greatest assist man in NBA history when he passed one legend and tied another in 1994-1995. On February 1, 1995, Utah's star point guard rifled a pass to teammate Karl Malone who hit a jumper from the corner. It was the 9,922nd assist of Stockton's career, moving him past the legendary Magic Johnson into first place on the all-time list. Stockton finished the year with an NBA best 1,011 assists, tying the record of another great, Bob Cousy, by leading the league for an eighth straight season. He also has the three highest single-season assist totals ever, his best being

1,164 in 1990-1991. A hard-nosed ballhawk who has also led the league in steals twice, Stockton still finds time to score in double figures consistently. He made the All-NBA first team in 1994-1995, has been an All-NBA second team choice five times, and finished the 1994-1995 season with 10,394 career assists.

## Chris Webber

6'10", 260-pound forward/center. Born March 1, 1973, Detroit, Michigan. One of the "Fab Five" freshman at Michigan who helped the Wolverines to two straight NCAA championship games, Webber became the number-one draft choice in 1993 of the Orlando Magic, who then traded him to the Warriors for another rookie, Anfernee Hardaway. Webber then went on to become NBA Rookie of the Year, averaging 17.5 points and grabbing 694 rebounds in 1993-1994. His 164 blocks were ninth best in the league. A powerful inside player, he can only get better as the years pass and is expected to be one of the top players in the league. Because of a contract dispute he was traded to the Washington Bullets at the start of the 1994-1995 season and missed a good part of the year to injury.

## Dominique Wilkins

**"The Human Highlight Film"** 6'8", 215-pound forward. Born January 12, 1960, Paris, France. One of the great pure scorers in NBA history, Wilkins is a player with the reputation for making so many impossible shots that he was given his odd nickname. Dominique spent the first 11 seasons and part of a 12th with the Atlanta Hawks before being traded to the Clippers during the 1993-1994 season. He played with the Boston Celtics in 1994-1995. He has taken one scoring title and would have had more had it not been for Michael Jordan. But Nique has already scored 25,389 points for a 25.8 average during his great career, and his average is fifth best on the NBA's all-time list. A consistent player throughout his career, Dominique was still good enough to average 17.8 points a game for the Celtics at age 35.

# Great NBA Coaches

## CHAPTER 10

There has always been a debate about how much the men behind the benches have to do with a team winning or losing. It's the same in all sports. In basketball, there was a time when coaches weren't allowed to talk with their teams during timeouts. But that era is long gone.

NBA coaches have always had to be motivators, strategists, and sometimes simply cheerleaders. Of course, it helps if there are Magic Johnsons, Larry Birds, Bill Russells, or Michael Jordans on the team. But certain coaches have compiled winning records over long periods of time and sometimes without the benefit of great teams or top players.

Let's take a brief look at some of the finer NBA coaches over the years and the records they have compiled.

# Al Attles

Born November 7, 1936, Newark, New Jersey. Attles spent his entire career in the Warrior organization, both as a player and a coach. He played from 1960-1961 to 1970-1971 and coached the team from 1969-1970 through 1982-1983, 14 years behind the bench. Often coaching mediocre teams, Attles had a record of 557 wins, 518 losses, but he did lead the Warriors to one NBA title in 1975.

# Red Auerbach

Born September 20, 1917, Brooklyn, New York. Mr. Boston Celtics, Auerbach coached the Celts for 16 of his 20 coaching years, spending his first four years with Washington and then Tri-Cities in the earliest days of the NBA. With the Celtics he was amazingly successful, winning nine NBA titles and a record eight in a row. His final coaching record is an impressive 938 wins, 479 losses. Known for lighting his victory cigar when his team had a game in the bag, Auerbach has remained with the Celtics, first as general manager and later as team president.

# Billy Cunningham

Born June 3, 1943, Brooklyn, New York. A Hall of Fame player with the Philadelphia 76ers, Cunningham later took over the coaching reins for the team for eight seasons between 1977-1978 and 1984-1985. During that time he coached the Sixers to the NBA finals on three occasions, finally getting a championship ring when his 1982-1983 Sixer team defeated the Lakers in four straight games. He retired with an impressive winning percentage of .698 and a record of 454-196. He was later one of the partners who brought the NBA to Miami with the Heat.

*CHUCK DALY*

# Chuck Daly

Born July 30, 1930, St. Mary's, Pennsylvania. Though he just retired after the 1993-1994 season, Daly is already considered an NBA coaching great. He put in a dozen years with Cleveland (one year), Detroit (nine years), and New Jersey (two years). His 1988-1989 and 1989-1990 Piston teams won NBA titles as Daly brilliantly geared the team to the talent available. He used a different style his final two years with the Nets and made them winners too. His final NBA coaching record was 564-379.

*COTTON FITZSIMMONS*

## Cotton Fitzsimmons

Born October 7, 1931, Hannibal, Missouri. A fine coach who never won an NBA title, Fitzsimmons nevertheless coached Phoenix, Atlanta, Buffalo, Kansas City, San Antonio, and Phoenix again to 805 victories from 1969-1970 through 1991-1992. Prior to that, he had a 222-60 record in 11 years of college coaching, so he's always been a winner. His pro teams made it to the Western Conference finals three times but always came up short. His total NBA coaching record was 805-745.

## Tom Heinsohn

Born August 26, 1934, Jersey City, New Jersey. A Hall of Fame forward with the Boston Celtics, Heinsohn averaged 18.6 points a game in a nine-year career. He spent another nine years coaching the Celts, from 1969-1970 through 1977-1978. A fiery, emotional coach, he had the Celtics between the Bill Russell and Larry Bird eras yet won a pair of NBA titles in 1974 and 1976. His final coaching record was 427-263.

## Red Holzman

Born August 10, 1920, Brooklyn, New York. A player in the early days of the NBL and NBA, Holzman later coached for 18 years, four seasons with the Hawks and then 14 with the New York Knicks. He was the architect of the Knick ballclubs that won NBA titles in 1970 and 1973. Holzman taught the Knicks a brilliant brand of team basketball, the likes of which has arguably not been seen since. His final coaching record was 696-604.

# K. C. Jones

Born May 25, 1932, Taylor, Texas. Another Hall of Fame player with the great Boston Celtic teams of the late 1950s and 1960s, K. C. Jones coached the Bullets, Celtics, and SuperSonics for ten years. He was with the Celtics for five years (1984-1985 through 1988-1989), coaching the team to a pair of NBA titles and into the championship series two other years. He also took the Bullets to the final round in 1975. His final coaching record was 522-252.

*K. C. JONES*

# John Kundla

Born July 3, 1916, Star Junction, Pennsylvania. The highly successful coach of the old Minneapolis Lakers, the first dynasty in NBA history, Kundla guided the George Mikan-led Lakers to five NBA titles in six years. All told, he coached 11 years in Minneapolis, with an NBA record of 423-302. He later coached for nine more years at the University of Minnesota.

# Joe Lapchick

Born April 12, 1900, Yonkers, New York. Died August 10, 1970. A fine pro player with the Original Celtics and other early teams, Lapchick spent 29 years behind the bench, 20 of them with St. John's University and nine with the New York Knicks. He coached the Knicks from 1948-1949 through 1955-1956, St. John's before and after. His college mark was an outstanding 334-130, while he was 326-247 with the Knicks. Colorful and exciting, Lapchick took the Knicks to the NBA final round in 1951.

# Doug Moe

Born September 21, 1938, Brooklyn, New York. A star player at the University of North Carolina and then in the ABA, Moe became a coach in 1976-1977, working behind the bench for 15 years, ten of them with the Denver Nuggets. He also had stops in San Antonio and Philadelphia. His Denver teams were characterized by a run-and-gun style that emphasized offense rather than defense. He was often criticized for his style, but the fans loved it. While he never won an NBA title, his overall coaching record was a successful 628-529.

# Jack Ramsay

Born February 21, 1925, Philadelphia, Pennsylvania. A college and pro coach for 32 years, Ramsay was always a winner. His 11-year record at St. Joseph's of Pennsylvania was 234-72. His 21-year NBA career saw him coach at Philadelphia, Buffalo, Portland, and Indiana. He led the 1976-1977 Trail Blazers to the NBA title, and his overall pro coaching record was 864-783. He is now a television basketball analyst.

There are several current NBA coaches who will someday enter the list of outstanding mentors. Here are the top men still active today.

# Larry Brown

*LARRY BROWN*

Born September 14, 1940, Brooklyn, New York. Known as the traveling man because of his habit of changing jobs and swinging between college and the pros, Brown has been a winner everywhere. He has coached at UCLA and Kansas, getting to the final game with the Bruins and winning an NCAA title with his 1988 Kansas team. His college record is 177-61. With the pros, he coached for years in the old ABA (229-107), and in the NBA he has been in Denver, New Jersey, San Antonio, Los Angeles (Clippers), and Indiana. His NBA record in 12 years through 1994-1995 is 533-409.

## Phil Jackson

Born September 17, 1945, Deer Lodge, Montana. Jackson completed just his sixth season with the Chicago Bulls in 1994-1995, and he has already won three NBA titles. Many say that's because he had Michael Jordan. But without Jordan in 1993-1994, the Bulls were still 55-27 and came within a whisker of beating the Knicks in the conference semifinals. Had they won, many felt the team

*PHIL JACKSON*

would have taken a fourth straight title. Through 1994-1995, Jackson's record is an impressive 344-150, for a fine .696 winning percentage.

## Don Nelson

Born May 15, 1940, Muskegon, Michigan. There are some who already call Nelson a coaching genius. The former Laker and Celtic player coached at Milwaukee and Golden State for 18 years and has shown the uncanny ability to make whatever talent he is given into winners. Though he has never won an NBA title, he is a three-time NBA Coach of the Year, and his teams have had just five losing seasons. Nelson resigned as coach of the Warriors midway through the 1994-1995 season. He subsequently signed to succeed Pat Riley as coach of the New York Knicks in 1995-1996. His coaching record through 1994-1995 is 817-607.

# Pat Riley

**PAT RILEY**

Born March 20, 1945, Rome, New York. In 13 years with the Lakers and Knicks, Riley has been a winner and a champion. He guided the Magic Johnson/Kareem Abdul-Jabbar Lakers to four NBA titles in seven final round appearances. In 1994, he had the Knicks in the final round, where they lost to Houston in seven tough games. Tough and demanding, Riley's record through 1994-1995 is 756-299, a winning percentage of .717. He resigned as the Knicks' coach after the 1994-1995 season but was expected to coach elsewhere in the coming years.

# Lenny Wilkens

Born October 28, 1937, Brooklyn, New York. Another Hall of Fame player who has made a very successful transition to coach,

**LENNY WILKENS**

Wilkens has coached for 22 years at Seattle, Portland, Cleveland, and now Atlanta. His SuperSonics team of 1979 won the NBA title after being beaten in the final round the year before. His coaching record through 1994-1995 is 968-814. Wilkens is now the winningest coach of all time, having passed Red Auerbach early in the 1994-1995 season.

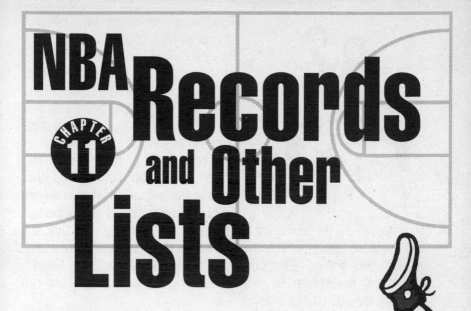

# NBA Records and Other Lists

## CHAPTER 11

**B**asketball is largely a game of numbers. The team that scores the most points wins. The player who scores the most points is the scoring champ. It's impossible to give every NBA record, every stat, and every list. But here are some of the great records, the all-time "bests" and near bests, and the players who set the marks.

# The NBA's Winningest Teams

The two most successful franchises in NBA history are the Boston Celtics, with 16 championships, and the Minneapolis/ Los Angeles Lakers, with 11. No other team has won more than three.

How has your favorite team done over the years? Here are the total NBA records for all the current franchises. Remember, some teams have been in the league longer than others. Total franchise records are included. In other words, the record for the Philadelphia 76ers includes that of the Syracuse Nats since it is the same franchise. No defunct franchises are included, and no ABA records are included. The teams are listed by winning percentage. Records include regular season only and run through the 1994-1995 season.

## NBA Team Records

| Team | Won | Lost | Percentage |
|---|---|---|---|
| **1.** Boston Celtics | 2,389 | 1,416 | .628 |
| **2.** Los Angeles Lakers | 2,239 | 1,456 | .606 |
| **3.** Milwaukee Bucks | 1,246 | 968 | .563 |
| **4.** Philadelphia 76ers | 2,017 | 1,613 | .556 |
| **5.** San Antonio Spurs | 855 | 703 | .549 |
| **6.** Phoenix Suns | 1,205 | 1,009 | .544 |
| **7.** Portland Trail Blazers | 1,085 | 965 | .529 |
| **8.** Chicago Bulls | 1,244 | 1,133 | .523 |
| **9.** Seattle SuperSonics | 1,189 | 1,107 | .518 |
| **10.** New York Knickerbockers | 1,932 | 1,869 | .508 |
| **11.** Atlanta Hawks | 1,838 | 1,794 | .506 |
| **12.** Denver Nuggets | 781 | 777 | .501 |

## NBA Team Records, continued

| | Team | Won | Lost | Percentage |
|---|---|---|---|---|
| 13. | Utah Jazz | 862 | 860 | .501 |
| 14. | Houston Rockets | 1,120 | 1,176 | .488 |
| 15. | Golden State Warriors | 1,842 | 1,958 | .485 |
| 16. | Detroit Pistons | 1,737 | 1,957 | .470 |
| 17. | Washington Bullets | 1,295 | 1,482 | .466 |
| 18. | Sacramento Kings | 1,692 | 2,003 | .458 |
| 19. | Orlando Magic | 218 | 274 | .443 |
| 20. | Cleveland Cavaliers | 906 | 1,144 | .442 |
| 21. | Indiana Pacers | 685 | 873 | .440 |
| 22. | Dallas Mavericks | 515 | 715 | .419 |
| 23. | New Jersey Nets | 630 | 928 | .404 |
| 24. | Charlotte Hornets | 231 | 343 | .402 |
| 25. | Los Angeles Clippers | 749 | 1,301 | .365 |
| 26. | Miami Heat | 205 | 369 | .357 |
| 27. | Minnesota Timberwolves | 126 | 366 | .256 |

It's interesting to note that just 13 of the 27 franchises have winning records. Part of that is due to all the recent expansion. New teams traditionally lose big their first few years in the league.

But a number of longtime franchises, such as the Warriors, Pistons, Bullets, and Kings, have losing records over the years, while the Knicks, long considered a flagship franchise, have only topped the .500 mark because of their recent teams.

There are a number of defunct teams that had winning records before disbanding. The old Chicago Stags were 145-92, the original Washington Capitols were 157-114, and the St. Louis Bombers were 122-115. That just points out the instability of the early NBA. Sometimes even successful teams couldn't survive. In today's game, a winning team is almost always guaranteed a big profit.

One other irony. As of 1995, the most successful franchise in NBA history was in a rebuilding stage. The Celtics were just 35-47 in 1994-

1995. But this club has never been down for long, so watch their progress over the next several seasons.

# Combined All-Time Scoring Leaders

Though there have been many other professional basketball leagues since the early days, the only one remotely recognized by the NBA is the American Basketball Association, which operated from 1968 through 1976. At that point, four ABA teams (the Denver Nuggets, San Antonio Spurs, New Jersey Nets, and Indiana Pacers) were absorbed into the NBA.

The NBA still lists ABA records separately in giving stats for players who performed in both leagues. But they also give a line to combined stats. There have been a number of very great players who either started their careers in the ABA or jumped to the ABA and then later returned to the NBA, including Moses Malone, Julius Erving, Dan Issel, Rick Barry, and George Gervin.

In looking at pro basketball's all-time scoring leaders, the NBA does list the combined records for the ABA and NBA. Here are pro basketball's all-time top 20 scoring leaders. The stats run through the 1994-1995 season. Scoring is by total points, not average.

## Pro Basketball's Top 20 Scorers By Total Points

| Player | Years | Games | Points | Average |
| --- | --- | --- | --- | --- |
| **1.** Kareem Abdul-Jabbar | 20 | 1,560 | 38,387 | 24.6 |
| **2.** Wilt Chamberlain | 14 | 1,045 | 31,419 | 30.1 |
| **3.** Julius Erving | 16 | 1,243 | 30,026 | 24.2 |
| **4.** Moses Malone* | 21 | 1,455 | 29,580 | 20.3 |
| **5.** Dan Issel | 15 | 1,218 | 27,482 | 22.6 |
| **6.** Elvin Hayes | 16 | 1,303 | 27,313 | 21.0 |

## Pro Basketball's Top 20 Scorers
## By Total Points, continued

| Player | Years | Games | Points | Average |
|---|---|---|---|---|
| 7. Oscar Robertson | 14 | 1,040 | 26,710 | 25.7 |
| 8. George Gervin | 14 | 1,060 | 26,595 | 25.1 |
| 9. John Havlicek | 16 | 1,270 | 26,395 | 20.8 |
| 10. Alex English | 15 | 1,193 | 25,613 | 21.5 |
| 11. Dominique Wilkins* | 13 | 984 | 25,389 | 25.8 |
| 12. Rick Barry | 14 | 1,020 | 25,279 | 24.8 |
| 13. Jerry West | 14 | 932 | 25,192 | 27.0 |
| 14. Artis Gilmore | 17 | 1,329 | 24,941 | 18.8 |
| 15. Robert Parish* | 19 | 1,494 | 23,180 | 15.5 |
| 16. Adrian Dantley | 15 | 955 | 23,177 | 24.3 |
| 17. Elgin Baylor | 14 | 846 | 23,149 | 27.4 |
| 18. Michael Jordan* | 10 | 684 | 21,998 | 32.2 |
| 19. Larry Bird | 13 | 897 | 21,791 | 24.3 |
| 20. Hal Greer | 15 | 1,122 | 21,586 | 19.2 |

*\* Denotes active player*

There is one thing that truly stands out when looking at this list. That is the accomplishment of Michael Jordan in just ten years. If he plays another six years and averages 30 points per game for 82 games, he would score another 14,760 points. That would give him more than 36,000 points, putting him solidly into second place behind Kareem.

As it is, Jordan has the highest average per game among the top 20 scorers. Let's see on the next page how the top ten would look if the list were based on average and not total points.

## Pro Basketball's Top Ten Scorers By Average

| Player | Average |
|---|---|
| **1.** Michael Jordan* | 32.2 points per game |
| **2.** Wilt Chamberlain | 30.1 points per game |
| **3.** Elgin Baylor | 27.4 points per game |
| **4.** Jerry West | 27.0 points per game |
| **5.** Dominique Wilkins* | 25.8 points per game |
| **6.** Oscar Robertson | 25.7 points per game |
| **7.** George Gervin | 25.1 points per game |
| **8.** Rick Barry | 24.8 points per game |
| **9.** Kareem Abdul-Jabbar | 24.6 points per game |
| **10.** Adrian Dantley | 24.3 points per game |
| **10.** Larry Bird | 24.3 points per game |

* Denotes active player

Who, then, is the greatest scorer? Is it the guy who played the most years and had the most points? Or is it the player whose career might have been shorter but who averaged more points per game? The immediate answer is that all of these men were great scorers.

Think about it some more. The players who stay in the league the longest invariably tail off in their final seasons. In his first nine years, Kareem Abdul-Jabbar scored 20,238 points in 693 games for a 29.2 average—over four points better than his final average. Wilt Chamberlain, on the other hand, scored 25,434 points in 706 games for a 36.0 average in his first nine seasons. After that, Wilt didn't emphasize scoring as much.

If you look at Wilt's physical attributes and what he did early in his career, including that 50.4 average in 1961-1962, then the Big Dipper was probably the greatest pure scorer the game has ever seen. In close, he was virtually unstoppable. As for the most spectacular scorer, nearly everyone agrees that Michael Jordan heads that list.

But the real truth is the immediate answer given before. All of these men were great scorers.

# Postseason Awards

As in other sports, the NBA has several prestigious postseason awards that are always awaited with anticipation. Perhaps the top prize is the Maurice Podoloff Trophy, given to the man considered the league's Most Valuable Player. Maurice Podoloff was the NBA's first commissioner. The award was first given following the 1955-1956 season.

Unlike baseball, where a player can occasionally rise to have one incredible season, win the MVP, and then become mediocre again, in the NBA it's always the superstar player who takes home the MVP. Here are the winners since the Podoloff Trophy was first presented.

## NBA Most Valuable Players

| Year | Player | Position | Team |
|------|--------|----------|------|
| 1955-1956 | Bob Pettit | Forward | St. Louis Hawks |
| 1956-1957 | Bob Cousy | Guard | Boston Celtics |
| 1957-1958 | Bill Russell | Center | Boston Celtics |
| 1958-1959 | Bob Pettit | Forward | St. Louis Hawks |
| 1959-1960 | Wilt Chamberlain | Center | Philadelphia Warriors |
| 1960-1961 | Bill Russell | Center | Boston Celtics |
| 1961-1962 | Bill Russell | Center | Boston Celtics |
| 1962-1963 | Bill Russell | Center | Boston Celtics |
| 1963-1964 | Oscar Robertson | Guard | Cincinnati Royals |
| 1964-1965 | Bill Russell | Center | Boston Celtics |
| 1965-1966 | Wilt Chamberlain | Center | Philadelphia 76ers |
| 1966-1967 | Wilt Chamberlain | Center | Philadelphia 76ers |
| 1967-1968 | Wilt Chamberlain | Center | Philadelphia 76ers |
| 1968-1969 | Wes Unseld | Center | Baltimore Bullets |
| 1969-1970 | Willis Reed | Center | New York Knicks |
| 1970-1971 | Lew Alcindor (Kareem Abdul-Jabbar) | Center | Milwaukee Bucks |

# NBA Most Valuable Players, continued

| Year | Player | Position | Team |
|------|--------|----------|------|
| 1971-1972 | Kareem Abdul-Jabbar | Center | Milwaukee Bucks |
| 1972-1973 | Dave Cowens | Center | Boston Celtics |
| 1973-1974 | Kareem Abdul-Jabbar | Center | Milwaukee Bucks |
| 1974-1975 | Bob McAdoo | Center | Buffalo Braves |
| 1975-1976 | Kareem Abdul-Jabbar | Center | Los Angeles Lakers |
| 1976-1977 | Kareem Abdul-Jabbar | Center | Los Angeles Lakers |
| 1977-1978 | Bill Walton | Center | Portland Trail Blazers |
| 1978-1979 | Moses Malone | Center | Houston Rockets |
| 1979-1980 | Kareem Abdul-Jabbar | Center | Los Angeles Lakers |
| 1980-1981 | Julius Erving | Forward | Philadelphia 76ers |
| 1981-1982 | Moses Malone | Center | Houston Rockets |
| 1982-1983 | Moses Malone | Center | Philadelphia 76ers |
| 1983-1984 | Larry Bird | Forward | Boston Celtics |
| 1984-1985 | Larry Bird | Forward | Boston Celtics |
| 1985-1986 | Larry Bird | Forward | Boston Celtics |
| 1986-1987 | Magic Johnson | Guard | Los Angeles Lakers |
| 1987-1988 | Michael Jordan | Guard | Chicago Bulls |
| 1988-1989 | Magic Johnson | Guard | Los Angeles Lakers |
| 1989-1990 | Magic Johnson | Guard | Los Angeles Lakers |
| 1990-1991 | Michael Jordan | Guard | Chicago Bulls |
| 1991-1992 | Michael Jordan | Guard | Chicago Bulls |
| 1992-1993 | Charles Barkley | Forward | Phoenix Suns |
| 1993-1994 | Hakeem Olajuwon | Center | Houston Rockets |
| 1994-1995 | David Robinson | Center | San Antonio Spurs |

A closer look at the MVP prize reveals some interesting things. For openers, Kareem Abdul-Jabbar is the only six-time winner of the prize. Bill Russell won it five times, Wilt Chamberlain four. They are arguably the three most dominant centers in the history of the game.

Of the 40 MVP awards through 1994-1995, 25 have gone to centers, seven to forwards, and eight to guards. From 1959-1960 through 1979-1980, centers won the prize 20 times in 21 years, including 16 in a row. But the pendulum swung back in the 1980s and early 1990s, when Larry Bird, Magic Johnson, Michael Jordan, and Charles Barkley combined to take the prize ten years in a row.

Perhaps the game had changed. In the 1980s, the dominant player was a forward or guard of multiple skills, a player good enough to play almost any position on the court—except center. A championship team didn't have to be built around a superstar center.

But things may be changing again. Hakeem Olajuwon deservedly won the prize in 1993-1994 and David Robinson took it in 1994-1995. Waiting in the wings are centers Shaquille O'Neal, Patrick Ewing, and Alonzo Mourning. It will be interesting to watch in upcoming years to see if yet another MVP pattern emerges.

# Finals MVPs

The award for the Most Valuable Player in the NBA finals wasn't presented until 1969. Some of the same names appear as in the list of Podoloff Trophy winners, but the best-of-seven final series affords some lesser known players a chance to shine. Over the long season, the MVP has always been a superstar. But check out the finals MVPs on the next page. There are some surprising names.

# NBA Finals Most Valuable Players

| Year | Player | Position | Team |
|------|--------|----------|------|
| 1969 | Jerry West | Guard | Los Angeles Lakers |
| 1970 | Willis Reed | Center | New York Knicks |
| 1971 | Lew Alcindor (Kareem Abdul-Jabbar) | Center | Milwaukee Bucks |
| 1972 | Wilt Chamberlain | Center | Los Angeles Lakers |
| 1973 | Willis Reed | Center | New York Knicks |
| 1974 | John Havlicek | Guard | Boston Celtics |
| 1975 | Rick Barry | Forward | Golden State Warriors |
| 1976 | Jo Jo White | Guard | Boston Celtics |
| 1977 | Bill Walton | Center | Portland Trail Blazers |
| 1978 | Wes Unseld | Center | Washington Bullets |
| 1979 | Dennis Johnson | Guard | Seattle SuperSonics |
| 1980 | Magic Johnson | Guard | Los Angeles Lakers |
| 1981 | Cedric Maxwell | Forward | Boston Celtics |
| 1982 | Magic Johnson | Guard | Los Angeles Lakers |
| 1983 | Moses Malone | Center | Philadelphia 76ers |
| 1984 | Larry Bird | Forward | Boston Celtics |
| 1985 | Kareem Abdul-Jabbar | Center | Los Angeles Lakers |
| 1986 | Larry Bird | Forward | Boston Celtics |
| 1987 | Magic Johnson | Guard | Los Angeles Lakers |
| 1988 | James Worthy | Forward | Los Angeles Lakers |
| 1989 | Joe Dumars | Guard | Detroit Pistons |
| 1990 | Isiah Thomas | Guard | Detroit Pistons |
| 1991 | Michael Jordan | Guard | Chicago Bulls |
| 1992 | Michael Jordan | Guard | Chicago Bulls |
| 1993 | Michael Jordan | Guard | Chicago Bulls |
| 1994 | Hakeem Olajuwon | Center | Houston Rockets |
| 1995 | Hakeem Olajuwon | Center | Houston Rockets |

In the finals, in 27 years of the award, ten centers have won, five forwards, and 12 guards. Of course, six of the 12 guards were named Magic and Michael. But in a short series, it seems that a backcourtman can often take the game in his own hands. Dennis Johnson, Joe Dumars, and Isiah Thomas were all fine players, big game players, and their selection is not surprising.

One other interesting number. Only nine times in the 27 years of the finals MVP has the regular season Most Valuable Player duplicated that prize in the finals. Of course, the regular season MVP hasn't always been in the finals, but in many cases he has. And if it weren't for Michael Jordan and Hakeem Olajuwon often receiving the finals MVP in the last several years, that number would appear much more significant.

# Rookie of the Year

The Rookie of the Year award is another prestigious award, a prize that top rookies vie for each season. Many of the top rookies have gone on to great careers. A few have disappointed. See how many of the names on the next page you know and how many went on to become true NBA superstars. The prize was first given in 1952-1953 and the trophy is named after Eddie Gottlieb, a basketball pioneer and coach of the Philadelphia Warriors the first nine years of NBA play. He was later the league's schedule maker.

# NBA Rookies of the Year

| Year | Player | Position | Team |
|------|--------|----------|------|
| 1952-1953 | Don Meineke | Forward | Fort Wayne Pistons |
| 1953-1954 | Ray Felix | Center | Baltimore Bullets |
| 1954-1955 | Bob Pettit | Forward | Milwaukee Hawks |
| 1955-1956 | Maurice Stokes | Forward | Rochester Royals |
| 1956-1957 | Tom Heinsohn | Forward | Boston Celtics |
| 1957-1958 | Woody Sauldsberry | Forward | Philadelphia Warriors |
| 1958-1959 | Elgin Baylor | Forward | Minneapolis Lakers |
| 1959-1960 | Wilt Chamberlain | Center | Philadelphia Warriors |
| 1960-1961 | Oscar Robertson | Guard | Cincinnati Royals |
| 1961-1962 | Walt Bellamy | Center | Chicago Packers |
| 1962-1963 | Terry Dischinger | Forward | Chicago Zephyrs |
| 1963-1964 | Jerry Lucas | Center/Forward | Cincinnati Royals |
| 1964-1965 | Willis Reed | Center | New York Knicks |
| 1965-1966 | Rick Barry | Forward | San Francisco Warriors |
| 1966-1967 | Dave Bing | Guard | Detroit Pistons |
| 1967-1968 | Earl Monroe | Guard | Baltimore Bullets |
| 1968-1969 | Wes Unseld | Center | Baltimore Bullets |
| 1969-1970 | Lew Alcindor (Kareem Abdul-Jabbar) | Center | Milwaukee Bucks |
| 1970-1971 | Dave Cowens<br>Geoff Petrie | Center<br>Guard | Boston Celtics<br>Portland Trail Blazers |
| 1971-1972 | Sidney Wicks | Forward | Portland Trail Blazers |
| 1972-1973 | Bob McAdoo | Center | Buffalo Braves |

| Year | Player | Position | Team |
|------|--------|----------|------|
| 1973-1974 | Ernie DiGregorio | Guard | Buffalo Braves |
| 1974-1975 | Keith Wilkes | Forward | Golden State Warriors |
| 1975-1976 | Alvan Adams | Center | Phoenix Suns |
| 1976-1977 | Adrian Dantley | Forward | Buffalo Braves |
| 1977-1978 | Walter Davis | Forward | Phoenix Suns |
| 1978-1979 | Phil Ford | Guard | Kansas City Kings |
| 1979-1980 | Larry Bird | Forward | Boston Celtics |
| 1980-1981 | Darrell Griffith | Guard | Utah Jazz |
| 1981-1982 | Buck Williams | Forward | New Jersey Nets |
| 1982-1983 | Terry Cummings | Forward | San Diego Clippers |
| 1983-1984 | Ralph Sampson | Center | Houston Rockets |
| 1984-1985 | Michael Jordan | Guard | Chicago Bulls |
| 1985-1986 | Patrick Ewing | Center | New York Knicks |
| 1986-1987 | Chuck Person | Forward | Indiana Pacers |
| 1987-1988 | Mark Jackson | Guard | New York Knicks |
| 1988-1989 | Mitch Richmond | Guard | Golden State Warriors |
| 1989-1990 | David Robinson | Center | San Antonio Spurs |
| 1990-1991 | Derrick Coleman | Forward | New Jersey Nets |
| 1991-1992 | Larry Johnson | Forward | Charlotte Hornets |
| 1992-1993 | Shaquille O'Neal | Center | Orlando Magic |
| 1993-1994 | Chris Webber | Forward/Center | Golden State Warriors |
| 1994-1995 | Grant Hill | Forward | Detroit Pistons |
| | Jason Kidd | Guard | Dallas Mavericks |

Another interesting list. It is certainly loaded with players who have become superstars and all-time greats: Bob Pettit, Elgin Baylor, Oscar Robertson, Wilt Chamberlain, Kareem Abdul-Jabbar, Patrick

Ewing, Larry Johnson, Shaquille O'Neal. But there are also those who never quite lived up to rookie expectations.

Some are slowed by injury; others just don't have the drive or desire to live up to the promise their Rookie of the Year awards have shown. Players like Woody Sauldsberry, Terry Dischinger, Sidney Wicks, Ernie DiGregorio, Ralph Sampson, and Chuck Person are some examples of players who certainly had talent but never quite fulfilled the promise of those first seasons.

More interesting, perhaps, are the names of some great players who weren't Rookies of the Year. Here are a few examples, with the player who *was* Rookie of the Year that year instead.

## NBA Players Who Were Not Rookies of the Year

| Year | Nonwinner | Award Winner |
|---|---|---|
| 1956-1957 | Bill Russell | Tom Heinsohn |
| 1960-1961 | Jerry West | Oscar Robertson |
| 1962-1963 | John Havlicek, Dave DeBusschere | Terry Dischinger |
| 1963-1964 | Nate Thurmond | Jerry Lucas |
| 1656-1966 | Billy Cunningham | Rick Barry |
| 1966-1967 | Cazzie Russell | Dave Bing |
| 1967-1968 | Walt Frazier | Earl Monroe |
| 1968-1969 | Elvin Hayes | Wes Unseld |
| 1970-1971 | Pete Maravich, Bob Lanier | Geoff Petrie, Dave Cowens |
| 1977-1978 | Marques Johnson, Bernard King | Walter Davis |
| 1979-1980 | Magic Johnson | Larry Bird |
| 1980-1981 | Kevin McHale | Darrell Griffith |
| 1981-1982 | Isiah Thomas | Buck Williams |
| 1982-1983 | Dominique Wilkins, James Worthy | Terry Cummings |

## NBA Players Who Were Not Rookies of the Year, continued

| Year | Nonwinner | Award Winner |
|------|-----------|--------------|
| 1984-1985 | Hakeem Olajuwon, Charles Barkley | Michael Jordan |
| 1985-1986 | Joe Dumars | Patrick Ewing |
| 1989-1990 | Tim Hardaway | David Robinson |
| 1992-1993 | Alonzo Mourning | Shaquille O'Neal |
| 1993-1994 | Anfernee Hardaway | Chris Webber |
| 1994-1995 | Glenn Robinson | Grant Hill, Jason Kidd |

Quite a list of impressive players. Imagine a team with Magic Johnson and Isiah Thomas at guard, Hakeem Olajuwon at center, and Charles Barkley and Elvin Hayes at forward. That's about as good as it gets. Here's another one: Jerry West and Walt Frazier at guard, Bill Russell at center, and Kevin McHale and Billy Cunningham at forward. Try a third team: Pete Maravich and John Havlicek at guard, Nate Thurmond or Bob Lanier at center, and Bernard King and Dominique Wilkins at forward.

There are three incredible basketball teams made up of players who, in their first season, weren't judged good enough to be Rookie of the Year. That's how tough it sometimes can be to pick the best rookie.

# Defensive Player of the Year

Though this award has been presented only since 1983, it has become one of the most prestigious prizes in the game. It's no secret that great defensive teams with outstanding defensive players win championships.

In the 13 years the award has been given, only two recipients have been members of the NBA championship team, Dennis Rodman in 1989-1990 and Hakeem Olajuwon in 1993-1994. The complete list of Defensive Player of the Year winners is on the next page.

## NBA Defensive Players of the Year

| Year | Player | Position | Team |
|------|--------|----------|------|
| 1982-1983 | Sidney Moncrief | Guard | Milwaukee Bucks |
| 1983-1984 | Sidney Moncrief | Guard | Milwaukee Bucks |
| 1984-1985 | Mark Eaton | Center | Utah Jazz |
| 1985-1986 | Alvin Robertson | Guard | San Antonio Spurs |
| 1986-1987 | Michael Cooper | Guard | Los Angeles Lakers |
| 1987-1988 | Michael Jordan | Guard | Chicago Bulls |
| 1988-1989 | Mark Eaton | Center | Utah Jazz |
| 1989-1990 | Dennis Rodman | Forward | Detroit Pistons |
| 1990-1991 | Dennis Rodman | Forward | Detroit Pistons |
| 1991-1992 | David Robinson | Center | San Antonio Spurs |
| 1992-1993 | Hakeem Olajuwon | Center | Houston Rockets |
| 1993-1994 | Hakeem Olajuwon | Center | Houston Rockets |
| 1994-1995 | Dikembe Mutombo | Center | Denver Nuggets |

In the first six years the award was given, it was won by guards five times. In the last seven years, five centers and two forwards have won, no guards. That and the fact that only two NBA champion players have won in the same year their teams have won indicate that the award is given to the player who is judged to play the best defense in the league, not necessarily the one on the best team.

# Number One Overall Draft Picks

The NBA draft gives the poorer teams an opportunity to have the early choice of the best college players available each year. And the team that gets the first pick overall has a chance to take the collegian they feel will make the most impact on their team. So the first pick overall is an important decision.

Prior to 1966, the draft didn't have quite the same significance. That's because territorial picks were allowed. A team had the rights to college players whose schools were in their territory. So there was no way any other team could pick the great Oscar Robertson in 1960. He went to the University of Cincinnati, giving the Cincinnati Royals the first chance to pick him, even if they didn't pick first in the draft.

In recent years, there have been several versions of a draft lottery. That means the teams not making the playoffs all have a shot at getting the number one pick, though the team with the poorest record has the best chance. And every team with a chance wants that number one pick.

Here are the top draft picks overall since the end of territorial choices (before 1966). See how many you know and how you think they have helped their teams.

## Number One NBA Draft Picks

| Year | Player, College | Position | Pro Team |
|------|-----------------|----------|----------|
| 1966 | Cazzie Russell, Michigan | Guard | New York Knicks |
| 1967 | Jimmy Walker, Providence | Guard | Detroit Pistons |
| 1968 | Elvin Hayes, Houston | Forward | Houston Rockets |
| 1969 | Lew Alcindor (Kareem Abdul-Jabbar), UCLA | Center | Milwaukee Bucks |
| 1970 | Bob Lanier, St. Bonaventure | Center | Detroit Pistons |
| 1971 | Austin Carr, Notre Dame | Guard | Cleveland Cavaliers |
| 1972 | LaRue Martin, Loyola-Chicago | Center | Portland Trail Blazers |
| 1973 | Doug Collins, Illinois State | Guard | Philadelphia 76ers |
| 1974 | Bill Walton, UCLA | Center | Portland Trail Blazers |
| 1975 | David Thompson, North Carolina State | Guard | Atlanta Hawks |
| 1976 | John Lucas, Maryland | Guard | Houston Rockets |
| 1977 | Kent Benson, Indiana | Center | Milwaukee Bucks |
| 1978 | Mychal Thompson, Minnesota | Center | Portland Trail Blazers |
| 1979 | Magic Johnson, Michigan State | Guard | Los Angeles Lakers |

## Number One NBA Draft Picks, continued

| Year | Player, College | Position | Pro Team |
|---|---|---|---|
| 1980 | Joe Barry Carroll, Purdue | Center | Golden State Warriors |
| 1981 | Mark Aguirre, DePaul | Forward | Dallas Mavericks |
| 1982 | James Worthy, North Carolina | Forward | Los Angeles Lakers |
| 1983 | Ralph Sampson, Virginia | Center | Houston Rockets |
| 1984 | Hakeem Olajuwon, Houston | Center | Houston Rockets |
| 1985 | Patrick Ewing, Georgetown | Center | New York Knicks |
| 1986 | Brad Daugherty, North Carolina | Center | Cleveland Cavaliers |
| 1987 | David Robinson, Navy | Center | San Antonio Spurs |
| 1988 | Danny Manning, Kansas | Forward | Los Angeles Clippers |
| 1989 | Pervis Ellison, Louisville | Center | Sacramento Kings |
| 1990 | Derrick Coleman, Syracuse | Forward | New Jersey Nets |
| 1991 | Larry Johnson, UNLV | Forward | Charlotte Hornets |
| 1992 | Shaquille O'Neal, LSU | Center | Orlando Magic |
| 1993 | Chris Webber, Michigan | Center/ Forward | Orlando Magic |
| 1994 | Glenn Robinson, Purdue | Forward | Milwaukee Bucks |
| 1995 | Joe Smith, Maryland | Center/ Forward | Golden State Warriors |

There are certainly many familiar names in the list. But of 30 first picks, only eight of the players have been good enough to be named Rookie of the Year. However, up to 1989, only three of the first rounders won the top rookie prize. Then, five straight top choices won the top rookie award: David Robinson, Coleman, Johnson, O'Neal, and Webber. (Robinson was the top choice in 1987, but because of a Naval commitment, he didn't play until 1989.)

Arguably, you can probably count ten superstars among the 30 top choices, and that includes young players Coleman, Johnson, and O'Neal. They still have to do it over a longer period of time. Hayes, Alcindor (Abdul-Jabbar), Lanier, Magic Johnson, Olajuwon, Ewing, and David Robinson can probably be given the superstar label. Walton would have undoubtedly also been a superstar had his career not been limited by foot injuries.

Others—such as Russell, Carr, Collins, David Thompson, Lucas, Mychal Thompson, Aguirre, Worthy, Daugherty, and Manning—were all outstanding players, just a notch below the elite group. Manning may still make it.

Number one choices who have to be classified as disappointing were Walker, Martin, Benson, Carroll, and Ellison. These players did not reach the expectations NBA teams had for them. Ellison is still active and has a chance.

In recent years, the crop of college players has been so strong that a number one choice is almost a "can't miss." The years 1990 to 1994 have produced Derrick Coleman, Larry Johnson, Shaquille O'Neal, Chris Webber, and Glenn Robinson. The first three are already impact players. Webber was Rookie of the Year in 1994, and Glenn Robinson was college basketball's Player of the Year. He is fully expected to take his place very soon among the NBA's elite.

# Let's Go to the Record Book

A number of great NBA records have already been mentioned in other sections of this book. But here's another quick trip through the record book with some of the amazing marks set down through the years.

# On the Court With Wilt

No one spent more time on a basketball court than Wilt Chamberlain. In his long career he averaged 45.8 minutes on court during each game. That's just a little over two minutes on the bench. And in one season, 1961-1962, Wilt averaged 48.5 minutes for 80 games. That's a half a minute over the maximum, because Wilt also played in several overtime games. In fact, he played the complete 48 minutes 79 times that year, sitting in only one game. And 47 of those complete games came in a row, another NBA mark.

Another reason Wilt didn't have to sit was that he was rarely in foul trouble. Despite being one of the great defensive centers of all time, Wilt had the agility and skill to keep from fouling. In fact, he also set another incredible record. In 1,045 regular season games and another 160 playoff games, Wilt Chamberlain never fouled out. Not once!

# Mr. Consistency

Here's one that will surprise a lot of people. Which player holds the NBA record for scoring 2,000 or more points the most consecutive seasons? The answer is Alex English, one of the NBA's most well kept superstar secrets. English had 2,000 or more points for eight straight years while playing for the Denver Nuggets from 1981-1982 to 1988-1989.

# Ice-Cold Superstar

Point guard Tim Hardaway of the Golden State Warriors is considered one of the finer players in the NBA. Yet on December 27, 1991, Hardaway set a record that he would never want to beat. In an overtime game at San Antonio, Hardaway shot the ball 17 times ... and made none, the most field goal attempts in a game without one going through the hoop.

# Long-Range Bombers

Beginning in the 1979-1980 season, the NBA instituted a three-point field goal for a shot taken behind a line 23'9" from the center of the basket (since changed to 22 feet from the basket). The three-point line is marked on the court around the hoop from one side of the basket to the other. Long-range bombing is a great way for a team to open up a bigger lead or close a gap quickly.

Most teams try to have one or more outstanding three-point shooters on the club. The most successful so far has been Dale Ellis, who has played for Dallas, Seattle, Milwaukee, and San Antonio since 1983-1984. Since his rookie year, Ellis has connected on 1,119 three-pointers in 2,783 tries. That's the most of any player in history.

The single season record is held by John Starks of New York, who canned 217 of 611 "tres" in 1994-1995. His 611 attempts is also an NBA mark.

Other players also set records in 1994-1995. Jeff Hornacek of Utah redefined the meaning of being "in the zone" on November 23, 1994, when he set a record by hitting eight straight three-pointers without a miss in a game against Seattle. Dana Barros of the 76ers set a new NBA mark by canning at least one tre in 58 consecutive games from December 23, 1994, to April 23, 1995. On January 29, 1995, the Phoenix Suns set a new record for long-range firing by hoisting up 39 three-pointers in a game against the Knicks. In the second half alone, the Suns fired 28 times from long range. And in a game on April 11, 1995, Dallas and Houston set a combined mark for three-point bombing when they sent the basketball flying toward the hoop 64 times from downtown.

# Canning Free Throws

To some players, a free throw is like trying to shoot a beachball through a tin can. To others, it's like trying to shoot a baseball through a hula-hoop. But even when the top foul shooters have a streak going, the pressure mounts. The ball seems bigger, the hoop smaller.

In 1980-1981, Calvin Murphy of Houston set a record by canning 78 free throws in a row. Then in 1992-1993, Mark Price of Cleveland, who has the all-time best NBA free throw percentage, made a run at Murphy's mark. He reached 77 straight, then missed.

Finally, also during the 1992-1993 season, Micheal Williams of the lowly Minnesota Timberwolves began making free throws. The streak reached 50, then 60, and finally 70. With the pressure mounting, Williams tied Murphy's record, then broke it! When he finally missed, he had brought the new consecutive free throw mark to an astounding 84 in a row.

# Grab That Rebound

There were probably more rebounds to be had in the 1950s and 1960s because shooting percentages were lower and not as many players slam dunked. Or maybe the rebounders back then were better. But the top five all-time rebounders all come from that era.

Wilt Chamberlain tops the list, averaging 22.9 rebounds for every game of his long career. Bill Russell is second. He averaged 22.5 boards per game.

Next comes a surprise. Third is Bob Pettit, a 6'9" forward, who grabbed an average of 16.2 rebounds during his Hall of Fame career. Jerry Lucas, a 6'8" center/forward, also had a great nose for the ball, averaging 15.6 rebounds during his career. And center Nate Thurmond, who might have done even better if it weren't for a succession of leg and knee injuries, still averaged 15.0 caroms a game during his time in the NBA.

# Steals and Blocks

These are two relatively new statistics that weren't kept until the 1973-1974 season, so the great players from the 1950s and 1960s never got a chance to compete in these categories. It's hard to figure anyone blocking more shots than Bill Russell, but no one will ever know for sure.

As it stands today, basketball's biggest one-season thief was Alvin Robertson of the San Antonio Spurs. In 1985-1986, Robertson was credited with

301 steals, an average of 3.7 thefts per game. For a single game, the top performance came from forward Larry Kenon. Playing for the San Antonio Spurs against Kansas City on December 26, 1976, Kenon swiped the basketball 11 times.

The single-season leader in blocked shots might surprise some. It's not Olajuwon, Robinson, or Ewing. It is Mark Eaton, the former 7'4" center of the Utah Jazz. Eaton was not especially quick nor was he a great leaper. But he had great timing and in 1985-1986 blocked 456 shots, an average of 5.56 a game.

For one game, the record is held by 7'0" Elmore Smith. Playing for the Lakers against the Trail Blazers on October 28, 1973, Smith blocked an incredible 17 shots. Imagine being able to do that every night.

# Best and Worst

The best single-season record compiled in the NBA goes to the 1971-1972 Los Angeles Lakers, who finished the season at 69-13. The record for futility goes to the 1972-1973 Philadelphia 76ers. Just six years after posting a great 68-13 season, the franchise had fallen on hard times and finished the season with an awful 9-73 mark. Next comes the 1992-1993 Dallas Mavericks. That club was almost as bad, finishing with an 11-71 record. Those aren't easy seasons to finish.

# Short Takes

The 1990-1991 Philadelphia 76ers played in a record 14 overtime games.

The highest-scoring team in NBA history was the 1981-1982 Denver Nuggets. They averaged 126.5 points a game. They also allowed their opponents 126.0 points a game, pretty much a standoff.

The highest-scoring game in NBA history occurred on December 13, 1983, a triple-overtime thriller between Detroit and Denver. The Pistons won it, 186-184.

The largest margin of victory ever occurred on December 17, 1991, when the Cleveland Cavaliers defeated the Miami Heat, 148-80, a difference of 68 points. No last-minute rallies here.

# The CHAPTER 12 Harlem Globetrotters

*T*hey take to the court to the upbeat tune of "Sweet Georgia Brown," form a circle at midcourt, and proceed to do magic with the basketball. It is a warm-up routine that has been seen for nearly half a century, an entertaining example of basketball wizardry as the ball zips between players in every conceivable way. It's a now-you-see-it, now-you-don't example of how basketball skills can be used for pure entertainment.

You may have guessed that we're describing the Harlem Globetrotters, a team usually made up of African-American players. They are basketball's premier entertainers and over the years have been one of its greatest ambassadors. The Trotters' routine is comedy. They play it strictly for laughs while utilizing outstanding basketball talent from fine players. But it wasn't always that way. When they started, the Trotters were out to earn respect.

# The New York Renaissance

The Trotters were not the first all African-American basketball team or the only one. In the early days of pro basketball, a man named Robert Douglas started an all African-American team named the New York Renaissance. The team barnstormed the country from 1922 to 1949, taking on all comers. They often faced long bus rides, cold sandwiches, and racial discrimination. Despite harsh and sometimes dangerous conditions, the team compiled an amazing 2,588-539 record.

During one 86-day stretch in 1932-1933, the Rens won an incredible 88 straight basketball games. And at a 1939 tournament billed as the World Professional Tournament, the Rens defeated the NBL champion Oshkosh All-Stars, 34-25, to become world champs. That year, the team had a 112-7 record, making them basketball's best.

Several of the Ren players, as well as founder and coach Douglas, are in basketball's Hall of Fame.

# The Trotters Are Born

*ABE SAPERSTEIN*

The Harlem Globetrotters were organized in 1927 by a man named Abe Saperstein, who had been coaching an all African-American team in the Chicago. After a dispute with the team's owner, Saperstein decided to put his own team together, which he named the Harlem Globetrotters. Harlem was the name of an African-American neighborhood in New York City, but Saperstein was from Chicago.

"That was the trick," Saperstein explained. "'Harlem' lets people know we're a black team. And 'Harlem Globetrotters' makes it sound as if we've been around. Who knows? Maybe someday we really will travel around the world."

The team began barnstorming, and soon they were beating most of the teams they played. Then in 1929, Saperstein signed a great player and showman named Inman Jackson. Saperstein decided to use all his talents, and the Trotters began to put comedy routines into their easier games.

# Early Routines

**INMAN JACKSON**

The comedy started in games when the Trotters had a big lead and didn't have to worry about losing. It all started with Inman Jackson. He was one of the few players back then who could palm a basketball. He would swing the ball around and around with one hand and not drop it. Fans always roared when he would fake a one-handed pass and not let go of the ball.

He was also able to spin the basketball on his fingertips for minutes at a time. Fans would also love watching this, clapping and yelling for more. And he could swing the ball behind his back and between his legs as his opponents tried to take it from him.

Jackson also began developing routines where he would fake one way, then another, as the man guarding him lunged and lunged. Finally, Jackson would put the ball on top of the bewildered man's head and walk away. The fans would roar.

When Abe Saperstein saw how the fans loved Inman Jackson's routines, he began getting other players into the act. In the early days, opponents didn't always like the Trotters' routines. They thought the fans were laughing at *them*, so there were occasional fights. After all, the object of the game was still to see which team would win.

# World Champs

In 1940 the Trotters proved they could play serious basketball. They entered a big pro tournament in Chicago, the winner to be declared World Champion. The Trotters went to work. Playing only serious basketball, they beat the Kenosha Royals, 50-26. Then they beat the New York Renaissance in a great game, 37-36.

Next came the semifinals, and the Trotters whipped the Syracuse Reds, 34-24. In the finals, they went up against the hometown Chicago Bruins. It was still the days of low-scoring games, and in the third quarter the Trotters held a 20-13 lead. But suddenly the Bruins got hot and went on a 16-1 run, taking a 29-21 lead with just five minutes left.

Playing their best basketball, the Trotters began hitting their shots once more and stopping the Bruins cold. They scored the last ten points of the game to win the championship, 31-29. They had proved that their clowning was just entertainment. When they wanted to, they could play basketball as well as or better than any team of the day.

*REECE "GOOSE" TATUM*

*MARQUES HAYNES*

# Goose and Marques

A new era started for the Globetrotters in the 1940s. In 1941, Abe Saperstein discovered a player named Reece Tatum. But everyone called him "Goose." Goose Tatum was not only a talented player but had a natural ability to entertain. He was 6'3" and had long arms and huge hands. Shortly after he joined the team he entered the service during World War II. When he returned, the Trotters really began to flourish.

By 1947 the Trotters were using the "Sweet Georgia Brown" theme song, and other new players had joined the team. One was Marques Haynes, who was billed as the World's Greatest Dribbler. Haynes would invariably go into his dribbling routine while all five players on the other team tried to take the ball from him.

He would dribble while sitting, lying flat on the court, kneeling, and, of course, standing and moving. Tatum, meanwhile, had perfected and embellished the early comedy routines developed by Inman Jackson. Other players joined the team, including Nat "Sweetwater"

Clifton, who would later become one of the first African-American players in the NBA. Another was Leon Hilliard, who could regularly hit a two-handed set shot from way, way out, also electrifying the crowds.

The Trotters became a unique team, giving fans pure basketball entertainment against different foes but eventually traveling with their own setup team to act as their foils.

# Worldwide Basketball, Globetrotter Style

**CURLY NEAL**

Abe Saperstein was right. The Harlem Globetrotters did begin to hopscotch the world, bringing their entertaining basketball routines to happy fans everywhere. And in doing so, they became one of the first ambassadors of the American court game, spreading basketball to all corners of the world.

Other players followed the great tradition. Eventually Meadowlark Lemon took over for Goose Tatum and Curly Neal became the team's new dribbling sensation. Even Wilt Chamberlain played with the Trotters for a year while waiting to enter the NBA. Other famous athletes have also taken a turn traveling with the Trotters. Some of them include basketball great Connie Hawkins, St. Louis Cardinal star pitcher Bob Gibson, and boxing champ Sugar Ray Robinson.

Abe Saperstein died in 1966, but the Trotters continue to be a worldwide basketball attraction—incredible ambassadors of basketball and goodwill.

# Some Great

# Great

## CHAPTER 13

# Early

# College Teams

By 1915 the Amateur Athletic Union met with the YMCAs and the International Athletic Association (the early name for the NCAA) and standardized the rules for amateur play everywhere. So, college basketball was basically the same game all over the country by 1920. Here are some of the special moments and special people who made early college ball so exciting.

As college basketball grew and prospered, the sport began developing more of a personality. There was more press, more games being broadcast on radio, and more players, coaches, and teams becoming known across the country. What was once strictly a regional sport was beginning to spread.

The successful teams wanted to try their luck against other successful teams, even if those clubs were on the other side of the country. It seemed just a matter of time before someone would begin to think in terms of a national tournament—leading up to the start of the National Invitation Tournament (NIT) in 1938 and the NCAA Tournament in 1939.

# The Eyes of Texas

Between 1913 and 1917, the eyes of Texas were upon not the traditionally powerful Longhorn football team but rather the basketball team. The team didn't even have an arena then. They played all their home games outdoors, as did many schools that were located in warm-weather areas back then.

The team began winning at the tail end of the 1912-1913 season, taking their final three games that year. Over the next three seasons, the Longhorn teams had records of 11-0, 14-0, and 12-0. (The seasons were somewhat shorter then.) When they won their next four games the following year, the winning streak reached 44 straight games—the longest in college ball to that time.

Texas was finally beaten by Rice, 28-14, ending the streak. Oddly enough, the 44-game win streak was done with four different coaches. Perhaps the best was R. B. Henderson, who coached the 12-0 season of 1915-1916. Henderson taught a wide-open offensive game and watched with a smile as his team ran up 560 points to just 185 for the opposition.

The most lopsided game that year was the very first one. In that contest, Henderson's Longhorns walloped San Marcos Baptist by the incredible score of 102-1.

# Other Unbeatens

Texas wasn't the only unbeaten team of that era. Wisconsin was undefeated in 1914, while Illinois and Virginia were perfect in 1915. Oregon State had an unblemished record in 1918, Navy in 1919, and

Texas A&M in 1920. Montana State was another top team, going 19-1 in 1917 and finishing with a perfect 13-0 mark in 1920. Between 1923 and 1928, the Bobcats compiled an impressive 144-31 record under coach Ott Romney.

The U.S. Military Academy (Army) also took the new game to heart. The Cadets were 17-0 in 1923 and ran up a 31-game winning streak before losing. North Carolina and Texas were unbeaten in 1924. Each had 23-0 records as the seasons began getting longer.

Before long, fans were clamoring to see their favorite teams play schools from other areas. The rules continued to change to make for a smoother, faster game. It's too bad some of these early unbeaten teams couldn't have met each other to see which was the best.

# Bigger and Better

Even though there were fine college teams all around the country, it was the New York area that took the lead in helping the still young sport to grow. One of the great early New York rivalries was between New York University (NYU) and City College of New York (CCNY). During the 1920 season, both schools had outstanding teams. When they were ready to do battle, NYU had an 11-1 mark while CCNY was 13-2.

The problem was that NYU didn't have its own gym and was always searching for a place to play. There was even a time when the team played a couple of its games on the deck of a barge floating on the Hudson River. This time NYU and CCNY decided to play at the 168th Street Regiment Armory.

When word of the game spread, fans rushed to get tickets. By the opening tap, there were nearly 10,000 fans jammed into the Armory, making it one of the largest crowds to watch a college basketball game to that time. NYU had the better of the action, running away with a 39-21 victory. The importance of the game—the outcome—was that it turned people on to the tremendous drawing potential of basketball.

# Slow Games and Low Scores Lead to New Rules

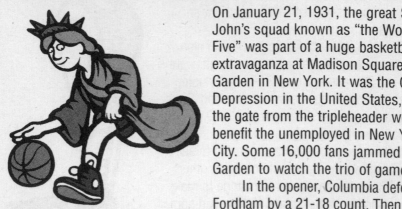

On January 21, 1931, the great St. John's squad known as "the Wonder Five" was part of a huge basketball extravaganza at Madison Square Garden in New York. It was the Great Depression in the United States, and the gate from the tripleheader would benefit the unemployed in New York City. Some 16,000 fans jammed the Garden to watch the trio of games.

In the opener, Columbia defeated Fordham by a 21-18 count. Then Manhattan came on and whipped NYU, 16-14. The Wonder Five were saved for last, taking on CCNY. CCNY scored the first basket of the game, then didn't score another point from the field until the final minute of the game.

The Wonder Five won it, 17-9. That sounded more like a football score than a basketball score. The tripleheader collected some $20,000 for the unemployed, but many of the fans were disappointed by the slow pace and low scores of all three games.

It was apparent that college basketball could attract huge crowds, but something had to be done to speed up the game. By the 1932-1933 season the center line was painted across the court and teams had ten seconds to bring the ball over. The three-second rule went into effect in 1935-1936. Offensive players could no longer camp in the foul lane. And finally, prior to the 1937-1938 season, the last of the archaic rules bit the dust. There was no longer a center jump after each basket. The sport was moving into the modern era.

# Irish Eyes Are Smiling

The 1930s were a time of transition for college basketball. The rules were changing to speed the game up. At the same time, more and more fans began to show an interest in the sport. There was a feeling that the big time was right around the corner.

Perhaps the man who most helped turn that corner was Ned Irish. Irish was introduced to the potential of college ball while he was still a young reporter for the *New York World Telegram*. He helped promote the famous 1931 tripleheader at Madison Square Garden. After seeing that, he felt that the sport shouldn't be confined to tiny, overcrowded gyms, where sometimes thousands of people couldn't get in.

Irish decided to become a full-time basketball promoter. He felt that fans would welcome big-time doubleheaders at Madison Square Garden. Besides seeing their favorite teams collide in great rivalries, they would also be getting two games for the price of one. He began pressing the Garden for dates to stage his double bills.

The first was held on December 29, 1934. St. John's played Westminster of Pennsylvania in the first game, while NYU took on Notre Dame in the second. All four teams were having outstanding seasons, and 16,188 fans paid their way into the Garden to witness this historic basketball event. Both New York teams were beaten that night, but otherwise the event was a huge success.

After that, teams from all over the country wanted to come to the Garden. Large crowds meant more money for their schools and their basketball programs. Thanks to Ned Irish and Madison Square Garden, the days of hiding top-notch basketball in small gyms was just about over.

# Stanford vs. LIU

One of the great early confrontations in college ball came on December 30, 1936, when Stanford and its great star Hank Luisetti traveled cross-country to meet Long Island University in Madison

Square Garden. The LIU Blackbirds, under coach Clair Bee, were riding a 43-game winning streak over three seasons and had a great team, led by 6'6" center Art Hillhouse. Some 18,000 fans crowded into the Garden to root for LIU and see Luisetti, who had a one-handed shot that he fired on the run as well as standing still.

Luisetti dominated the game at both ends of the court. Using his one-hander, instead of the two-handed shot that most players were still using, from both in close and from long range, Luisetti scored 15 points and led his team to a convincing 45-31 victory, ending the Blackbirds' win streak.

New York fans were thrilled by Luisetti's performance. Even though he was the enemy, the fans appreciated a great show, just as they do today. As Luisetti left the court and perhaps changed how New York fans viewed basketball forever, the huge Garden throng gave him a thunderous ovation.

Now the stage was set for college basketball to move into its next phase, the creation of the NIT and NCAA tournaments.

# The Great College Tournaments

## CHAPTER 14

B eginning in 1938 and 1939, college basketball had a new
stage: the great postseason
tournaments, the NIT (National
Invitation Tournament) and NCAA
(National Collegiate Athletic
Association). They were designed to
give the best teams a chance to play
each other with the winner judged the
best team in the land.

At first, fans didn't quite accept the concept of choosing the top team. There were two tournaments. Sometimes the same teams participated in both. But after a few years, it was the NCAA Tournament that emerged as college basketball's premier event, with the winner declared the clear-cut national champion. Of course, it wasn't always the best team that won, just as it isn't in other sports, especially where one game decides a title.

Today, Final Four weekend is one of the major events in all of sports. The four teams making the NCAA semifinals already have received much prestige, not to mention dollars for their schools. The tournament now receives huge media coverage with the final game on prime-time television for the whole nation to see.

Naturally, it wasn't always that big. But here are brief capsules of the NCAA Tournament since 1939, followed by lists of the NIT winners.

# The NCAA Tournament

At the beginning, the NIT was a bigger tournament than the NCAA because it was played at Madison Square Garden in New York before capacity crowds and with extended media coverage. The NCAA was played in smaller arenas and took longer to grow. But college coaches and administrators always felt it was more of a national tournament, with the early rounds staged all over the country. So they kept working to make it bigger and more successful.

At the outset, the NIT favored taking independent teams into its tourney, while the NCAA entries were usually affiliated with conferences and regions. During the first 12 years of the NCAA Tournament, there were only eight teams participating, one from each of the eight districts in which the selection committee divided the country.

# 1939

**Finals site:** Evanston, Illinois. **Winner:** Oregon. **Runner-up:** Ohio State. **Outstanding Player:** None selected.

By way of a historical note, the eight teams in the first NCAA Tournament were Brown, Villanova, Ohio State, Oklahoma, Texas, Wake Forest, Utah State, and Oregon. It finally came down to Oregon and Ohio State with some 5,000 fans in attendance. Oregon had a 6'8" center and two 6'4½" forwards, nicknamed "the Tall Firs." It was that height that finally won it, 46-33.

• • • • • • • • • • • • • • • • • • • • • • • • • • •

# 1940

**Finals site:** Kansas City, Missouri. **Winner:** Indiana. **Runner-up:** Kansas. **Outstanding Player:** Marv Huffman, Indiana.

The final was played between two schools that were already developing a great basketball tradition. The Hoosiers dominated the game and won easily, 60-42.

• • • • • • • • • • • • • • • • • • • • • • • • • • •

# 1941

**Finals site:** Kansas City, Missouri. **Winner:** Wisconsin. **Runner-up:** Washington State. **Outstanding Player:** John Kotz, Wisconsin.

Wisconsin had a 12-game winning streak coming into the tournament but barely made it through the first round, beating Dartmouth, 51-50. In the final, Gene Englund put the clamps on State's 6'7" center, Paul Lindeman, and scored 13 points of his own. Wisconsin won it, 39-34.

• • • • • • • • • • • • • • • • • • • • • • • • • • •

# 1942

**Finals site:** Kansas City, Missouri. **Winner:** Stanford. **Runner-up:** Dartmouth. **Outstanding Player:** Howard Dallmar, Stanford.

Stanford had a sophomore star, Jim Pollard, but he came down with the flu in Kansas City and couldn't play in the final against Dartmouth. Even without Pollard, Stanford won easily, 53-38, as Howard Dallmar led the way with 15 points.

• • • • • • • • • • • • • • • • • • • • • • • • • • •

# 1943

**Finals site:** New York City. **Winner:** Wyoming. **Runner-up:** Georgetown. **Outstanding Player:** Kenny Sailors, Wyoming.

World War II had taken many top players, but DePaul came in with a 6'10" freshman named George Mikan. The Blue Demons, however, lost to Georgetown in the semifinals. Wyoming took the other semi, beating Texas, and then defeated Georgetown in the final, 46-34, with MVP Kenny Sailors scoring 16 points.

• • • • • • • • • • • • • • • • • • • • •

# 1944

**Finals site:** New York City. **Winner:** Utah. **Runner-up:** Dartmouth. **Outstanding Player:** Arnie Ferrin, Utah.

Utah won the tournament under strange circumstances. The Utes got an NIT bid and were eliminated there in the first round. Then an automobile accident involving the Arkansas team caused them to withdraw from the NCAA Tournament. Utah became a last-minute replacement because they were passing through the regional site in Kansas City on the way home from the NIT. The Utes then won in the semifinals to earn a trip back to New York. Waiting was Dartmouth. But Arnie Ferrin scored 22 points in the final as Utah surprised everyone with a 42-40 victory, one of the most unexpected in NCAA history.

• • • • • • • • • • • • • • • • • • • • •

# 1945

**Finals site:** New York City. **Winner:** Oklahoma A&M. **Runner-up:** New York University. **Outstanding Player:** Bob Kurland, Oklahoma A&M.

The Oklahoma A&M Aggies had 6'10" Bob "Foothills" Kurland. Meeting the Aggies in the final was local favorite New York University, led by Sid Tanenbaum and freshman Dolph Schayes. But in the final it was Kurland dominating with 22 points and some tough defense to help the Aggies to a close 49-45 victory.

• • • • • • • • • • • • • • • • • • • • •

# 1946

**Finals site:** New York City. **Winner:** Oklahoma A&M. **Runner-up:** North Carolina. **Outstanding Player:** Bob Kurland, Oklahoma A&M.

The Aggies became the first repeat champion and Bob Kurland the first repeat Outstanding Player. In the final, North Carolina's skinny 6'6" center, Bones McKinney, gave Kurland fits. Both finally fouled out, and the Aggies needed a last-second hoop to cement a 43-40 victory. Kurland had 72 points in three tournament games.

# 1947

**Finals site:** New York City. **Winner:** Holy Cross. **Runner-up:** Oklahoma. **Outstanding Player:** George Kaftan, Holy Cross.

A new champion was crowned as Holy Cross, led by 6'4" center George Kaftan, topped Oklahoma in the title game. Kaftan scored 18 to lead the Crusaders to a 58-47 victory.

# 1948

**Finals site:** New York City. **Winner:** Kentucky. **Runner-up:** Baylor. **Outstanding Player:** Alex Groza, Kentucky.

Kentucky coach Adolph Rupp unleashed center Alex Groza, guard Ralph Beard, and forward "Wah Wah" Jones on the rest of the country and few could stop them. Baylor was no match for the Wildcats in the final. Kentucky won, 58-42. It was the first of five NCAA Tournament wins for the Wildcats.

# 1949

**Finals site:** Seattle, Washington. **Winner:** Kentucky. **Runner-up:** Oklahoma A&M. **Outstanding Player:** Alex Groza, Kentucky.

Kentucky met a stubborn Oklahoma A&M team in the final but won it by a 46-36 score to repeat as champs. Groza had 25 points in the game.

# 1950

**Finals site:** New York City. **Winner:** CCNY. **Runner-up:** Bradley.
**Outstanding Player:** Irwin Dambrot, CCNY.

It was an incredible year for coach Nat Holman's City College team. First the Beavers won the NIT, defeating Bradley in the final. From there, both teams entered the NCAA and wound up in the title game again, the only time that has ever happened. CCNY won a close game, 71-68. Irwin Dambrot had 15 and a key block to win the Outstanding Player title and make CCNY the only team to win both the NIT and NCAA titles in the same year.

· · · · · · · · · · · · · · · · · · · · · · · · · · · · · · ·

# 1951

**Finals site:** Minneapolis, Minnesota. **Winner:** Kentucky. **Runner-up:** Kansas State. **Outstanding Player:** None selected.

The field was expanded to 16 teams, but an old friend won it. Adolph Rupp and Kentucky took their third title in four years. This time the Wildcats were led by 7'0" center Bill Spivey and forwards Cliff Hagan and Frank Ramsey. Now a team had to win four times to become champion, but Kentucky did it, besting Kansas State in the finals, 68-58.

· · · · · · · · · · · · · · · · · · · · · · · · · · · · · ·

# 1952

**Finals site:** Seattle, Washington. **Winner:** Kansas. **Runner-up:** St. John's (N.Y.). **Outstanding Player:** Clyde Lovellette, Kansas.

This was a tournament dominated by Kansas center Clyde Lovellette, a 6'9", 270-pound mountain. In a second-round game against St. Louis, big Clyde set a tournament scoring record with 44 points. In the finals, the Jayhawks met a good St. John's team. With Lovellette pounding the ball inside, Kansas won easily, 80-63. Lovellette set a tournament record for points (141) and rebounds (69).

· · · · · · · · · · · · · · · · · · · · · · · · · · · · · · ·

# 1953

**Final Four site:** Kansas City, Missouri. **Winner:** Indiana. **Runner-up:** Kansas. **Outstanding Player:** B. H. Born, Kansas.

High scoring was beginning to be the norm in college basketball. In the early rounds of the tournament, Bob Houbregs of Washington erased Clyde Lovellette's year-old record by scoring 45 points against Seattle. Sophomore Bob Pettit of LSU had games of 28 and 29 points. But in the final it was Indiana, led by Don Schlundt's 30 points, that edged out Kansas, 69-68. It was the first time both the semifinals and finals were played at the same site—hence, the Final Four.

# 1954

**Final Four site:** Kansas City, Missouri. **Winner:** La Salle. **Runner-up:** Bradley. **Outstanding Player:** Tom Gola, La Salle.

Kentucky was unbeaten in the regular season, but before the tournament, three star players were declared ineligible, so Kentucky didn't even enter. The tournament belonged to La Salle's 6'6" junior center, Tom Gola. Against North Carolina State, he had 26 points and 26 rebounds. Against Navy, he had 22 points and 24 rebounds. And in the finals against Bradley, the All-American scored 19 more as La Salle won easily, 92-76.

# 1955

**Final Four site:** Kansas City, Missouri. **Winner:** San Francisco. **Runner-up:** La Salle. **Outstanding Player:** Bill Russell, San Francisco.

San Francisco's 6'10" junior, Bill Russell, became the most dominant center in college basketball history. Aided by guard K. C. Jones, Russell and the Dons lost only a single game early in the season, then began their march through the NCAA Tournament. In the final, Jones had 24 points, Russell 23, and the Dons easily beat defending champ La Salle, 77-63.

# 1956

**Final Four site:** Evanston, Illinois. **Winner:** San Francisco. **Runner-up:** Iowa. **Outstanding Player:** Hal Lear, Temple.

It was an undefeated year for Bill Russell and the San Francisco Dons. Even when K. C. Jones used up his eligibility before the tournament, no team could stop San Francisco. In the finals, they took a very good Iowa team, 83-71. Russell had 26 points in his final collegiate game, and the Dons had a collegiate record 55-game win streak. But the Outstanding Player was Temple's Hal Lear, who scored a record 48 points against SMU in the consolation game.

# 1957

**Final Four site:** Kansas City, Missouri. **Winner:** North Carolina. **Runner-up:** Kansas. **Outstanding Player:** Wilt Chamberlain, Kansas.

A great year for the NCAA. College basketball had a new giant, 7'1" Wilt Chamberlain, a sophomore at Kansas. But the North Carolina Tar Heels were unbeaten. It was inevitable that these two teams would meet in the final, and the game was a classic, going into triple-overtime. Joe Quigg of Carolina finally won it by calmly making two free throws, giving the Tar Heels the title, 54-53, and a 32-0 season. Chamberlain wound up with 23 points and 14 rebounds.

# 1958

**Final Four site:** Louisville, Kentucky. **Winner:** Kentucky. **Runner-up:** Seattle. **Outstanding Player:** Elgin Baylor, Seattle.

College basketball was filled with great stars and future NBAers: Chamberlain, Oscar Robertson, Jerry West, Guy Rodgers, and Elgin Baylor. It finally came down to hometown Kentucky against Seattle. And it was Adolph Rupp's Wildcats who became the first team to win four titles. They rallied from a 39-36 halftime deficit to win the championship, 84-72, behind Vern Hatton's 30 points. Baylor had 25 points and 19 rebounds for Seattle. And in a regional consolation game, Cincinnati's Oscar Robertson scored an NCAA record 56 points.

# 1959

**Final Four site:** Louisville, Kentucky. **Winner:** California. **Runner-up:** West Virginia. **Outstanding Player:** Jerry West, West Virginia.

With Oscar Robertson and Jerry West both leading their teams to the Final Four, fans hoped to see these two great guards in a champi-

onship showdown. But the University of California Bears upset the apple cart. First they whipped Cincinnati in the semis, 64-58. Then they did the same to West Virginia in the final. The Bears held a 12-point lead in the second half, only to see West (28 points) hit clutch shot after clutch shot in the final minutes. But Cal held on to win a 71-70 squeaker.

· · · · · · · · · · · · · · · · · · · · · · · ·

# 1960

**Final Four site:** San Francisco, California. **Winner:** Ohio State. **Runner-up:** California. **Outstanding Player:** Jerry Lucas, Ohio State.

There was a new kid on the block, an Ohio State team that featured sophomore stars Jerry Lucas and John Havlicek. Cincinnati and Oscar Robertson came in the favorites with a 26-1 mark. But at the Final Four, Pete Newell's California team put the clamps on Robertson and Cincinnati, 77-69. Then Ohio State rolled over California for the title, 75-55. All five Buckeye starters were in double figures.

· · · · · · · · · · · · · · · · · · · · · · · ·

# 1961

**Final Four site:** Kansas City, Missouri. **Winner:** Cincinnati. **Runner-up:** Ohio State. **Outstanding Player:** Jerry Lucas, Ohio State.

Ohio State seemed even stronger in 1961. Waiting for the Buckeyes in the final was none other than cross-state rival Cincinnati. It went into overtime where Cincinnati pulled out a 70-65 upset victory. Lucas had 27 points and 12 rebounds to become the Outstanding Player, but the Bearcats had still pulled off a major upset.

· · · · · · · · · · · · · · · · · · · · · · · ·

# 1962

**Final Four site:** Louisville, Kentucky. **Winner:** Cincinnati. **Runner-up:** Ohio State. **Outstanding Player:** Paul Hogue, Cincinnati.

Cincinnati and Ohio State returned to the finals. But in a semifinal win over Wake Forest, Lucas suffered a leg injury. He wasn't at full strength in the final, and Cincinnati center Paul Hogue had a great game. Cincinnati repeated with a 71-59 victory. Lucas managed 11 points and 16 rebounds, but Hogue scored 22 and had 19 boards.

· · · · · · · · · · · · · · · · · · · · · · · ·

# 1963

**Final Four site:** Louisville, Kentucky. **Winner:** Loyola-Chicago. **Runner-up:** Cincinnati. **Outstanding Player:** Art Heyman, Duke.

Cincinnati was back looking for three in a row. The Bearcats' opponents were the surprising Ramblers from Loyola-Chicago in a game between the nation's highest scoring team (Loyola) and the nation's best defensive team (Cincinnati). Loyola hung tough, sending the game into overtime. In OT the two teams traded hoops until the final seconds when Loyola's Vic Rouse rebounded a missed shot and put it back in for a 60-58 Loyola win.

# 1964

**Final Four site:** Kansas City, Missouri. **Winner:** UCLA. **Runner-up:** Duke. **Outstanding Player:** Walt Hazzard, UCLA.

This was the year coach John Wooden brought his UCLA Bruins to the finals for the first time. The unbeaten Bruins' strength was an electric backcourt of Walt Hazzard and Gail Goodrich. In the final, the Bruins ran off 16 straight points to open a 50-38 halftime lead over Duke and cruise to a 98-83 victory. Goodrich had 27 points and Kenny Washington 26.

# 1965

**Final Four site:** Portland, Oregon. **Winner:** UCLA. **Runner-up:** Michigan. **Outstanding Player:** Bill Bradley, Princeton.

This UCLA team breezed through the early rounds of the tourney, then blasted Wichita State in the semifinals, 108-89. In the other semifinal, powerful Michigan with Cazzie Russell topped Princeton, 93-76, despite 29 points from Bill Bradley. In the final, Goodrich exploded for 42 points as the Bruins made it two straight, 91-80. Bradley scored 58 points in the consolation game against Wichita State.

# 1966

**Final Four site:** College Park, Maryland. **Winner:** Texas Western. **Runner-up:** Kentucky. **Outstanding Player:** Jerry Chambers, Utah.

This one was dubbed the "Last Chance Tournament." UCLA wasn't there, but the Bruins had a 7'2" freshman named Lew Alcindor who was so good that most everyone was conceding the next three years to UCLA. The finals ended up a battle between Texas Western and Kentucky. Adolph Rupp was going for title number five, but the Miners spoiled the party with a 72-65 triumph. Though his team lost in the semifinals and in the consolation game, Utah's Jerry Chambers was the Outstanding Player with a record 143 points in four tourney games, a 35.7 average.

# 1967

**Final Four site:** Louisville, Kentucky. **Winner:** UCLA. **Runner-up:** Dayton.
**Outstanding Player:** Lew Alcindor, UCLA.

To no one's surprise, UCLA and Lew Alcindor were everything everyone expected, rolling through the season unbeaten and continuing their dominance in the tournament. In Alcindor's first varsity game ever, he had scored 56 points. In his final game of the year for the national championship, he scored just 20 but pulled down 18 rebounds as his team did the rest. The backcourt of Mike Warren and Lucius Allen had 36 between them as the Bruins topped Dayton, 79-64.

# 1968

**Final Four site:** Los Angeles, California. **Winner:** UCLA. **Runner-up:** North Carolina. **Outstanding Player:** Lew Alcindor, UCLA.

This was the year the NCAA outlawed dunking in an attempt to neutralize Alcindor's dominance. It didn't work. The Bruins lost just a single game and the big guy was better than ever. In the tournament final, UCLA easily topped a very good North Carolina team, 78-55. Alcindor had 34 points and 16 rebounds.

# 1969

**Final Four site:** Louisville, Kentucky. **Winner:** UCLA. **Runner-up:** Purdue.
**Outstanding Player:** Lew Alcindor, UCLA.

As expected, Alcindor and UCLA dominated for a third straight year. In the final against Rick Mount and Purdue, Alcindor closed out his college career with a 37-point, 20-rebound performance to lead his club to a 92-72 win, the Bruins' fifth national championship. Alcindor was the Outstanding Player for an unprecedented third straight year and would go on to NBA fame as Kareem Abdul-Jabbar.

• • • • • • • • • • • • • • • • • • • • • • • • • •

# 1970

**Final Four site:** College Park, Maryland. **Winner:** UCLA. **Runner-up:** Jacksonville. **Outstanding Player:** Sidney Wicks, UCLA.

Just when everyone thought the UCLA dynasty was over, junior forwards Sidney Wicks and Curtis Rowe took over, joined by outstanding guards John Vallely and Henry Bibby. Their opponent in the final game was Jacksonville, with 7'2" center Artis Gilmore. Jacksonville led most of the first half until the 6'9" Wicks used his quickness to shut down the big center, and the Bruins rolled to an 80-69 triumph, making it four in a row. Rowe had 19 points, while Wicks had 17 points and 18 rebounds.

• • • • • • • • • • • • • • • • • • • • • • • • • •

# 1971

**Final Four site:** Houston, Texas. **Winner:** UCLA. **Runner-up:** Villanova. **Outstanding Player:** Howard Porter, Villanova.

The Bruins did it again. Villanova fought hard in the finals but trailed all the way. The Bruins won it, 68-62, as center Steve Patterson played the game of his life with 29 points. UCLA had won its fifth straight title. And waiting in the wings for 1972 was a 6'11" center named Bill Walton.

• • • • • • • • • • • • • • • • • • • • • • • • • •

# 1972

**Final Four site:** Los Angeles, California. **Winner:** UCLA. **Runner-up:** Florida State. **Outstanding Player:** Bill Walton, UCLA.

Sophomore Bill Walton turned out to be another crown jewel. He didn't score like Alcindor, but he was a better rebounder and passer. Add forward Keith Wilkes (later known as Jamal Wilkes), the continued fine play of Henry Bibby, and a strong bench, and the result was an unbeaten season. UCLA faced the Florida State Seminoles in the final. The Bruins withstood a late FSU rally to win, 81-76. Despite foul trouble, Walton finished with 24 points and 20 rebounds, while Wilkes had 23 points.

• • • • • • • • • • • • • • • • • • • • • • • • •

# 1973

**Final Four site:** St. Louis, Missouri. **Winner:** UCLA. **Runner-up:** Memphis State. **Outstanding Player:** Bill Walton, UCLA.

No team could touch UCLA, which went unbeaten again and by the end of the season had put together a record-setting win streak that had reached 75 games. In the tournament final, their opponent was Memphis State, which had star guard Larry Finch and forward Larry Kenon. But this one was all Walton. The big redhead scored 44 points on 21 of 22 shooting from the field as the Bruins made it seven straight titles, 87-66. There was another unbeaten team this year: North Carolina State with the sensational David Thompson. But they had been ineligible for postseason play this time around.

• • • • • • • • • • • • • • • • • • • • • • • •

# 1974

**Final Four site:** Greensboro, North Carolina. **Winner:** North Carolina State. **Runner-up:** Marquette. **Outstanding Player:** David Thompson, North Carolina State.

Early in the season, UCLA defeated North Carolina State, 84-66. The Bruins' win streak reached 88 games before Notre Dame staged a furious last-minute rally and beat them. But by tournament time, the Bruins and Walton were again favored. North Carolina State, however, hadn't lost since the early UCLA game, and the two teams met in the semifinals. The 6'4" Thompson was an amazing player, and 7'4" Tom Burleson had the size to stay with Walton. The game was a classic, going into double-overtime, where N.C. State somehow staged an incredible rally and won the game, 80-77. In the final, State had enough juice left to top Marquette, 76-64.

• • • • • • • • • • • • • • • • • • • • • • • •

# 1975

**Final Four site:** San Diego, California. **Winner:** UCLA. **Runner-up:** Kentucky. **Outstanding Player:** Richard Washington, UCLA.

With the tournament expanding to 32 teams and UCLA without an Alcindor or a Walton, it looked wide open. What a shock when the Final Four rolled around and there was UCLA again. In the semis against Louisville, the game went into overtime, and a clutch baseline jumper by Richard Washington gave UCLA a 75-74 victory. In the finals, there was Kentucky again. It was still just a 76-75 game with seven minutes left. But the Bruins got some of the old magic again and won it, 92-85. It was UCLA and John Wooden's tenth title in 12 years, a record that may never be broken.

• • • • • • • • • • • • • • • • • • • • • • • •

# 1976

**Final Four site:** Philadelphia, Pennsylvania. **Winner:** Indiana. **Runner-up:** Michigan. **Outstanding Player:** Kent Benson, Indiana.

Bob Knight's Indiana Hoosiers ripped through the regular season unbeaten and came into the tournament the obvious favorite. In the final, Michigan was up by a 35-29 count at the half. But after intermission, Indiana's Scott May and Kent Benson turned on the juice, and the Hoosiers won going away, 86-68. May had 26, Benson 25.

• • • • • • • • • • • • • • • • • • • • • • • •

# 1977

**Final Four site:** Atlanta, Georgia. **Winner:** Marquette. **Runner-up:** North Carolina. **Outstanding Player:** Butch Lee, Marquette.

The Marquette Warriors came into the tournament with seven losses, more than any winning team in tournament history to date. But some of the favored teams were upset in the earlier rounds, and powerful North Carolina had several players hurt. In the final, Marquette raced to a 39-27 halftime lead, only to see Walter Davis lead Carolina back to a 45-43 advantage. But the Warriors retook the lead, winning 67-59, as retiring coach Al McGuire wept on the bench. He and his team finally had a title.

• • • • • • • • • • • • • • • • • • • • • • • •

# 1978

**Final Four site:** St. Louis, Missouri. **Winner:** Kentucky. **Runner-up:** Duke. **Outstanding Player:** Jack Givens, Kentucky.

Kentucky, with just two losses, came to the table as the favorite. Joe B. Hall's Wildcats were going for their fifth title, the first without Adolph Rupp behind the bench. In the final against Duke, Kentucky forward Jack "Goose" Givens had one of those magical games that happen once in a lifetime. The lefty forward had 41 points on 18 of 27 shooting from the field, leading the Wildcats to a 94-88 win and a fifth title.

• • • • • • • • • • • • • • • • • • • • • • • • •

# 1979

**Final Four site:** Salt Lake City, Utah. **Winner:** Michigan State. **Runner-up:** Indiana State. **Outstanding Player:** Earvin "Magic" Johnson, Michigan State.

In the eyes of many, this was the game that really put the Final Four on the map. It was the year that 6'9" sophomore point guard Earvin "Magic" Johnson led Michigan State into the final against undefeated Indiana State. Indiana State was as much a one-man team as ever made it to the finals. That one man was 6'9" Larry Bird. The two players would forever be linked by this game and later as pros. The field was expanded to 40 teams, but it all came down to Magic and Bird. Michigan State used its speed to win it, 75-64, as Magic scored 24 points. Bird was "held" to 19 points and 13 rebounds. Magic and Bird then marched off to the NBA.

• • • • • • • • • • • • • • • • • • • • • • • • •

# 1980

**Final Four site:** Indianapolis, Indiana. **Winner:** Louisville. **Runner-up:** UCLA. **Outstanding Player:** Darrell Griffith, Louisville.

In a year of tournament upsets, the Final Four consisted of teams that had lost a total of 29 games. Only Louisville, with just three losses, seemed to be a major force. In the final, coach Denny Crum's Cardinals ran into an old adversary, UCLA. UCLA had a 28-26 lead at the half, but Louisville rallied behind All-American Darrell Griffith (23 points) and won its first title, 59-54.

• • • • • • • • • • • • • • • • • • • • • • • • •

# 1981

**Final Four site:** Philadelphia, Pennsylvania. **Winner:** Indiana. **Runner-up:** North Carolina. **Outstanding Player:** Isiah Thomas, Indiana.

It was another year of upsets, something that seemed to be happening more and more. In the final it was the slick play of guard Isiah Thomas (23 points) that enabled Bobby Knight's Hoosiers to win a second title, 63-50. Indiana came in with nine losses, the most ever to that point for a winning team.

• • • • • • • • • • • • • • • • • • • • • • •

# 1982

**Final Four site:** New Orleans, Louisiana. **Winner:** North Carolina. **Runner-up:** Georgetown. **Outstanding Player:** James Worthy, North Carolina.

An outstanding tournament from start to finish with coach Dean Smith finally winning it all after six previous trips to the Final Four. But the Tar Heels didn't have an easy time. In the semifinals they had to beat a good Houston team, 68-63, then had to meet the Georgetown Hoyas, led by 7'0" freshman center Patrick Ewing. But Carolina had a freshman star of its own, Michael Jordan, and two outstanding big men in James Worthy and Sam Perkins. The Hoyas led, 62-61, with less than a minute left. Then Jordan hit the winning shot with 15 seconds left to cement a 63-62 win.

• • • • • • • • • • • • • • • • • • • • • • •

# 1983

**Final Four site:** Albuquerque, New Mexico. **Winner:** North Carolina State. **Runner-up:** Houston. **Outstanding Player:** Hakeem Olajuwon, Houston.

Houston came in with a 27-2 record, a 7'0" center named Hakeem Olajuwon, and a running, dunking team nicknamed Phi Slamma Jamma. North Carolina State came in at 20-10 and was given little chance to get past the regionals. Guess what? These were the two teams that met for the title. Coach Jim Valvano's Wolfpack slowed the pace, hit their shots, and had a shocking 33-25 halftime lead. The Cougars opened the second half with a 15-2 run and appeared ready to break it open. But the Wolfpack fought back to tie it at 52-all. With time running down, State's Lorenzo Charles grabbed an airball and jammed it home as the buzzer sounded. Upset city, 54-52, in one of the most memorable games ever.

• • • • • • • • • • • • • • • • • • • • • • • • • •

# 1984

**Final Four site:** Seattle, Washington. **Winner:** Georgetown. **Runner-up:** Houston. **Outstanding Player:** Patrick Ewing, Georgetown.

This one was billed as the battle of the 7' centers, Patrick Ewing and Hakeem Olajuwon. Olajuwon was hurt by foul trouble and Ewing concentrated on defense. Neither big man had a great game. But the more balanced Georgetown team won it, 84-75, behind 19 points by Reggie Williams.

• • • • • • • • • • • • • • • • • • • • • • • • • •

# 1985

**Final Four site:** Lexington, Kentucky. **Winner:** Villanova. **Runner-up:** Georgetown. **Outstanding Player:** Ed Pinckney, Villanova.

Maybe the greatest upset of them all. Powerful Georgetown was expected to repeat. Villanova, at 19-10, wasn't even supposed to be there. It was agreed that Villanova would have to play a perfect game to beat Patrick Ewing and company. Guess what? They did. Rollie Massimino's Wildcats hit 22 of 28 shots from the floor, Gary McLain's ballhandling broke the Georgetown press, and Ed Pinckney outplayed Ewing. Nova won the game, 66-64, in a thrilling finish.

• • • • • • • • • • • • • • • • • • • • • • • • • •

# 1986

**Final Four site:** Dallas, Texas. **Winner:** Louisville. **Runner-up:** Duke. **Outstanding Player:** Pervis Ellison, Louisville.

Once again the tournament expanded, this time to 64 teams. The Final Four had become one of the great sporting events in the world, and now more teams had a chance to win the title. But when the smoke cleared and 62 of the teams had been eliminated, only Louisville and Duke remained. Duke had lost just twice in the regular season, Louisville seven times. But that was before a 6'9" freshman center took over. His name was Pervis Ellison and his nickname was "Never Nervous." Ellison scored 25 points, grabbed 11 rebounds, and made the big plays down the stretch. Louisville won its second title, 72-69.

• • • • • • • • • • • • • • • • • • • • • • •

# 1987

**Final Four site:** New Orleans, Louisiana. **Winner:** Indiana. **Runner-up:** Syracuse. **Outstanding Player:** Keith Smart, Indiana.

Bobby Knight continued his magic touch in the finals. It was the first year of the three-point field goal and Indiana hit the long shot as well as anyone. Syracuse—with Derrick Coleman, Rony Seikaly, and Sherman Douglas—was the Hoosier opponent, and the game went down to the wire. The Orangemen held a 73-72 lead with time running down. But Keith Smart hit a baseline jumper to win it for Indiana, 74-73.

• • • • • • • • • • • • • • • • • • • • • • •

# 1988

**Final Four site:** Kansas City, Missouri. **Winner:** Kansas. **Runner-up:** Oklahoma. **Outstanding Player:** Danny Manning, Kansas.

In the eyes of many, 6'11" Danny Manning of Kansas was the best player in the country. Yet come tournament time, the Jayhawks had 11 losses, and no team with that many defeats had ever won the title. But the Jayhawks reached the final, where they were underdogs to high-scoring Oklahoma. The game was 50-50 at the half. It wasn't until the final seconds that Manning's heroics led to an 83-79 Kansas victory. Manning had 31 points and 18 rebounds.

• • • • • • • • • • • • • • • • • • • • • • •

# 1989

**Final Four site:** Seattle, Washington. **Winner:** Michigan. **Runner-up:** Seton Hall. **Outstanding Player:** Glen Rice, Michigan.

It was Michigan and Seton Hall for the title, a great game that went into overtime, the first OT final since 1963. The game ended when Michigan's Rumeal Robinson was fouled on a drive and calmly sank the two free throws to give his team an 80-79 victory in one of the most exciting finals in years. Glen Rice scored 31 points.

• • • • • • • • • • • • • • • • • • • • • • •

# 1990

**Final Four site:** Denver, Colorado. **Winner:** Nevada-Las Vegas.
**Runner-up:** Duke. **Outstanding Player:** Anderson Hunt, Nevada-Las
Vegas.

There were great teams and superb players everywhere, but the
real powerhouse was the University of Nevada-Las Vegas, where coach
Jerry Tarkanian added junior transfer Larry Johnson to an already
strong team. The team faced Duke for the title. The game was a rout.
UNLV dominated, 103-73, the largest victory margin ever in a final.

# 1991

**Final Four site:** Indianapolis, Indiana. **Winner:** Duke. **Runner-up:** Kansas.
**Outstanding Player:** Christian Laettner, Duke.

The big news this time wasn't the final but the semifinal.
Nevada-Las Vegas came in unbeaten with the entire title team from
1990. But Duke, which had lost seven games during the season,
came in inspired. With 3:51 left, UNLV had a 74-71 lead, but point
guard Greg Anthony fouled out. It was 76-71 when Duke came back,
tying the game at 77-77. With 12 seconds left, Christian Laettner hit
two free throws, and that led to one of the great upsets in NCAA history, 79-77. In the finals, Duke topped Kansas, 72-65, to cement its
first title ever. But in the eyes of many, they had won it in the semis.

# 1992

**Final Four site:** Minneapolis, Minnesota. **Winner:** Duke. **Runner-up:**
Michigan. **Outstanding Player:** Bobby Hurley, Duke.

The Blue Devils made it two in a row, but coach Mike
Krzyzewski's ballclub took a backseat to Michigan, a team that cap-
tured the fancy of the fans. Michigan had a starting team of five
freshmen, featuring 6'10" forward Chris Webber and 6'8" point guard
Jalen Rose, tagged "the Fab Five." Waiting for them was Duke and its
veteran team. But the Fab Five hung tough and even had a 31-30
halftime lead. Then Christian Laettner took over, leading a 23-6 run in
the final seven minutes to put the game away, 71-51.

# 1993

**Final Four site:** New Orleans, Louisiana. **Winner:** North Carolina. **Runner-up:** Michigan. **Outstanding Player:** Donald Williams, North Carolina.

Dean Smith brought another powerful North Carolina team into the tournament. The Carolina coach had more tournament wins in 22 previous years than any other coach. But he had just one title and wanted a second. The Fab Five from Michigan were back, all sophomores now. In the final, North Carolina held off the Fab Five to win the title for Smith, 77-71.

· · · · · · · · · · · · · · · · · · · · · · · · · ·

# 1994

**Final Four site:** Charlotte, North Carolina. **Winner:** Arkansas. **Runner-up:** Duke. **Outstanding Player:** Corliss Williamson, Arkansas.

The Arkansas Razorbacks were the nation's number one team and had lost just three games all year. Coach Nolan Richardson and his team were determined to succeed where previous Razorback teams had failed. With President Bill Clinton (from Arkansas) looking on, Arkansas and Duke put on a show. Arkansas led, 34-33, at the half, but Duke exploded to a 48-38 advantage early in the second half. Then the Blue Devils went cold and Corliss Williamson led the Razorbacks' comeback. With Williamson getting 23, Arkansas won its first national crown, 76-72, much to the president's delight.

· · · · · · · · · · · · · · · · · · · · · · · · · ·

# 1995

**Final Four site:** Seattle, Washington. **Winner:** UCLA. **Runner-up:** Arkansas. **Outstanding Player:** Ed O'Bannon, UCLA.

It took 20 years, but the school that had won the most NCAA titles finally got another one. UCLA returned to former glory in winning its 11th national championship overall, its first without John Wooden at the helm. But coach Jim Harrick brought a typical Bruins team to the tournament, a quick-striking unit that lost just two games. The Bruins met defending champ Arkansas in the title game. With point guard Tyus Edney unable to play because of a wrist injury,

UCLA had to raise its game yet another level. For the first half, Corliss Williamson and the Razorbacks kept it close, the Bruins leading, 40-39. But after intermission, forward Ed O'Bannon came out refusing to lose. He wound up with 30 points, and the Bruins had yet another title, 89-78.

• • • • • • • • • • • • • • • • • • • • • • • • • •

# The All-Time NCAA Tournament Team

In 1989, in celebration of the 50th anniversary of the NCAA Tournament, a special blue ribbon panel of coaches and administrators selected an All-Time Final Four team. Here are the results of the poll. Alongside the names are the year or years in which the players selected excelled.

| The All-Time Team | |
| --- | --- |
| **Player** | **Year(s)** |
| Lew Alcindor, UCLA | 1967-1969 |
| Larry Bird, Indiana State | 1979 |
| Wilt Chamberlain, Kansas | 1957 |
| Magic Johnson, Michigan State | 1979 |
| Michael Jordan, North Carolina | 1982 |

# The National Invitation Tournament

The National Invitation Tournament began in 1938, a year before the NCAA Tournament started. The NIT was played exclusively in Madison Square Garden during the early years. It had as much prestige as the NCAA back then, and teams sometimes entered both tournaments, since the NIT was usually held first.

In 1950, City College of New York became the only school to win both tournaments in the same year. And their finals opponent each time was Bradley. Both schools played in each tourney.

As the years passed, the NCAA slowly became *the* postseason tournament, and the NIT began taking teams that were not invited to the NCAA. In recent times, early-round NIT games are played at various sites around the country. Only the semifinals and finals are played at Madison Square Garden.

Here, for the record, are the winners and losers from the NIT finals and the score.

## NIT Winners and Losers

| Year | Winner | Loser | Score |
|------|--------|-------|-------|
| 1938 | Temple | Colorado | 60-36 |
| 1939 | LIU-Brooklyn | Loyola (Ill.) | 44-32 |
| 1940 | Colorado | Duquesne | 51-40 |
| 1941 | LIU-Brooklyn | Ohio University | 56-42 |
| 1942 | West Virginia | Western Kentucky | 47-45 |
| 1943 | St. John's | Toledo | 48-27 |
| 1944 | St. John's | DePaul | 47-39 |
| 1945 | DePaul | Bowling Green | 71-54 |
| 1946 | Kentucky | Rhode Island | 46-45 |
| 1947 | Utah | Kentucky | 49-45 |
| 1948 | St. Louis | NYU | 65-52 |
| 1949 | San Francisco | Loyola (Ill.) | 48-47 |
| 1950 | CCNY | Bradley | 69-61 |
| 1951 | Brigham Young | Dayton | 62-42 |
| 1952 | La Salle | Dayton | 75-64 |
| 1953 | Seton Hall | St. John's | 58-46 |
| 1954 | Holy Cross | Duquesne | 71-62 |
| 1955 | Duquesne | Dayton | 70-58 |
| 1956 | Louisville | Dayton | 93-80 |
| 1957 | Bradley | Memphis State | 84-83 |
| 1958 | Xavier (Ohio) | Dayton | 78-74 (OT) |
| 1959 | St. John's | Bradley | 76-71 (OT) |
| 1960 | Bradley | Providence | 88-72 |
| 1961 | Providence | St. Louis | 69-52 |
| 1962 | Dayton | St. John's | 73-67 |

## NIT Winners and Losers, continued

| Year | Winner | Loser | Score |
|------|--------|-------|-------|
| 1963 | Providence | Canisius | 81-66 |
| 1964 | Bradley | New Mexico | 86-54 |
| 1965 | St. John's | Villanova | 55-51 |
| 1966 | Brigham Young | NYU | 97-84 |
| 1967 | Southern Illinois | Marquette | 71-56 |
| 1968 | Dayton | Kansas | 61-48 |
| 1969 | Temple | Boston College | 89-76 |
| 1970 | Marquette | St. John's | 65-53 |
| 1971 | North Carolina | Georgia Tech | 84-66 |
| 1972 | Maryland | Niagara | 100-69 |
| 1973 | Virginia Tech | Notre Dame | 92-91 (OT) |
| 1974 | Purdue | Utah | 97-81 |
| 1975 | Princeton | Providence | 80-69 |
| 1976 | Kentucky | North Carolina-Charlotte | 71-67 |
| 1977 | St. Bonaventure | Houston | 94-91 |
| 1978 | Texas | North Carolina State | 101-93 |
| 1979 | Indiana | Purdue | 53-52 |
| 1980 | Virginia | Minnesota | 58-55 |
| 1981 | Tulsa | Syracuse | 86-84 (OT) |
| 1982 | Bradley | Purdue | 67-58 |
| 1983 | Fresno State | DePaul | 69-60 |
| 1984 | Michigan | Notre Dame | 83-63 |
| 1985 | UCLA | Indiana | 65-62 |
| 1986 | Ohio State | Wyoming | 73-63 |
| 1987 | Southern Mississippi | La Salle | 84-80 |
| 1988 | Connecticut | Ohio State | 72-67 |
| 1989 | St. John's | St. Louis | 73-65 |

## NIT Winners and Losers, continued

| Year | Winner | Loser | Score |
|------|--------|-------|-------|
| 1990 | Vanderbilt | St. Louis | 74-72 |
| 1991 | Stanford | Oklahoma | 78-72 |
| 1992 | Virginia | Notre Dame | 81-76 (OT) |
| 1993 | Minnesota | Georgetown | 62-61 |
| 1994 | Villanova | Vanderbilt | 80-73 |
| 1995 | Virginia Tech | Marquette | 65-64 |

# Women's
## Chapter 15
# College
# Basketball

**W**omen's basketball today is a major collegiate sport. The colleges look to recruit the best women athletes just like they go after the top men. The interesting thing is that James Naismith, the man who created basketball, always felt women should play the game the same as the men. And for a while, they did.

The problem was that in the early days, the rules split off. The men played by one set of rules, the women by another. It wasn't until 1970 that the women began to play by nearly the same rules as the men. And that's when the women's game really began to grow.

# The Old Rules

The women's game from the earliest days was different. It started with nine players on a side. But each player was confined to a certain area of the court. The ball had to be passed to each area before a shot could be taken. So the ball moved, but the players really did not.

Soon after there was a six-player version. But it too was not the same as the men's game. Three guards stayed at one end of the court for defense. The three other players, called the forwards, were at the other end. Their job was to take the shots.

There was also a rule against dribbling. Later, it was changed to let a player bounce the ball once before a pass or shot. However, as late as the 1950s, women's basketball permitted only two bounces—no sustained dribbling. Even in the 1960s, when the men's game was flourishing, the women were allowed only three bounces.

# Women's Hoop Comes of Age

It was in 1970 that the women finally began to play five to a side. Up to then, it was still six. Then in the mid-1970s, a new rule was passed that provided money for women's athletic programs. Women's teams could now have uniforms, full-time coaches, major schedules, and athletic scholarships. The women's game had finally come of age.

# Into the Garden

The first women's game at Madison Square Garden in New York City came in February 1975. There were some 12,000 fans on hand to see national champion Immaculata College of Pennsylvania play Queens College that night. That's pretty much big time.

The skills of the women players were changing now. Maybe they weren't as tall as the men, but the guards could dribble, the forwards could rebound, the centers could block shots. And everyone could hit a jumper. The Association for Intercollegiate Athletics for Women (AIAW) began holding its own national championship tournament in 1972. The NCAA began officially keeping records in 1982.

# The First Women's Powerhouse

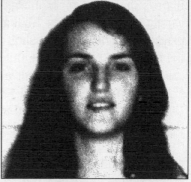

*THERESA SHANK*

Immaculata was a small women's college in Pennsylvania that from 1972 to 1974 won three straight national titles, beating West Chester University, Queens College, and Mississippi College in the title games. Back then, the traditional large schools weren't a factor.

Still, between 1970 and 1974, the Mighty Macs of Immaculata compiled an amazing 64-2 record, a mark worthy of UCLA or Duke. The star of the team for several of those seasons was a 5'11" center named Theresa Shank. At that time, she was one of the taller players in the women's game and definitely one of the best. Coach Cathy Rush also deserved credit for the success of the Macs.

# Other Stars

*ANN MEYERS*

After Immaculata's three-year run, Delta State of Mississippi took over as the top team, winning the next three AIAW titles through 1977. The Lady Statesmen also had a top center, 6'3" Lusia Harris. She was so good that the New Orleans Jazz of the NBA made her one of their draft picks.

The first women to receive an athletic scholarship to UCLA was Ann Meyers. She was the sister of All-American Dave Meyers, who played during the UCLA dynasty days under John Wooden. Ann Meyers became a great star on the women's side, making the

All-American team four times and leading the Lady Bruins to the AIAW championship in 1978.

# The Blaze

Her name was Carol Blazejowski and she was known simply as "the Blaze." She played for Montclair State College in New Jersey for three varsity seasons between 1976 and 1978. The Blaze was a smooth player with a deadly jump shot. She could also handle the ball, drive to the hoop, and play defense, much like the superstars among the men.

On March 6, 1977, Montclair State took part in a doubleheader at Madison Square Garden with 12,336 fans on hand. Playing against Queens College, the Blaze had a quiet first half, scoring just 14 points. But after intermission she was unstoppable, hitting on jumpers and drives. The Blaze connected on 17 of 21 field goals after intermission and finished the game with 52 points. At that time, it was the most points scored in the new Garden (built in 1968) by a man or a woman.

In 101 games over three years, Carol Blazejowski scored 3,199 points for a 31.7 average, which is still unofficially the best career average among women. It's unofficial because official NCAA records for women didn't begin until 1982.

Carol Blazejowski was the first winner of the Wade Trophy, started in 1978 and given to the best woman college player in the land. She is still considered by many the best pure scorer among the women who have played the college game.

*NANCY LIEBERMAN*

# Nancy Lieberman

While she was still in high school, Nancy Lieberman was good enough to make the U.S. Olympic team. From there, the 5'10" point guard went to Old Dominion in Norfolk, Virginia, and led her team to the AIAW title in 1979. Lieberman was a two-time winner of the Wade Trophy and a real pioneer in women's basketball.

She played a major role in starting a women's professional basketball league in the early 1980s. The league didn't last long, but Lieberman helped show that it could work someday. She also had the courage to try out with an NBA team and later played with a team that traveled as the opponents for the Harlem Globetrotters.

And those who saw her in her days at Old Dominion remember a point guard who ran the offense like any superstar point guard anywhere.

# Lynette Woodard

*LYNETTE WOODARD*

Simply a great basketball player, Lynette Woodard was a four-time All-American at Kansas from 1978 to 1981. In four years, she scored a record 3,659 points, hitting an incredible 52.5 percent of her shots and averaging 26.3 points a game. She also grabbed 1,734 rebounds.

In addition to her basketball accomplishments, Lynette Woodard also hit the books. She was a two-time academic All-American as well.

# Cheryl Miller

*CHERYL MILLER*

Basketball fans all know about Reggie Miller of the Indiana Pacers. He had a great 1993-1994 season and was even better in the playoffs. Reggie is now considered perhaps the best shooting guard in the NBA. But those who know the Millers say Reggie is the *second best* basketball player in his family. The best was his sister, Cheryl.

In four years at the University of Southern California, 1983 to 1986, Cheryl scored 3,018 points for a 23.6 average. She also won all the major Player of the Year awards, including the Naismith Trophy three straight times.

# Rebecca Lobo

**REBECCA LOBO**

Happiness for a college basketball player is being named Player of the Year after your team completes a perfect unbeaten season and wins the national championship. That's what happened to Rebecca Lobo, the 6'4" forward for the University of Connecticut's Lady Huskies. A two-time Academic All-American on the hardwood, Lobo averaged over 17 points and ten rebounds a game. As a senior, she was second in the nation in blocked shots with 3.5 a game. Lobo is a player and person of character. For five summers during her teens, she worked in the tobacco fields of Southwick, Massacusetts, as a test of her own dedication. And while leading the Lady Huskies to an unbeaten season, her schoolwork was so outstanding that she was encouraged to apply for a Rhodes Scholarship, one of the highest academic honors in the world. At UConn in 1995, Lobo simply ruled the roost on the basketball court.

# The NCAA Tournament for Women

In 1982 the NCAA finally caught up with the times and saw how big college basketball for women had become. It finally started a postseason tournament to crown a women's national champion. There are three separate tournaments for Division I, II, and III schools. As with the men, Division I gets the most exposure and the largest number of fans.

The field has expanded from 32 to 48 teams, and the tournament grows each year. Here are the tournament winners, beginning with the AIAW finals in 1972 and then the NCAA finals in 1982. The AIAW also had a tournament in 1982, but most Division I teams had already moved over to the NCAA tourney.

## AIAW Winners and Runners-Up

| Year | Winner | Runner-up | Score |
|------|--------|-----------|-------|
| 1972 | Immaculata | West Chester | 52-48 |
| 1973 | Immaculata | Queens College | 59-52 |
| 1974 | Immaculata | Mississippi College | 68-53 |
| 1975 | Delta State | Immaculata | 90-81 |
| 1976 | Delta State | Immaculata | 69-64 |
| 1977 | Delta State | Louisiana State | 68-55 |
| 1978 | UCLA | Maryland | 90-74 |
| 1979 | Old Dominion | Louisiana Tech | 75-65 |
| 1980 | Old Dominion | Tennessee | 68-53 |
| 1981 | Louisiana Tech | Tennessee | 79-59 |
| 1982 | Rutgers | Texas | 83-77 |

## NCAA Women's Winners and Runners-Up

| Year | Winner | Runner-up | Score |
|------|--------|-----------|-------|
| 1982 | Louisiana Tech | Cheyney | 76-62 |
| 1983 | USC | Louisiana Tech | 69-67 |
| 1984 | USC | Tennessee | 72-61 |
| 1985 | Old Dominion | Georgia | 70-65 |
| 1986 | Texas | USC | 97-81 |
| 1987 | Tennessee | Louisiana Tech | 67-44 |
| 1988 | Louisiana Tech | Auburn | 56-54 |
| 1989 | Tennessee | Auburn | 76-60 |
| 1990 | Stanford | Auburn | 88-81 |
| 1991 | Tennessee | Virginia | 70-67 (OT) |
| 1992 | Stanford | Western Kentucky | 78-62 |
| 1993 | Texas Tech | Ohio State | 84-82 |
| 1994 | North Carolina | Louisiana Tech | 60-59 |
| 1995 | Connecticut | Tennessee | 70-64 |

# The Wade Trophy

The Wade Trophy is voted on by the National Association for Girls and Women in Sports and awarded for academics and community service as well as player performance. It was first presented in 1978 in the name of the former Delta State coach, Margaret Wade.

## Wade Trophy Winners

| Year | Winner | School |
|------|--------|--------|
| 1978 | Carol Blazejowski | Montclair State |
| 1979 | Nancy Lieberman | Old Dominion |
| 1980 | Nancy Lieberman | Old Dominion |
| 1981 | Lynette Woodard | Kansas |
| 1982 | Pam Kelly | Louisiana Tech |
| 1983 | LaTaunya Pollard | Long Beach State |
| 1984 | Janice Lawrence | Louisiana Tech |
| 1985 | Cheryl Miller | USC |
| 1986 | Kamie Ethridge | Texas |
| 1987 | Shelly Pennefather | Villanova |
| 1988 | Teresa Weatherspoon | Louisiana Tech |
| 1989 | Clarissa Davis | Texas |
| 1990 | Jennifer Azzi | Stanford |
| 1991 | Daedra Charles | Tennessee |
| 1992 | Susan Robinson | Penn State |
| 1993 | Karen Jennings | Nebraska |
| 1994 | Carol Ann Shudlick | Minnesota |
| 1995 | Rebecca Lobo | Connecticut |

# The Naismith Trophy

This Player of the Year award is voted on by a panel of coaches, sportswriters, and broadcasters. It was first presented in 1983 in the name of the inventor of basketball, James Naismith.

| Naismith Trophy Winners | | |
|---|---|---|
| Year | Winner | School |
| 1983 | Anne Donovan | Old Dominion |
| 1984 | Cheryl Miller | USC |
| 1985 | Cheryl Miller | USC |
| 1986 | Cheryl Miller | USC |
| 1987 | Clarissa Davis | Texas |
| 1988 | Sue Wicks | Rutgers |
| 1989 | Clarissa Davis | Texas |
| 1990 | Jennifer Azzi | Stanford |
| 1991 | Dawn Staley | Virginia |
| 1992 | Dawn Staley | Virginia |
| 1993 | Sheryl Swoopes | Texas Tech |
| 1994 | Lisa Leslie | USC |
| 1995 | Rebecca Lobo | Connecticut |

# Top All-Time Scorers

Though women basketball stars are still not as well known as their male counterparts, on the next page are the top career and season scorers, by average, since the NCAA began keeping records in 1982. Remember, the great players who came prior to 1982 are not on this list. If they were, for instance, Carol Blazejowski would still be number one among career point getters with her 31.7 career average.

## Top Women's Career Scorers

| Player and School | Years | Points | Average |
|---|---|---|---|
| Patricia Hoskins, Mississippi Valley State | 1985-1989 | 3,122 | 28.4 |
| Sandra Hodge, New Orleans | 1981-1984 | 2,860 | 26.7 |
| Lorri Bauman, Drake | 1981-1984 | 3,115 | 26.0 |
| Valorie Whiteside, Appalachian State | 1984-1988 | 2,944 | 25.4 |
| Joyce Walker, Louisiana State | 1981-1984 | 2,906 | 24.8 |
| Tarcha Hollis, Grambling | 1988-1991 | 2,058 | 24.2 |
| Karen Pelphrey, Marshall | 1983-1986 | 2,746 | 24.1 |
| Erma Jones, Bethune-Cookman | 1982-1984 | 2,095 | 24.1 |
| Cheryl Miller, USC | 1983-1986 | 3,018 | 23.6 |
| Chris Starr, Nevada-Reno | 1983-1986 | 2,356 | 23.3 |

## Top Women's Single Season Scorers

| Player and School | Year | Games | Points | Average |
|---|---|---|---|---|
| Patricia Hoskins, Mississippi Valley State | 1989 | 27 | 908 | 33.6 |
| Andrea Congreaves, Mercer | 1992 | 28 | 925 | 33.0 |
| Deborah Temple, Delta State | 1984 | 28 | 873 | 31.2 |
| Wanda Ford, Drake | 1986 | 30 | 919 | 30.6 |
| Anucha Browne, Northwestern | 1985 | 28 | 855 | 30.5 |
| LeChandra LeDay, Grambling | 1988 | 28 | 850 | 30.4 |
| Kim Perrot, Southwestern Louisiana | 1990 | 28 | 839 | 30.0 |
| Tina Hutchinson, San Diego State | 1984 | 30 | 898 | 29.9 |
| Jan Jensen, Drake | 1991 | 30 | 888 | 29.6 |
| Genia Miller, California State-Fullerton | 1991 | 33 | 969 | 29.4 |

# College Basketball's

## CHAPTER 16

# Basketball's Record Breakers

C ollege basketball has had its share of great records. Some have been broken again and again over the years, while others have stayed on the books for many years. There is an old saying about sports records—that they are made to be broken. Of course, every now and then there's a record that looks as if it will last forever.

Take a look at some of these amazing records that have been set over the years and see what you think. Will any player today or any team today break them? That's always a great sports argument. Unless specified otherwise, all records are in Division I play.

# Hot as a Pistol

Pistol Pete Maravich was a great NBA player, a scoring champion, and a Hall of Famer. But before he ventured onto the NBA hardwood for the first time, the Pistol was the greatest scoring machine college basketball has ever known. His first varsity season at Louisiana State was 1967-1968. He was a skinny, 6'5" sophomore whose father, Press, was coach of the team.

All he did that year was lead the nation in scoring with a record-breaking 43.8 average. The next year he led the nation with a 44.2 average, and in his senior year he led again with a 44.5 mark. By the time he graduated in 1970, he had set the following records, none of which have ever been broken:

- Most points in a single season: 1,381
- Highest single season scoring average: 44.5
- Most points in a career: 3,667
- Highest scoring average for a career: 44.2
- Most games scoring 50 or more points, season: 10
- Most games scoring 50 or more points, career: 28

In addition to these incredible marks, the Pistol holds numerous miscellaneous scoring and shooting records, such as the most field goal attempts in a season (1,168), the most made (522), the most attempts in a career (3,166), the most made (1,387), and the most free throws made in a game (30 made in 31 attempts).

Sure, someone may come along and top some or all of the Pistol's marks. But they have stood for a quarter-century now. Pete Maravich was one of a kind, a wizard with a basketball who had a nose for the basket and simply went out and made it happen.

# Selvy Hits the Century Mark

One of the great records in NBA basketball history was set by Wilt Chamberlain in 1962 when he went out against the Knicks and scored 100 points in a single game. Well, it happened once before that in the college ranks. Frank Selvy, a 6'3" guard at Furman, turned the trick against Newberry on February 13, 1954.

Selvy was in the middle of a season in which he would average 41.7 points a game, a total topped only by the three great seasons of Pete Maravich. And on this night against Newberry, Selvy was absolutely out of this world. He started quickly, scoring 24 points in the first ten minutes of action. By halftime, he had run his total to 37. With ten minutes left, he had 62 points and counting.

Now his Furman teammates began feeding him the ball, and Selvy continued to score. With 35 seconds left, he already had a new record of 90 points. But he wasn't ready to quit. Somehow, he managed eight more points in 30 seconds. Now there were five seconds left and Furman had the ball again. Selvy's only chance was a last-second heave from just inside the half-court line. Swish! It went in. Selvy had scored an amazing 100 points. To this day, the record stands proudly and may never be broken.

# Robby the Rejecter

*DAVID ROBINSON*

Blocked shots were not an official NCAA statistic until 1986. So no one will ever know how many Bill Russell and Wilt Chamberlain blocked when they were All-American college players. But the greatest shot blocker since the stats were kept was none other than David Robinson when he played at Navy.

The future superstar of the San Antonio Spurs grew several inches while at the Academy. His final two years he was 6'11" and then 7'0". Those were the years shot blocking became an official stat.

In 1986, Robinson set a record by blocking 207 shots in 35 games, an average of 5.91 per game. He added 144 blocks the next season, giving him 351 in 67 games. That gave him a record average of 5.24 blocks in his career. By the way, the player who came closest to Robinson's single season record was Shaquille O'Neal. Playing for Louisiana State in 1992, the Shaq averaged 5.23 blocks per game. But Robinson is still tops. It was a risk for anyone taking the ball into the paint against the Admiral.

# Single Game Highs

Here are a few single game records that will really amaze you.

In February 1953, Bill Chambers of William & Mary grabbed 51 rebounds in a game against Virginia.

Three players share the record for the most assists in a game. Tony Fairley of Charleston South, Avery Johnson of Southern, and Sherman Douglas of Syracuse all had the hot passing hand and garnered 22 assists in a single game. Johnson and Douglas went on to become point guards in the NBA.

Avery Johnson also holds the record for the best assist average for a single season. In 1988 the slick point guard had 399 assists in 30 games for an average of 13.3 per outing.

David Robinson of Navy and Shawn Bradley of Brigham Young share the record of 14 blocked shots in a single game. Bradley was a 7'6" freshman when he tied Robinson's mark on December 7, 1990. Robinson had set his mark January 4, 1986.

Mookie Blaylock of Oklahoma had the fastest hands in college ball. On two occasions, Blaylock had 13 steals in a single game, once during the 1987 season and again in 1988.

The three-point field goal changed the strategy of college basketball. Dave Jamerson of Ohio University really took advantage of the new rule when he drilled 14 three-pointers in 17 tries in a game against Charleston on December 21, 1989.

When Frank Selvy scored his record 100 points for Furman in 1954, he also set a record by hitting 41 field goals that magical night.

# The L-Train Rolls

Talk about great college careers. There have been a number of players who have scored more than 2,000 points and grabbed more than 1,000 rebounds during their NCAA years. The player who stands first with the greatest combination of points and rebounds is Lionel Simmons, who played four years for La Salle until 1990.

The 6'7" Simmons scored 3,217 points and grabbed 1,429 rebounds in 131 games. That's an average of 24.5 points and 10.9 rebounds per game, quite a combination for a player who went on to become a fine pro.

# Scoring and Rebounding

While Lionel Simmons set a standard for combined scoring and rebounding totals in a career, only seven players in NCAA history have averaged more than 20 points and 20 rebounds for their careers. These players didn't play four full varsity years or their totals might have surpassed those of Simmons.

The great Elgin Baylor of Seattle was the only player to average more than 30 points and 20 boards. He scored at a 31.3 clip and rebounded at a 20.0 norm. The others were Walter Dukes of Seton Hall (23.5 points, 21.1 rebounds), Bill Russell of San Francisco (20.7 points, 20.3 rebounds), Paul Silas of Creighton (20.5 points, 21.6 rebounds), Julius Erving of Massachusetts (26.3 points, 20.2 rebounds), Artis Gilmore of Jacksonville (24.3 points, 22.7 rebounds), and Kermit Washington of American (20.1 points, 20.2 rebounds).

All were the real thing. Baylor, Russell, Gilmore, Silas, and Erving became super pros. Dukes and Washington also had solid NBA careers.

# The Win Streak

During the glory years of UCLA, when John Wooden's teams were winning a record ten NCAA titles in 12 years, including an incredible seven in a row, the team set another record that will be hard to beat. Beginning on January 30, 1971, and extending through January 17, 1974, the Bruins won an amazing 88 games in a row.

They did it playing a tough schedule and the pressure-packed NCAA playoffs as well. And when it ended, it took an incredible finish. On January 19, 1974, the Bruins were beating the Fighting Irish of Notre Dame, 70-59, with just three minutes left in the game. It looked like a sure shot for number 89.

But suddenly Notre Dame caught fire. In those final three minutes of action, the Irish reeled off 12 unanswered points to win the game, 71-70, and thus end the longest winning streak in college basketball history.

# Don't Play the Wildcats at Home

The University of Kentucky had some great teams in the 1940s. Adolph Rupp, known as the Baron, ruled his Wildcats with an iron hand. And when the team played before its basketball-crazed home fans at Lexington, they must have felt like supermen.

From January 4, 1943, to January 8, 1955, a period of 12 years, the Wildcats never lost a home game. They won 129 consecutive home victories, a record. The amazing streak was ended by Georgia Tech, but not without a fight. The Yellow Jackets topped the Wildcats, 59-58.

# The Longest Game Ever

Overtime games are always exciting, but they don't occur too often. A double-overtime game is even more of a rarity, and triple-over-time—well, that happens only occasionally. But the record for the most overtimes in a game is hard to believe.

It happened on December 21, 1981, when the University of Cincinnati went up against the Bradley Braves. The two teams were evenly matched that night, so evenly matched that the game was tied at the end of regulation. It was also tied at the end of the first over-time period, the second overtime period, the third overtime period ... why bore you with details?

It took seven full, five-minute overtimes for Cincinnati to finally win, 75-73. With 35 extra minutes of action, you would think the teams would have been over 100 points. But the longest game in college history was basically a defensive battle.

# Run and Shoot, Shoot, Shoot

Both Loyola Marymount and U.S. International had the same philosophy: run and shoot, and forget about defense. Whenever these two schools got together it was a scoring bonanza. In fact, the combination set several scoring records that seem hard to believe.

When the two teams met on January 5, 1991, Loyola set the record for most points by a team in a single game. They scored 186 points in whipping International, 186-140.

When the two teams met on January 31, 1989, they set a record for points by two teams, 331. Loyola won that game, 181-150. That also gave U.S. International the record for the most points ever by a losing team, 150.

When Loyola played Gonzaga on February 18, 1989, they set a record for most points by two teams in a half, 172. The game was tied at 86-86 at intermission.

And when U.S. International played Oklahoma on November 29, 1989, they allowed the Sooners to score the most points by a team in a half. Oklahoma scored 97 points in 20 minutes, while International patiently waited its turn.

Oh, yes, one final mark. In 1990, Loyola Marymount scored 3,918 points in 32 games, an average of 122.4 points per game. Like we said, run and shoot, then do it again.

# Playoff Marks

Come NCAA Tournament time, everything is on the line and the best players try to take their games up a notch. Here are some playoff records set by players whose names are probably very familiar to fans everywhere.

The most total points scored in the NCAA playoffs was amassed by Duke's Christian Laettner, who scored 407 points in 23 tournament games over four years from 1989 to 1992.

The highest average in the tournament belongs to Austin Carr of Notre Dame. Playing in seven tournament games from 1969 to 1971, Carr scored 289 points for a 41.3 average.

Elvin Hayes of Houston had the most total rebounds in tournament play, grabbing 222 boards in 13 playoff games between 1966 and 1968.

Jumpin' Johnny Green of Michigan State holds the rebounding average record, grabbing 19.7 caroms in his tourney games between 1957 and 1959.

Austin Carr holds the NCAA single game scoring mark, having tallied 61 points in a game against Ohio University in 1970.

Carr played in three tournament games that same year and set a record by averaging 52.7 points over that trio of contests.

Elvin Hayes played in five games during the 1968 NCAA tourney and grabbed 97 rebounds for a record 19.4 per game in a single tournament.

Back in 1956, Fred Cohen of Temple set a single game playoff record when he pulled down 34 rebounds in a game against Connecticut.

Shawn Bradley of Brigham Young holds the record for the most blocked shots in a playoff game when he rejected ten against West Virginia in 1991.

David Robinson holds the series rejection record, swatting 23 shots for Navy during a four-game stretch in 1986.

Glen Rice of Michigan set a tournament record when he nailed 27 three-point field goals during Michigan's six-game run to the title in 1989.

Playing 14 tournament games for Syracuse from 1985-1986 to 1988-1989, Sherman Douglas set an NCAA mark by dishing off for 106 assists.

# Amazing College Basketball Moments

## CHAPTER 17

**T**he world of college basketball is filled with events and moments that just happen without planning and sometimes without warning. Any time you attend a game, something strange, unexpected, or amazing can happen. Some make you laugh, others leave you wide-eyed and wondering how they could happen. Still others might leave you somewhat embarrassed.

Let's take a look at some of the more unusual happenings from the world of college hoops. See how many you knew about before.

# Total Collapse

The most amazing last-minute collapse of a team came on January 6, 1990, when Shasta College of Redding, California, was playing Butte Community College of Oroville, California. With 1:17 left in the game, Shasta had a seemingly insurmountable 89-71 lead. That's when it started. By the time the clock was down to 1:02, the lead was down to 89-79.

Shasta's starters were rushed back into the game, but the onslaught continued. With 36 seconds left the lead had been trimmed to six. Butte's full-court press had Shasta shaken. With 29 seconds left the lead was down to three. Shasta had committed five turnovers since the 1:17 mark, and then a 25-foot Butte shot swished for a three-pointer to tie the game. Shasta had blown an 18-point lead in just 77 seconds.

It went into overtime and somehow Shasta suddenly put it together and raced to a 103-92 lead with just 1:54 left in OT. But once again Butte made a run and tied the game in the closing seconds. Double-overtime. This time Butte went out and won the game, 116-115.

What a collapse. Not only had Shasta blown an 18-point lead in 77 seconds, but they also blew an 11-point lead in overtime with less than two minutes left. The old saying must be true. It ain't over till the fat lady sings.

# See the Ball

Sounds easy, but seeing the ball wasn't for Kevin Golden of DePauw University in a 1986 game with Dayton. Golden wore contact lenses and before going to sleep in his hotel room, he removed them and put them in a glass of water next to his bed. When he woke up in the morning the glass was there, but the water and the contacts were gone.

It was a mystery until Golden checked with his roommate, Andy Laux. When he heard the story, Laux clutched at his throat. It seems he had awakened in the middle of the night with a big thirst. He saw the full glass of water and glugged it down. And along with the water, he had swallowed Golden's contacts.

# The Best Teams to Go Nowhere

It would seem that the NCAA Tournament should feature the best possible teams it can get. But there have been a number of powerhouse teams that haven't gone to the tournament for one reason or another. Here are what are judged the five best teams that didn't go the tournament.

The **Kentucky Wildcats of 1954** were a 25-0 team that many thought would win it all. In fact, some said it was Adolph Rupp's greatest team. But on the eve of the tournament the NCAA stepped in and said that Wildcat stars Frank Ramsey, Cliff Hagan, and Lou Tsioropoulos had enough credits to graduate and were ineligible. Not wanting to be embarrassed, coach Adolph Rupp said his team would not enter.

The **Maryland Terps of 1974** were a 23-5 team featuring Len Elmore, Tom McMillen, and John Lucas. They almost beat UCLA early in the season, then finally lost to North Carolina State in the finals of the Atlantic Coast Conference Tournament, 103-100, in one of the greatest games ever. The rules at the time said that only one ACC team could go, so Maryland got shut out.

The **North Carolina State Wolfpack of 1973** was another unbeaten team that featured All-American David Thompson, 7'4" center Tom Burleson, and 5'6" point guard Monte Towe. The Wolfpack won 27 straight during the regular season but were on probation and couldn't go to the tourney. Off probation a year later, they lost one regular season game to UCLA, got revenge in the semifinals, and won it all.

The **Southern California Trojans of 1971** were an outstanding 24-2 team but a notch below perennial king UCLA, which gave the Trojans their only two losses. The Bruins represented the conference, and so Southern Cal stayed home.

The **La Salle Explorers of 1969** were another team that was hit by probation. But this

Explorer unit, led by Ken Durrett and Larry Cannon, rivaled the La Salle teams of Tom Gola 15 years earlier. Unfortunately, they never got a chance to prove their mettle in the NCAA playoffs.

# It Runs in the Family ... Almost

There have been a number of outstanding college basketball performers who followed in the footsteps of a family member who was an outstanding athlete, but not in the same sport. Here are a few college players whose family traditions might surprise you.

**Pat Riley** was a star player for Adolph Rupp's Kentucky teams of the mid-1960s. He later rose to fame as a championship coach with the Los Angeles Lakers and then as coach of the New York Knicks. His father, Lee, was a major league player with the Philadelphia Phillies in 1944, and his brother, also called Lee, was a defensive back with four AFL and NFL teams from 1955 to 1962.

**Alex Groza** and **Ralph Beard** were the All-American stars on Kentucky's NCAA title teams of 1948 and 1949. Each had a famous brother who passed up the hardwood for other sports. Lou Groza was a tackle and longtime placekicker for the NFL Cleveland Browns. Known as "the Toe," he was a nine-time Pro Bowler and is in the Pro Football Hall of Fame. Frank Beard took

a less violent route. He became a fine professional golfer who spent years on the PGA tour.

**Grant Hill**, twice an NCAA champ with the Duke Blue Devils and the 1994-1995 NBA Rookie of the Year, is the son of Calvin Hill. Calvin Hill graduated from Yale and became an outstanding running back with the Dallas Cowboys in the early 1970s.

**Thomas Hill**, no relation to Grant and Calvin, was another star on Duke's title teams of the 1990s. His father, Thomas Hill, Sr., was an outstanding track and field performer who won a bronze medal in the 110-meter hurdles at the 1972 Olympics.

**Kelly Tripucka** was a star at Notre Dame in the late 1970s and then went on to play in the NBA. His father, Frank, was an outstanding quarterback at Notre Dame in the latter 1940s, leading the Irish to a 9-0-1 record his senior year of 1948. He then played pro football until 1963.

**Bill Walton** was, of course, a great center at UCLA. But not many know that his brother, Bruce, was an offensive lineman with the Dallas Cowboys from 1973 through 1975.

**Kiki Vandeweghe**, the top scorer and rebounder on the 1980 UCLA team that was in the NCAA final, has a real family tradition. His father, Ernie, played for the New York Knicks. His brother, Bruk, has been on the Pro Beach Volleyball Tour. His sister, Tauna, was a member of the 1976 U.S. Olympic swimming team, competing in the 100-meter backstroke. To top it off, their mother, Colleen, was once Miss America. Now that's quite a family.

# An Amazing Transition

Perhaps no player in the history of college basketball made the kind of transition to the NBA that was made by the Big O, Oscar Robertson. Robertson was one of the greatest collegiate players of all time. In three varsity seasons at the University of Cincinnati, the Big O scored 2,973 points for an average of 33.8 per game. In his senior year, this three-time All-American averaged 33.7 points and 14.1 rebounds a game, shooting 52.6 percent from the field and 75.6 percent from the foul line. Drafted by the Cincinnati Royals in 1960, the Big O moved on to the pros, where he would have to play a much longer schedule against bigger and stronger men. Most college players need a period of adjustment. Not Oscar. In his first year the 6'5" guard averaged 30.5 points and 10.1 rebounds and shot 47.3 percent from the field and 82.2 from the line. The Big O could simply play against anyone.

# Chalk One Up to the Fans

On January 25, 1989, Vanderbilt had a two-point lead over Florida with one second left. They only had to inbound the ball and the game

was over. But suddenly Vanderbilt's home fans began firing yellow tennis balls on the court, trying to hit Florida center Dwayne Schintzius, who had some preseason publicity when he tried to clobber a fellow student with a tennis racket.

The fans fired the tennis balls with glee, but Vandy coach C. M. Newton wasn't smiling. He ran out on the court, trying to stop the storm of tennis balls. Too late. The ref invoked a rule stating that it's a technical foul if hometown fans throw objects on the court. And a technical foul in college ball means two shots.

Ironically, it was the target of their missiles, Dwayne Schintzius, who hit both free throws to force the game into overtime. Then in OT, Schintzius scored seven straight points to lead Florida to an 81-78 victory.

Not only did the tennis-ball stunt cost Vandy a victory, but Florida went on to win the SEC championship on the strength of that one win. They finished 13-5 while Vandy was 12-6 in conference play. Without the tennis-ball incident, the records would have been reversed.

# The Worst Shellacking

On January 29, 1974, tiny Englewood Cliffs College went up against Essex County Community College, both in New Jersey. Essex had a real powerhouse team, while the Englewood Cliffs program was barely hanging on.

It was apparent in the opening four minutes that the game was no contest. Essex raced to a quick 26-0 lead. If you could throw in the towel and go home, the Cliffs might have done just that. But they kept playing and by halftime trailed, 110-29. Some of the Essex players wanted to take it easy after that until a radio announcer informed them they were in striking distance of the single game collegiate scoring record of 202 points.

"I didn't want to embarrass Englewood," said Essex coach Cleo Hill. "But the kids asked me to let them have a shot at the record and I said OK."

So the onslaught continued. They would score, steal the ball, score again, steal the ball, score ... well, you get the idea. When it ended, the Wolverines of Essex had broken the record and in doing so administered the biggest beating in college history, winning 210-67.

# Hondo's Decision

Ohio State star John Havlicek went on to become an even bigger star in the NBA than he was with the Buckeyes. But it almost didn't happen. The reason was simple. The 6'5" Havlicek was such a great athlete and strong player that the Cleveland Browns made him their seventh-round pick in the 1962 NFL draft. They wanted him as a wide receiver.

Hondo didn't play a down of football at Ohio State, although he did play two years of baseball as a first baseman. Yet when the Browns drafted him, he went out for the team.

Being the great athlete he was, Hondo made it right up to the last cut. Finally the Browns had to choose between Havlicek and Gary Collins. It worked out for everyone. Collins became an outstanding receiver who caught five TD passes in three NFL title games, while Hondo went on to play 16 seasons with the Boston Celtics and retired as an all-time great.

# Surprise Star

Everyone knows about the UCLA dynasty, ten NCAA titles in 12 years, led by stars like Walt Hazzard, Gail Goodrich, Lew Alcindor, Bill Walton, Sidney Wicks, Keith Wilkes, and many others. They were players who knew how to rise to the occasion and come up big in the biggest games.

But on the first of those ten title teams, the 1964 Bruins, the player who rose to the occasion took everyone by surprise. He might be the most unlikely star in NCAA history. Kenny Washington was the sixth man on that UCLA team who had averaged just 6.1 points during the season. But in the final game with Duke, coach John Wooden inserted the ballhawking Washington to help with a trapping zone press.

The strategy worked, slowing down the Duke offense. But the surprise was Washington's scoring. He erupted for 26 points as UCLA won, 98-83. In doing that, he became the only player with a single-digit scoring average during the regular season to score more than 25 points in an NCAA championship game.

A year later, Washington almost duplicated the feat. He averaged just 8.9 points over the 1965 season, then scored 17 as the Bruins topped Michigan for their second title. Big game player. That was Kenny Washington.

# Too Much Happiness

On March 2, 1988, the Fairfield (Connecticut) University Stags were playing highly favored St. Peter's in the first round of the Metro Atlantic Athletic Conference Tournament. The game was unexpectedly close and as the final seconds ticked away, Fairfield's Harold Brantley took a long pass and went in for the hoop that gave the Stags a 60-59 lead and an apparent victory.

At that point, an ecstatic Fairfield coach Mitch Buonaguro raced onto the court in celebration. He jumped in the air, did a victory dance, and began hugging his players. Meanwhile, St. Peter's coach Tom Fiore was telling the refs there was one second left and Buonaguro should be called for a technical for running onto the court.

The technical was called, and Willie Haynes of St. Peter's made both free throws. St. Peter's then inbounded, and another foul was called. Two more free throws made the final score 63-60.

The Peacocks had scored four points in the final second, thanks largely to a coach who was so happy for his team that he wanted to be on the court to share a special moment with them. It was a case of too much happiness just a little too soon.

# Mikan a Project?

The word for a player with undeveloped potential is a "project," a guy who might make it with a lot of work. It's hard to picture big George Mikan as a project. After all, the 6'10" center who became an All-American at DePaul in the mid-1940s has a special place in basketball history. He is considered the first dominant center. But the big men who came later had been playing the game for years. George Mikan, however, was considered a "glandular goon," a man too tall ever to be a great player.

As a freshman at DePaul, Mikan didn't begin dunking the ball and blocking shots. Instead, he jumped rope, ran figure eights around chairs, boxed, danced, and ran with the track team. He was, in effect, a project. Coach Ray Meyer knew he might be a special player, but it would take time. First, big George needed more speed, more quickness, more agility, and more hand-eye coordination. A project.

In fact, during the first month of basketball practice the man who would become *the* big man of his generation wasn't even allowed to touch a basketball. Not even once.

# The Alcindor Rule

This one is hard to believe, especially since you can't go to a basketball game today, from high school to the pros, without seeing players slam-dunk. It's part of the game. The NBA even has a slam-dunk contest as part of its all-star weekend.

Many players take pride in the variety of ways they can jam. It was already getting that way back in the middle 1960s when Lew Alcindor arrived at UCLA. Alcindor, who would later change his name to Kareem Abdul-Jabbar, was a 7'1" dominant center who helped the Bruins win three straight NCAA titles. Though he always had an all-around game, once he was in close, Alcindor simply had to go up and jam.

Then, in 1968, the dunk shot was made illegal. Players weren't even allowed to dunk in pregame warm-ups! Some called it the Alcindor rule, claiming the lords of the game outlawed the jam because Alcindor was such a dominant player it might even things up a bit. It didn't. All the rule did was take some of the luster off the game. There were many high flying players at the time who would take off on a breakaway and have to lay the ball off the glass or gingerly guide it over the rim.

This absurd rule lasted for nine years until 1977, when the dunk was again legalized. Imagine all the sensational slams that didn't happen during that time. And imagine telling the players today—Shaq, Dominique, L.J., Sir Charles, and all the collegians—that they weren't allowed to dunk.

# Bragging Rights

When the weekly basketball polls came out on February 14, 1995, college hoop fans had to look twice. For the first time in history, the same school was number one in both the men's and women's polls. The University of Connecticut Huskies were 19-1 atop the men's poll, while the Lady Huskies at 21-0 topped the women's poll. While the men's team didn't wind up number one, the Lady Huskies went all the way, winning the national championship and completing an unbeaten season. But for one shining moment, UConn had bragging rights to all of college basketball.

# These Guys Are Coaches?

The coach is supposed to be the guiding influence on the team, the teacher, the character builder, the man who turns boys into men and top-notch basketball players. Some coaches sit calmly on the bench, quietly giving instructions and trying to figure out the way for their teams to win. Others are more emotional, walking up and down, screaming and yelling at officials and players. But they are still coaches.

But there is another side to coaches: their nicknames. Try these on for size: Phog, Forddy, Frosty, Tippy, Slats, Bully, Doc, Peck, Doggie, Bebe, Bones, Bucky, Digger, Nibs, and Butch. Sounds like a bunch of kids in elementary school. But in reality, they are:

Forrest "Phog" Allen, Forrest "Forddy" Anderson, Forrest "Frosty" Cox, William "Tippy" Dye, Amory "Slats" Gill, H. C. "Bully" Gilstrap, E. O. "Doc" Hayes, Bernard "Peck" Hickman, Alvin "Doggie" Julian, Horace B. "Bebe" Lee, Horace "Bones" McKinney, Frank "Bucky" O'Conner, Richard "Digger" Phelps, C. M. "Nibs" Price, and Bill "Butch" van Breda Kolff.

Those are some strange nicknames, but there sure are a lot of victories crammed into them.

# A Look at the
# College Numbers

## CHAPTER 18

*T*his is for all you people who love numbers—the stats and lists, the all-time records and award winners. The best teams, national champions, and top coaches. Let's take a look at the history of college basketball through the numbers, at the players and teams that have excelled down through the years.

# The Coaches

In some ways, the names are always the same. Success just seems to follow certain coaches wherever they go, like Bobby Knight and Dean Smith. Others have had some ups and downs but also have the skills to win when given the talent. Here is a look at both former and current coaches' records.

The 20 winningest active coaches include those who have at least five years as a Division I coach. Once they have completed the five-year minimum, their additional records are included even if their team or previous team played in Division II. Records, however, include four-year colleges only. If a coach has been at more than one school, the current school is listed first. Only the total record is listed, and they run through the 1994-1995 season.

## Winningest Active College Coaches By Number of Victories

| Coach | School(s) | Years | Won | Lost | Pct. |
|---|---|---|---|---|---|
| 1. Dean Smith | North Carolina | 34 | 830 | 236 | .779 |
| 2. James Phelan | Mount St. Mary's (Md.) | 41 | 737 | 392 | .653 |
| 3. Don Haskins | Texas-El Paso | 34 | 665 | 298 | .691 |
| 4. Norm Stewart | Missouri, Northern Iowa | 34 | 660 | 319 | .674 |
| 5. Bobby Knight | Indiana, Army | 30 | 659 | 235 | .737 |
| 6. Lefty Driesell | James Madison, Maryland, Davidson | 33 | 657 | 302 | .685 |
| 7. Lou Henson | Illinois, New Mexico State, Hardin-Simmons | 33 | 645 | 318 | .670 |
| 8. Gene Bartow | Alabama-Birmingham, UCLA, Illinois, Memphis State, Valparaiso, Central Missouri | 33 | 631 | 339 | .651 |
| 9. Denny Crum | Louisville | 24 | 565 | 212 | .727 |

| | Coach | School(s) | Years | Won | Lost | Pct. |
|---|---|---|---|---|---|---|
| 10. | Gary Colson | Fresno State, New Mexico, Pepperdine, Valdosto State | 34 | 563 | 385 | .594 |
| 11. | Eddie Sutton | Oklahoma State, Kentucky, Arkansas, Creighton | 25 | 553 | 209 | .726 |
| 12. | Eldon Miller | Northern Iowa, Ohio State, Western Michigan, Wittenburg | 33 | 528 | 377 | .583 |
| 13. | Hugh Durham | Georgia, Florida State | 29 | 527 | 310 | .630 |
| 14. | John Thompson | Georgetown | 23 | 524 | 200 | .724 |
| 15. | John Chaney | Temple | 23 | 520 | 175 | .748 |
| 16. | Pete Carril | Princeton, Lehigh | 29 | 503 | 266 | .654 |
| 17. | Bill Foster | Virginia Tech, Miami (Fla.), Clemson, North Carolina-Charolotte, Shorter | 28 | 494 | 303 | .620 |
| 18. | Lute Olson | Arizona, Iowa, Long Beach State | 22 | 481 | 187 | .720 |
| 19. | Bob Hallberg | Illinois-Chicago | 24 | 474 | 255 | .650 |
| 20. | Tom Davis | Iowa | 22 | 458 | 250 | .646 |

As you can see from the table, a good number of these coaches are well known. Others, such as Phelan, Colson, and Hallberg, toil at smaller schools and don't have the national recognition. All they have done is simply win.

There are several outstanding coaches now filling the spots between 20 and 40. A number of them will undoubtedly crack the top 20 before they retire. Some of the better known include Jim Boeheim at Syracuse (454), Jim Calhoun at Connecticut (438), Dale Brown at LSU (426), Tom Penders at Texas (425), Mike Krzyzewski at Duke (422), and Bobby Crimins at Georgia Tech (375).

# Winning Percentage

The previous table was based on total victories. When you look at the list based on winning percentage, it changes. Percentages are computed through the 1994-1995 season, and the school listed is where the coaches are working now, though the records are for their total coaching travels.

## Winningest Active College Coaches By Percentage

| | Coach | School | Years | Won | Lost | Pct. |
|---|---|---|---|---|---|---|
| 1. | Roy Williams | Kansas | 7 | 184 | 51 | .783 |
| 2. | Dean Smith | North Carolina | 34 | 830 | 236 | .779 |
| 3. | Nolan Richardson | Arkansas | 15 | 371 | 119 | .757 |
| 4. | Jim Boeheim | Syracuse | 19 | 454 | 150 | .752 |
| 5. | John Chaney | Temple | 23 | 520 | 175 | .748 |
| 6. | Larry Hunter | Ohio | 19 | 414 | 145 | .741 |
| 7. | Bobby Knight | Indiana | 30 | 659 | 235 | .737 |
| 8. | Denny Crum | Louisville | 24 | 565 | 212 | .727 |
| 9. | Eddie Sutton | Oklahoma State | 25 | 553 | 209 | .726 |
| 10. | John Thompson | Georgetown | 23 | 524 | 200 | .724 |
| 11. | Lute Olson | Arizona | 22 | 481 | 187 | .720 |
| 12. | Pete Gillen | Providence | 10 | 219 | 88 | .713 |
| 13. | Rick Pitino | Kentucky | 13 | 283 | 117 | .708 |
| 14. | Steve Fisher | Michigan | 7 | 140 | 59 | .704 |
| 15. | Bob Huggins | Cincinnati | 14 | 306 | 130 | .702 |
| 16. | Roger Reid | Brigham Young | 6 | 136 | 58 | .701 |
| 17. | Mike Krzyzewski | Duke | 19 | 422 | 183 | .698 |
| 18. | Ralph Underhill | Wright State | 17 | 342 | 149 | .697 |
| 19. | Don Haskins | Texas-El Paso | 34 | 665 | 298 | .691 |
| 20. | Wimp Sanderson | Arkansas-Little Rock | 13 | 282 | 130 | .684 |

# The All-Time List

The following table lists the top ten all-time coaching winners by victories. The school listed is the one for which the coach is most well known. Records for active coaches are through the 1994-1995 season.

| Top Ten All-Time Winningest College Coaches By Number of Victories | |
| --- | --- |
| **Coach and School** | **Wins** |
| **1.** Adolph Rupp, Kentucky | 875 victories |
| **2.** Dean Smith*, North Carolina | 830 victories |
| **3.** Henry Iba, Oklahoma State | 767 victories |
| **4.** Ed Diddle, Western Kentucky | 759 victories |
| **5.** F. C. "Phog" Allen, Kansas | 746 victories |
| **6.** James Phelan*, Mount St. Mary's (Md.) | 737 victories |
| **7.** Ray Meyer, DePaul | 724 victories |
| **8.** Don Haskins*, Texas-El Paso | 665 victories |
| **9.** John Wooden, UCLA | 664 victories |
| **10.** Ralph Miller, Oregon State | 657 victories |
| * Denotes active coach. | |

# Some Other Coaching Numbers

Nine coaches have been behind the bench for more than 1,000 games. Hank Iba tops the list with 1,105. Dean Smith is the only active coach on the list with 1,066 through 1994-1995.

Phog Allen holds the record for coaching the most seasons. This all-time great was behind the bench for 48 seasons, nearly a half-century of coaching. Allen spent 39 of those years at Kansas.

The record for coaching the most years at one school is shared by Ed Diddle of Western Kentucky and Ray Meyer of DePaul. Both spent 42 seasons coaching at their respective colleges. Adolph Rupp was at Kentucky for 41 years.

The most traveled coaches were Elmer Ripley and Bob Vanetta. Ripley, a pioneer of the game, coached between 1923 and 1953, making stops at Wagner, Georgetown, Yale, Columbia, Notre Dame, John Carroll, and Army. Vanetta was behind the bench at Central Missouri State, Southwest Missouri State, Army, Bradley, Memphis State, Missouri, and Delta State between 1943 and 1973.

John Wooden stands alone when it comes to NCAA titles. The Wizard of Westwood led his team to the promised land ten times, a great coaching achievement. Of course, it didn't hurt that he had Lew Alcindor, Bill Walton, and a host of other great players to guide.

# Coach of the Year

This presents a slight problem in that there are now five different Coach of the Year awards presented in college basketball. United Press International was the first, starting in 1955. The United States Basketball Writers Association began presenting their own award in 1959. The Associated Press began in 1967, the National Association of Basketball Coaches in 1969, and finally, the Naismith Coach of the Year award was started in 1987. Because the UPI award was the first, that's the one we'll list beginning on the next page, starting in 1955.

# UPI Coach of the Year Award Winners

| Year | Coach | School |
|------|-------|--------|
| 1955 | Phil Woolpert | San Francisco |
| 1956 | Phil Woolpert | San Francisco |
| 1957 | Frank McGuire | North Carolina |
| 1958 | Tex Winter | Kansas State |
| 1959 | Adolph Rupp | Kentucky |
| 1960 | Pete Newell | California |
| 1961 | Fred Taylor | Ohio State |
| 1962 | Fred Taylor | Ohio State |
| 1963 | Ed Jucker | Cincinnati |
| 1964 | John Wooden | UCLA |
| 1965 | Dave Strack | Michigan |
| 1966 | Adolph Rupp | Kentucky |
| 1967 | John Wooden | UCLA |
| 1968 | Guy Lewis | Houston |
| 1969 | John Wooden | UCLA |
| 1970 | John Wooden | UCLA |
| 1971 | Al McGuire | Marquette |
| 1972 | John Wooden | UCLA |
| 1973 | John Wooden | UCLA |
| 1974 | Digger Phelps | Notre Dame |
| 1975 | Bobby Knight | Indiana |
| 1976 | Tom Young | Rutgers |
| 1977 | Bob Gaillard | San Francisco |
| 1978 | Eddie Sutton | Arkansas |
| 1979 | Bill Hodges | Indiana State |
| 1980 | Ray Meyer | DePaul |
| 1981 | Ralph Miller | Oregon State |
| 1982 | Norm Stewart | Missouri |
| 1983 | Jerry Tarkanian | Nevada-Las Vegas |
| 1984 | Ray Meyer | DePaul |

## UPI Coach of the Year Award Winners, continued

| Year | Coach | School |
|------|-------|--------|
| 1985 | Lou Carnesecca | St. John's (N.Y.) |
| 1986 | Mike Krzyzewski | Duke |
| 1987 | John Thompson | Georgetown |
| 1988 | John Chaney | Temple |
| 1989 | Bobby Knight | Indiana |
| 1990 | Jim Calhoun | Connecticut |
| 1991 | Rick Majerus | Utah |
| 1992 | Perry Clark | Tulane |
| 1993 | Eddie Fogler | Vanderbilt |
| 1994 | Norm Stewart | Missouri |
| 1995 | Leonard Hamilton | Miami (Fla.) |

# The Players: Scoring Leaders

The NCAA did not begin keeping individual scoring records until the 1947-1948 season. Here are the annual scoring champions since that time. The scoring champ is based on average, since all schools do not play the same number of games. Postseason games are also included. You'll notice the names of many great players here, but also the names of obscure players who performed at smaller schools and never went on to play professional ball.

## College Scoring Leaders

| Year | Player | School | Games | Points | Average |
|------|--------|--------|-------|--------|---------|
| 1948 | Murray Wier | Iowa | 19 | 399 | 21.0 |
| 1949 | Tony Lavelli | Yale | 30 | 671 | 22.4 |
| 1950 | Paul Arizin | Villanova | 29 | 735 | 25.3 |
| 1951 | Bill Mlkvy | Temple | 25 | 731 | 29.2 |
| 1952 | Clyde Lovellette | Kansas | 28 | 795 | 28.4 |
| 1953 | Frank Selvy | Furman | 25 | 738 | 29.5 |
| 1954 | Frank Selvy | Furman | 29 | 1,209 | 41.7 |

## College Scoring Leaders, continued

| Year | Player | School | Games | Points | Average |
|------|--------|--------|-------|--------|---------|
| 1955 | Darrell Floyd | Furman | 25 | 897 | 35.9 |
| 1956 | Darrell Floyd | Furman | 28 | 946 | 33.8 |
| 1957 | Grady Wallace | South Carolina | 29 | 906 | 31.2 |
| 1958 | Oscar Robertson | Cincinnati | 28 | 984 | 35.1 |
| 1959 | Oscar Robertson | Cincinnati | 30 | 978 | 32.6 |
| 1960 | Oscar Robertson | Cincinnati | 30 | 1,011 | 33.7 |
| 1961 | Frank Burgess | Gonzaga | 26 | 842 | 32.4 |
| 1962 | Billy McGill | Utah | 26 | 1,009 | 38.8 |
| 1963 | Nick Werkman | Seton Hall | 22 | 650 | 29.5 |
| 1964 | Howard Komives | Bowling Green | 23 | 844 | 36.7 |
| 1965 | Rick Barry | Miami (Fla.) | 26 | 973 | 37.4 |
| 1966 | Dave Schellhase | Purdue | 24 | 781 | 32.5 |
| 1967 | Jimmy Walker | Providence | 28 | 851 | 30.4 |
| 1968 | Pete Maravich | LSU | 26 | 1,138 | 43.8 |
| 1969 | Pete Maravich | LSU | 26 | 1,148 | 44.2 |
| 1970 | Pete Maravich | LSU | 31 | 1,381 | 44.5 |
| 1971 | Johnny Neumann | Mississippi | 23 | 923 | 40.1 |
| 1972 | Dwight Lamar | Southwest Louisiana | 29 | 1,054 | 36.3 |
| 1973 | William Averitt | Pepperdine | 25 | 848 | 33.9 |
| 1974 | Larry Fogle | Canisius | 25 | 835 | 33.4 |
| 1975 | Bob McCurdy | Richmond | 26 | 855 | 32.9 |
| 1976 | Marshall Rodgers | Pan American | 25 | 919 | 36.8 |
| 1977 | Freeman Williams | Portland State | 26 | 1,010 | 38.8 |
| 1978 | Freeman Williams | Portland State | 27 | 969 | 35.9 |
| 1979 | Lawrence Butler | Idaho State | 27 | 812 | 30.1 |
| 1980 | Tony Murphy | Southern-Baton Rouge | 29 | 932 | 32.1 |
| 1981 | Zam Fredrick | South Carolina | 27 | 781 | 28.9 |
| 1982 | Harry Kelly | Texas Southern | 29 | 862 | 29.7 |

| Year | Player | School | Games | Points | Average |
|------|--------|--------|-------|--------|---------|
| 1983 | Harry Kelly | Texas Southern | 29 | 835 | 28.8 |
| 1984 | Joe Jakubick | Akron | 27 | 814 | 30.1 |
| 1985 | Xavier McDaniel | Wichita State | 31 | 844 | 27.2 |
| 1986 | Terrance Bailey | Wagner | 29 | 854 | 29.4 |
| 1987 | Kevin Houston | Army | 29 | 953 | 32.9 |
| 1988 | Hersey Hawkins | Bradley | 31 | 1,125 | 36.3 |
| 1989 | Hank Gathers | Loyola Marymount | 31 | 1,015 | 32.7 |
| 1990 | Bo Kimble | Loyola Marymount | 32 | 1,131 | 35.3 |
| 1991 | Kevin Bradshaw | U.S. International | 28 | 1,054 | 37.6 |
| 1992 | Brett Roberts | Morehead State | 29 | 815 | 28.1 |
| 1993 | Greg Guy | Texas-Pan American | 19 | 556 | 29.3 |
| 1994 | Glenn Robinson | Purdue | 34 | 1,030 | 30.3 |
| 1995 | Kurt Thomas | Texas Christian | 27 | 781 | 28.9 |

# The All-Time Scorers

Let's take a look on the next page at the ten greatest collegiate scorers of all time, by both total points and average. Most of the names will be familiar to hoop fans, but there are a few surprises. Not all the players went on to become great pros.

## All-Time College Scorers By Total Points

| | Player | School | Years | Games | Total Points |
|---|---|---|---|---|---|
| 1. | Pete Maravich | LSU | 1968-1970 | 83 | 3,667 |
| 2. | Freeman Williams | Portland State | 1975-1978 | 106 | 3,249 |
| 3. | Lionel Simmons | La Salle | 1987-1990 | 131 | 3,217 |
| 4. | Harry Kelly | Texas Southern | 1980-1983 | 110 | 3,066 |
| 5. | Hersey Hawkins | Bradley | 1985-1988 | 125 | 3,008 |
| 6. | Oscar Robertson | Cincinnati | 1958-1960 | 88 | 2,973 |
| 7. | Danny Manning | Kansas | 1985-1988 | 147 | 2,951 |
| 8. | Alfredrick Hughes | Loyola (III.) | 1982-1985 | 120 | 2,914 |
| 9. | Elvin Hayes | Houston | 1966-1968 | 93 | 2,884 |
| 10. | Larry Bird | Indiana State | 1977-1979 | 94 | 2,850 |

## All-Time College Scorers By Average

| | Player | School | Years | Points | Average |
|---|---|---|---|---|---|
| 1. | Pete Maravich | LSU | 1968-1970 | 3,667 | 44.2 |
| 2. | Austin Carr | Notre Dame | 1969-1971 | 2,560 | 34.6 |
| 3. | Oscar Robertson | Cincinnati | 1958-1960 | 2,973 | 33.8 |
| 4. | Calvin Murphy | Niagara | 1968-1970 | 2,548 | 33.1 |
| 5. | Dwight Lamar | Southwest Louisiana | 1972-1973 | 1,862 | 32.7 |
| 6. | Frank Selvy | Furman | 1952-1954 | 2,538 | 32.5 |
| 7. | Rick Mount | Purdue | 1968-1970 | 2,323 | 32.3 |
| 8. | Darrell Floyd | Furman | 1954-1956 | 2,281 | 32.1 |
| 9. | Nick Werkman | Seton Hall | 1962-1964 | 2,273 | 32.0 |
| 10. | Willie Humes | Idaho State | 1970-1971 | 1,510 | 31.5 |

As you can see, there are differences in the two lists. In recent years, freshmen can play varsity ball, so some players have four full years to accumulate points. If Pete Maravich had played as a freshman, his record would have been out of sight.

Three members of the top ten by average played at the same time. Maravich, Calvin Murphy, and Rick Mount all played from 1968 to 1970. That's a lot of scoring. And from 1952 to 1956, Furman had five years of Frank Selvy and Darrell Floyd, both of whom finished in the top ten. Of the top ten, however, only Maravich, Carr, Robertson, and Murphy (the top four) repeated their scoring success in the NBA.

# Top Rebounders

Official rebounding records were not kept until the 1950-1951 season. Then, from 1956 to 1962, the NCAA did a strange thing. They based the rebounding championship on the highest percentage of recoveries out of all the rebounds made by both teams in all games. So the average for those years is a percentage and not rebounds per game. In 1963 it went back to boards per game, the way it should be.

Next to the scoring championship, the rebounding title is perhaps the most important individual stat. Only three players—Xavier McDaniel of Wichita State in 1985, the late Hank Gathers of Loyola Marymount in 1989, and Kurt Thomas of Texas Christian in 1995—have won both the scoring and rebounding titles in the same year. Check out these kings of the boards on the next page.

## College Rebounding Leaders

| Year | Player | School | Games | Rebounds | Average |
|------|--------|--------|-------|----------|---------|
| 1951 | Ernie Beck | Pennsylvania | 27 | 556 | 20.6 |
| 1952 | Bill Hannon | Army | 17 | 355 | 20.9 |
| 1953 | Ed Conlin | Fordham | 26 | 612 | 23.5 |
| 1954 | Art Quimby | Connecticut | 26 | 588 | 22.6 |
| 1955 | Charlie Slack | Marshall | 21 | 538 | 25.6 |
| 1956 | Joe Holup | George Washington | 26 | 604 | .256 |
| 1957 | Elgin Baylor | Seattle | 25 | 508 | .235 |
| 1958 | Alex Ellis | Niagara | 25 | 536 | .262 |
| 1959 | Leroy Wright | Pacific | 26 | 652 | .238 |
| 1960 | Leroy Wright | Pacific | 17 | 380 | .234 |
| 1961 | Jerry Lucas | Ohio State | 27 | 470 | .198 |
| 1962 | Jerry Lucas | Ohio State | 28 | 499 | .211 |
| 1963 | Paul Silas | Creighton | 27 | 557 | 20.6 |
| 1964 | Bob Pelkington | Xavier (Ohio) | 26 | 567 | 21.8 |
| 1965 | Toby Kimball | Connecticut | 23 | 483 | 21.0 |
| 1966 | Jim Ware | Oklahoma City | 29 | 607 | 20.9 |
| 1967 | Dick Cunningham | Murray State | 22 | 479 | 21.8 |
| 1968 | Neal Walk | Florida | 25 | 494 | 19.8 |
| 1969 | Spencer Haywood | Detroit | 22 | 472 | 21.5 |
| 1970 | Artis Gilmore | Jacksonville | 28 | 621 | 22.2 |
| 1971 | Artis Gilmore | Jacksonville | 26 | 603 | 23.2 |
| 1972 | Kermit Washington | American | 23 | 455 | 19.8 |
| 1973 | Kermit Washington | American | 22 | 439 | 20.0 |
| 1974 | Marvin Barnes | Providence | 32 | 597 | 18.7 |
| 1975 | John Irving | Hofstra | 21 | 323 | 15.4 |
| 1976 | Sam Pellom | Buffalo | 26 | 420 | 16.2 |
| 1977 | Glenn Moseley | Seton Hall | 29 | 473 | 16.3 |

## College Rebounding Leaders, continued

| Year | Player | School | Games | Rebounds | Average |
|------|--------|--------|-------|----------|---------|
| 1978 | Ken Williams | North Texas | 28 | 411 | 14.7 |
| 1979 | Monti Davis | Tennessee State | 26 | 421 | 16.2 |
| 1980 | Larry Smith | Alcorn State | 26 | 392 | 15.1 |
| 1981 | Darryl Watson | Mississippi Valley State | 27 | 379 | 14.0 |
| 1982 | LaSalle Thompson | Texas | 27 | 365 | 13.5 |
| 1983 | Xavier McDaniel | Wichita State | 28 | 403 | 14.4 |
| 1984 | Hakeem Olajuwon | Houston | 37 | 500 | 13.5 |
| 1985 | Xavier McDaniel | Wichita State | 31 | 460 | 14.8 |
| 1986 | David Robinson | Navy | 35 | 455 | 13.0 |
| 1987 | Jerome Lane | Pittsburgh | 33 | 444 | 13.5 |
| 1988 | Kenny Miller | Loyola (Ill.) | 29 | 395 | 13.6 |
| 1989 | Hank Gathers | Loyola Marymount | 31 | 426 | 13.7 |
| 1990 | Anthony Bonner | St. Louis | 33 | 456 | 13.8 |
| 1991 | Shaquille O'Neal | LSU | 28 | 411 | 14.7 |
| 1992 | Popeye Jones | Murray State | 30 | 431 | 14.4 |
| 1993 | Warren Kidd | Middle Tennessee State | 26 | 386 | 14.8 |
| 1994 | Jerome Lambert | Baylor | 24 | 355 | 14.8 |
| 1995 | Kurt Thomas | Texas Christian | 27 | 393 | 14.6 |

No collegian has averaged more than 20 rebounds a game since Kermit Washington in 1973. Yet there have been some great rebounders, like Olajuwon, Robinson, and O'Neal. As in the NBA, rebounding numbers have fallen. Perhaps it is because the shooting percentages are higher, there are more slam dunks, and, as a consequence, fewer rebounds to be had.

# Assists, Blocked Shots, and Steals

Though these are all major categories today, the NCAA didn't begin keeping stats until midway through the 1980s. Let's take a look anyway and see who the leaders have been since the stats were kept.

## College Assists Leaders

| Year | Player | School | Games | Assists | Average |
|------|--------|--------|-------|---------|---------|
| 1984 | Craig Lathen | Illinois-Chicago | 29 | 274 | 9.4 |
| 1985 | Rob Weingard | Hofstra | 24 | 228 | 9.5 |
| 1986 | Mark Jackson | St. John's (N.Y.) | 36 | 328 | 9.1 |
| 1987 | Avery Johnson | Southern-Baton Rouge | 31 | 333 | 10.7 |
| 1988 | Avery Johnson | Southern-Baton Rouge | 30 | 399 | 13.3 |
| 1989 | Glenn Williams | Holy Cross | 28 | 278 | 9.9 |
| 1990 | Todd Lehmann | Drexel | 28 | 260 | 9.3 |
| 1991 | Chris Corchiani | North Carolina State | 31 | 299 | 9.6 |
| 1992 | Van Usher | Tennessee Tech | 29 | 254 | 8.8 |
| 1993 | Sam Crawford | New Mexico State | 34 | 310 | 9.1 |
| 1994 | Jason Kidd | California | 30 | 272 | 9.1 |
| 1995 | Nelson Haggerty | Baylor | 28 | 284 | 10.1 |

## College Blocked Shots Leaders

| Year | Player | School | Games | Blocks | Average |
|------|--------|--------|-------|--------|---------|
| 1986 | David Robinson | Navy | 35 | 207 | 5.91 |
| 1987 | David Robinson | Navy | 32 | 144 | 4.50 |
| 1988 | Rodney Blake | St. Joseph's (Pa.) | 29 | 116 | 4.00 |
| 1989 | Alonzo Mourning | Georgetown | 34 | 169 | 4.97 |
| 1990 | Kenny Green | Rhode Island | 26 | 124 | 4.77 |
| 1991 | Shawn Bradley | Brigham Young | 34 | 177 | 5.21 |
| 1992 | Shaquille O'Neal | LSU | 30 | 157 | 5.23 |
| 1993 | Theo Ralliff | Wyoming | 28 | 124 | 4.43 |
| 1994 | Grady Livingston | Howard | 26 | 115 | 4.42 |
| 1995 | Keith Closs | Central Connecticut State | 26 | 139 | 5.35 |

## College Steals Leaders

| Year | Player | School | Games | Steals | Average |
|------|--------|--------|-------|--------|---------|
| 1986 | Darron Brittman | Chicago State | 28 | 139 | 5.0 |
| 1987 | Tony Fairley | Charleston South | 28 | 114 | 4.1 |
| 1988 | Aldwin Ware | Florida A&M | 29 | 142 | 4.9 |
| 1989 | Kenny Robertson | Cleveland State | 28 | 111 | 4.0 |
| 1990 | Ronn McMahon | Eastern Washington | 29 | 130 | 4.5 |
| 1991 | Van Usher | Tennessee Tech | 28 | 104 | 3.7 |
| 1992 | Victor Snipes | Northeastern Illinois | 25 | 86 | 3.4 |
| 1993 | Jason Kidd | California | 29 | 110 | 3.8 |
| 1994 | Shawn Griggs | Southwestern Lousiana | 30 | 120 | 4.0 |
| 1995 | Roderick Anderson | Texas | 30 | 101 | 3.4 |

The real shame of these stats that weren't kept sooner is that there is no way to compare the leaders of the last decade with those who came before. Did Bill Russell block more shots than Shaquille O'Neal? Did Bob Cousy have more assists than Mark Jackson? Did Walt Frazier accumulate more steals than Jason Kidd? We'll never know.

# Player of the Year

As with the Coach of the Year award, the college basketball Player of the Year prize presents a rather complex picture. That's because there are now six major groups giving out a Player of the Year trophy.

The first was United Press International, which began in 1955. Next came the United States Basketball Writers Association, which presented its first award in 1959. The Associated Press began giving out the Adolph Rupp Trophy in 1961. The James Naismith Award was first presented in 1969, while the National Association of Basketball Coaches began presenting the Eastman Award in 1975.

The prestigious John Wooden Award was first presented in 1977. Unlike the other five, candidates for the Wooden Award must have a minimum grade point average of 2.00 out of a possible 4.00. It's the only prize that takes into consideration academics as well as basketball skills.

For the sake of comparison, we will list the UPI winners, because that was the first, and also the Naismith and Wooden Award winners, since both are usually considered quite prestigious. In fact, they all are, but there are so many repeat winners that these three will give you a pretty good idea who the top players were.

## College Players of the Year

| Year | UPI Winner | Naismith Winner | Wooden Winner |
|------|-----------|-----------------|---------------|
| 1955 | Tom Gola, La Salle | | |
| 1956 | Bill Russell, San Francisco | | |
| 1957 | Chet Forte, Columbia | | |
| 1958 | Oscar Robertson, Cincinnati | | |

# College Players of the Year, continued

| Year | UPI Winner | Naismith Winner | Wooden Winner |
|------|-----------|-----------------|---------------|
| 1959 | Oscar Robertson, Cincinnati | | |
| 1960 | Oscar Robertson, Cincinnati | | |
| 1961 | Jerry Lucas, Ohio State | | |
| 1962 | Jerry Lucas, Ohio State | | |
| 1963 | Art Heyman, Duke | | |
| 1964 | Gary Bradds, Ohio State | | |
| 1965 | Bill Bradley, Princeton | | |
| 1966 | Cazzie Russell, Michigan | | |
| 1967 | Lew Alcindor, UCLA | | |
| 1968 | Elvin Hayes, Houston | | |
| 1969 | Lew Alcindor, UCLA | Lew Alcindor, UCLA | |
| 1970 | Pete Maravich, LSU | Pete Maravich, LSU | |
| 1971 | Austin Carr, Notre Dame | Austin Carr, Notre Dame | |
| 1972 | Bill Walton, UCLA | Bill Walton, UCLA | |
| 1973 | Bill Walton, UCLA | Bill Walton, UCLA | |
| 1974 | Bill Walton, UCLA | Bill Walton, UCLA | |

## College Players of the Year, continued

| Year | UPI Winner | Naismith Winner | Wooden Winner |
|------|-----------|-----------------|---------------|
| 1975 | David Thompson, North Carolina State | David Thompson, North Carolina State | |
| 1976 | Scott May, Indiana | Scott May, Indiana | |
| 1977 | Marques Johnson, UCLA | Marques Johnson, UCLA | Marques Johnson, UCLA |
| 1978 | Butch Lee, Marquette | Butch Lee, Marquette | Phil Ford, North Carolina |
| 1979 | Larry Bird, Indiana State | Larry Bird, Indiana State | Larry Bird, Indiana State |
| 1980 | Mark Aguirre, DePaul | Mark Aguirre, DePaul | Darrell Griffith, Louisville |
| 1981 | Ralph Sampson, Virginia | Ralph Sampson, Virginia | Danny Ainge, Brigham Young |
| 1982 | Ralph Sampson, Virginia | Ralph Sampson, Virginia | Ralph Sampson, Virginia |
| 1983 | Ralph Sampson, Virginia | Ralph Sampson, Virginia | Ralph Sampson, Virginia |
| 1984 | Michael Jordan, North Carolina | Michael Jordan, North Carolina | Michael Jordan, North Carolina |
| 1985 | Chris Mullin, St. John's (N.Y.) | Patrick Ewing, Georgetown | Chris Mullin, St. John's (N.Y.) |
| 1986 | Walter Berry, St. John's (N.Y.) | Johnny Dawkins, Duke | Walter Berry, St. John's (N.Y.) |
| 1987 | David Robinson, Navy | David Robinson, Navy | David Robinson, Navy |
| 1988 | Hersey Hawkins, Bradley | Danny Manning, Kansas | Danny Manning, Kansas |
| 1989 | Danny Ferry, Duke | Danny Ferry, Duke | Sean Elliott, Arizona |
| 1990 | Lionel Simmons, La Salle | Lionel Simmons, La Salle | Lionel Simmons, La Salle |

## College Players of the Year, continued

| Year | UPI Winner | Naismith Winner | Wooden Winner |
|------|------------|-----------------|---------------|
| 1991 | Shaquille O'Neal, Louisianna State | Larry Johnson, Nevada-Las Vegas | Larry Johnson, Nevada-Las Vegas |
| 1992 | Jim Jackson, Ohio State | Christian Laettner, Duke | Christian Laettner, Duke |
| 1993 | Calbert Cheaney, Indiana | Calbert Cheaney, Indiana | Calbert Cheaney, Indiana |
| 1994 | Glenn Robinson, Purdue | Glenn Robinson, Purdue | Glenn Robinson, Purdue |
| 1995 | Joe Smith, Maryland | Joe Smith, Maryland | Ed O'Bannon, UCLA |

# Defensive Player of the Year

This is a relatively new award, probably created because a similar prize had become very prestigious in the NBA. In college ball, it has been presented only since 1987. Here are the winners.

## College Defensive Players of the Year

| Year | Player | School |
|------|--------|--------|
| 1987 | Tommy Amaker | Duke |
| 1988 | Billy King | Duke |
| 1989 | Stacey Augmon | Nevada-Las Vegas |
| 1990 | Stacey Augmon | Nevada-Las Vegas |
| 1991 | Stacey Augmon | Nevada-Las Vegas |
| 1992 | Alonzo Mourning | Georgetown |
| 1993 | Grant Hill | Duke |
| 1994 | Jim Mc Ilvaine | Marquette |
| 1995 | Tim Duncan | Wake Forest |

# The All-Time Top Teams

A look at the winningest teams in college basketball provides no real surprises. It seems that the same teams are always in the top 20, are always making the regional finals or Final Four of the NCAA Tournament, and have been successful over a long period of time. If the program is in place with a solid coach, the winning seems to continue.

Here is a list of the top 20 all-time teams by victories through the 1994-1995 season. To qualify, schools must have a minimum of 25 years in Division I. See if your favorite team is on the list.

## All-Time Winningest College Teams By Number of Victories

| School | Years | Won | Lost | Percentage |
|--------|-------|-----|------|------------|
| 1. North Carolina | 85 | 1,626 | 577 | .738 |
| 2. Kentucky | 92 | 1,616 | 518 | .757 |
| 3. Kansas | 97 | 1,567 | 702 | .691 |
| 4. St. John's (N.Y.) | 88 | 1,508 | 666 | .694 |
| 5. Duke | 90 | 1,474 | 727 | .670 |
| 6. Temple | 99 | 1,435 | 780 | .648 |
| 7. Oregon State | 94 | 1,430 | 927 | .607 |
| 8. Pennsylvania | 95 | 1,408 | 796 | .639 |
| 9. Syracuse | 94 | 1,403 | 661 | .680 |
| 10. Notre Dame | 90 | 1,389 | 730 | .655 |
| 11. Indiana | 95 | 1,369 | 732 | .652 |
| 12. UCLA | 76 | 1,351 | 588 | .697 |
| 13. Washington | 93 | 1,332 | 861 | .607 |
| 14. Western Kentucky | 76 | 1,331 | 621 | .682 |
| 15. Princeton | 95 | 1,313 | 830 | .613 |
| 16. Purdue | 97 | 1,311 | 732 | .642 |
| 17. Fordham | 92 | 1,303 | 924 | .585 |
| 18. West Virginia | 86 | 1,292 | 787 | .621 |
| 19. Utah | 87 | 1,290 | 717 | .643 |
| 20. Bradley | 91 | 1,284 | 797 | .617 |

The teams are really bunched up here. While the same basic teams will probably be on the list in five years, the positions may change. North Carolina, at number one, has just ten more wins than number two Kentucky.

Now let's look at the top teams another way, by winning percentage. This may be a better barometer of the most successful teams. Notice that there are a few new entries here, teams that don't have enough total wins to crack the top 20 yet. But their percentage ranks them on the top 20 of this table. Take a look at the two tables and compare.

## All-Time Winningest College Teams By Percentage

| School | Years | Won | Lost | Percentage |
|---|---|---|---|---|
| 1. Kentucky | 92 | 1,616 | 518 | .757 |
| 2. Nevada-Las Vegas | 37 | 779 | 268 | .744 |
| 3. North Carolina | 85 | 1,626 | 577 | .738 |
| 4. UCLA | 76 | 1,351 | 588 | .697 |
| 5. St. John's (N.Y.) | 88 | 1,508 | 666 | .694 |
| 6. Kansas | 97 | 1,567 | 702 | .691 |
| 7. Western Kentucky | 76 | 1,331 | 621 | .682 |
| 8. Syracuse | 94 | 1,403 | 661 | .680 |
| 9. Duke | 90 | 1,474 | 727 | .670 |
| 10. DePaul | 72 | 1,166 | 582 | .667 |
| 11. Arkansas | 72 | 1,230 | 635 | .660 |
| 12. Notre Dame | 90 | 1,389 | 730 | .655 |
| 13. Louisville | 81 | 1,277 | 675 | .654 |
| 14. Indiana | 95 | 1,369 | 732 | .652 |
| 15. Weber State | 33 | 605 | 328 | .648 |
| 16. Temple | 99 | 1,435 | 780 | .648 |
| 17. La Salle | 65 | 1,069 | 589 | .645 |
| 18. Utah | 87 | 1,290 | 717 | .643 |
| 19. Illinois | 90 | 1,281 | 713 | .642 |
| 20. Purdue | 97 | 1,311 | 732 | .642 |

# Winning Streaks

UCLA's famed "Walton Gang," the team led by center Bill Walton, set the most amazing winning streak in college basketball when it triumphed in 88 straight games between 1971 and 1974. Let's take a quick look at some other major win streaks. The streaks include postseason games.

## Longest College Winning Streaks

| Team | Victories | Seasons | Ended By | Score |
|------|-----------|---------|----------|-------|
| 1. UCLA | 88 | 1971-1974 | Notre Dame | 71-70 |
| 2. San Francisco | 60 | 1955-1957 | Illinois | 62-33 |
| 3. UCLA | 47 | 1966-1968 | Houston | 71-69 |
| 4. Nevada-Las Vegas | 45 | 1990-1991 | Duke | 79-77 |
| 5. Texas | 44 | 1913-1917 | Rice | 24-18 |
| 6. Seton Hall | 43 | 1939-1941 | LIU | 49-26 |
| 7. LIU-Brooklyn | 43 | 1935-1937 | Stanford | 45-31 |
| 8. UCLA | 41 | 1968-1969 | USC | 46-44 |
| 9. Marquette | 39 | 1970-1971 | Ohio State | 60-59 |
| 10. Cincinnati | 37 | 1962-1963 | Wichita State | 65-64 |
| 10. North Carolina | 37 | 1957-1958 | West Virginia | 75-64 |

A couple of interesting observations. Look how long the Texas record, set from 1913 to 1917, lasted. It wasn't broken until the 1950s. Second, had the UCLA teams of 1966-1969 not lost to Houston in 1968, that club would have won 89 straight games and topped the next UCLA superteam by one. That shows again just how great the Alcindor-led and Walton-led Bruin teams really were.

People always talk about the home-court advantage in sports. In basketball, teams are often bolstered by loud, cheering crowds urging them on. It has made some teams nearly invincible at home. Here are some almost mind-boggling home court winning streaks. These clubs might have lost a few on the road, but at home no one wanted to play them.

# Longest College Home-Court Winning Streaks

| Team | Home Wins | Start | End |
|---|---|---|---|
| 1. Kentucky | 129 | 1943 | 1955 |
| 2. St. Bonaventure | 99 | 1948 | 1961 |
| 3. UCLA | 98 | 1970 | 1976 |
| 4. Cincinnati | 86 | 1957 | 1964 |
| 5. Marquette | 81 | 1967 | 1973 |
| 6. Arizona | 81 | 1945 | 1951 |
| 7. Lamar | 80 | 1978 | 1984 |
| 8. Long Beach State | 75 | 1968 | 1974 |
| 9. Nevada-Las Vegas | 72 | 1974 | 1978 |
| 10. Cincinnati | 68 | 1972 | 1978 |

# They Said It: Memorable Quotes

## CHAPTER 19

# Quotes From the World of Basketball

*D*own through the years, the sport of basketball has been defined by those who play it. A player's most meaningful statement is usually made on the court with the ball in his hands. But there have also been many things said off the court that also give the game and its players personality and yet another dimension.

Here are the words of the players and coaches down through the years, in both college and pro basketball, describing how they feel about themselves, the things they've seen and done, and their relation to their game.

"During the game, the fans were leaving. They wanted their money back. It was boring to watch a team sitting on the ball. It got so bad, people were reading newspapers in the stands. They had to do something."

Minneapolis guard Slater Martin describing the 1950 game in which the Fort Wayne Pistons stalled their way to a 19-18 victory over the Lakers—the game that helped bring about the 24-second rule several years later.

"You never worried about the games, you worried about how to get out of the place alive, especially if you won. We played with one referee, and his theory was, 'If you need any help, don't expect it from me. If you can't take care of yourself, you don't belong out there.' They believed in no blood, no foul."

John "Honey" Russell describing how it was to play in a hostile building during the early days of the pro game.

"Our fun comes when we put the trophy in the trophy case."

Longtime Kentucky coach Adolph Rupp's response when asked about his serious, no-nonsense approach to the game.

"It took us an hour to play each game. It will take a lifetime to forget them."

Coach Nat Holman addressing the media in 1950 after his CCNY team became the only team in history to win both the NIT and NCAA Tournament in the same year.

"I blame Jerry West for that disaster.
He was the one who fouled me and sent me to the line
with a three-to-make-two. I wouldn't
have blown the game if it hadn't been for West."

Chicago Bulls' rookie center Tom Boerwinkle after missing three straight last-second free throws in a 93-92 loss to the Los Angeles Lakers, a game that cost his team a shot at the 1969 playoffs.

"I cut down to six meals a day."

Charles Barkley on how he lost 40 pounds prior to his rookie NBA season with the Philadelphia 76ers.

"The team was like a slingshot. I was the fork,
K.C. was the rubber band."

San Francisco center Bill Russell describing how he and guard K. C. Jones helped the Dons dominate the college game in 1955 and 1956.

"The coaches were constantly drilling us
on executing the right way. It was backdoors, picks and
rolls, using the backboard for layups.
They kept banging the fundamentals of the game
into us. Make a mistake and you did it over.
And that was fine with me. I never wanted to leave the
court until I got things exactly right."

Former Celtic great Larry Bird on how he learned to play a complete team game in high school, lessons that carried over right into the pros.

"The referees have asked that, regardless of
how terrible the officiating is,
please don't throw things on the floor."

Oklahoma coach Billy Tubbs's announcement to the home
crowd during a big 1989 game against visiting Missouri.
His little extra comment on the quality of the officiating
cost the coach a technical foul.

"You can't be Dr. J or the Big E.
They're both taken. Can I call you Magic?"

*Lansing State Journal* sportswriter Fred Stabley speaking
to high school star Earvin Johnson after he scored 36
points, grabbed 18 rebounds, and handed out 16 assists.
Stabley wanted to give the youngster a nickname. Little
did he know it would become one of the most famous
nicknames in sports history.

"We were stunned. There was nothing to say.
We knew we had to chew this one
before we could swallow it.
We sat chewing and the taste was bad."

Chicago Bull coach Dick Motta after his team let the 24-sec-
ond clock run out without getting a shot while trailing by
one point in the closing seconds of the seventh game of a
semifinal playoff series with the Los Angeles Lakers in
1973.

"Who knows what would have happened if
my father hadn't talked to me? I was lucky enough to
have parents who cared. They always gave
me guidance and at the same time taught me
to work hard."

Michael Jordan on his late father's advice when he was
skipping classes in high school to play basketball.

"I got some towels and soaked them in vinegar.
Then I placed the towels along the sidelines
and when our boys ran by they would step on them.
The vinegar cut the wax and somehow we
managed to remain upright."

> Abe Saperstein on how he solved the problem of a wax-glazed floor so slippery his Harlem Globetrotter team couldn't keep from slipping—until the vinegar cure.

"I could see the object was to put the ball in
the basket. But the game was more difficult than
I could have imagined."

> Knick center Patrick Ewing upon seeing the game of basketball for the first time when he arrived in Cambridge, Massachusetts, from his native Jamaica when he was 12 years old.

"I'm getting awfully tired of this baloney.
Every kid who can dribble a ball gets called
as good as Cousy. Well, I've got news for you.
There ain't nobody as good as Cooz. There never was."

> Outspoken Celtic coach Red Auerbach praising his star guard, Bob Cousy, in the 1960s.

"George, I'm afraid you need glasses and I never heard
of a basketball player with glasses ever
amounting to anything. I'm sorry, but I'll have to cut
you from the squad."

> A high school coach at Joliet Catholic in Joliet, Illinois, dismissing young George Mikan as a nearsighted youngster who would never make a basketball player. Mikan subsequently wore his glasses for his entire Hall of Fame career.

"Russell is more effective against me than any other
defender in the NBA because he catches me
off guard with his moves. Sometimes, he's playing in
front to keep the ball from me.
Other times, he's in back of me. He keeps me guessing.
He plays me tight this time, loose the next.
I've always got to look around to find out where he is.
It means I'm concentrating on him
as much as my shot."

> Wilt Chamberlain on the defensive genius of his archrival,
> Bill Russell.

"I was just in the right place at the right time. I've hit
them harder than that before. A lot harder than that.
I was a little surprised, but when it started coming
down, I started running the other way."

> Shaquille O'Neal after his slam dunk in Phoenix in 1993
> caused the backboard stanchion to break and the entire
> basket and backboard to sink onto the court.

"It has to be one of the best two or three sporting
events in the country, and that's not going to change.
It's at least the equivalent of the World Series, better
than the Super Bowl. You've got to win six times and
you've got to win twice within three days to win the
championship."

> Indiana coach Bobby Knight on the significance of the
> NCAA Tournament and the difficulty in winning.

"It was almost as if he *willed*
himself taller."

The late James Jordan commenting on son Michael growing five inches, from 5'10" to 6'3", between his sophomore
and junior years in high school. No other male member of
the Jordan family was over 6' tall. Michael ended up 6'6".

"I don't think it makes a bit of difference who's
covering Oscar. You just don't stop him. The way we
work it here now, I let the guards decide
that among themselves. The way they've worked it out
is that the one with the worst excuse gets him."

Celtic player/coach Bill Russell on the impossible job of trying to keep the Royals' Oscar Robertson in check defensively.

"There was no way I could really make that shot.
I just threw the ball."

Frank Selvy on his last-second midcourt heave that went
in and gave him a record 100 points for Furman in a
1954 game against Newberry.

"For three years, everybody always said Lew did it.
Well, we just proved that four other
men from that team could play basketball."

UCLA forward Curtis Rowe after the Bruins had won their
fourth straight NCAA title, but the first without Lew
Alcindor (Kareem Abdul-Jabbar) at center.

"It's never been a monkey on my back. Kids shouldn't play for coaches. They play together and have fun. But it's also nice to say we finally played well in April."

Duke coach Mike Krzyzewski after his Blue Devils won their first national championship in 1991.

"The next time we went to Syracuse it seemed like everybody in the place was puffing on a smelly old stogie. By the third quarter there were layers of smoke hanging over the floor. We had to peek between layers just to find our way downcourt."

Vern Mikkelsen of the old Minneapolis Lakers describing the atmosphere at the State Fair Coliseum in Syracuse the game after the Lakers' George Mikan had complained that the arena was too smoky from cigarettes and cigars. The fans really gave him something to complain about.

"In this game it is the survival of the fittest. The strong survive; the weak do not."

Former Knick center Willis Reed on what it took to be a top pivotman in the NBA of the 1960s.

# Basketball

**CHAPTER 20**

# and the Olympics

*B*asketball became an Olympic sport for men in 1936 and for women in 1976. The U.S. men's teams have had, for the most part, tremendous success. For the women, the results have been good but not great. But the international competition has always been exciting.

Because basketball was created in Massachusetts, it's not surprising that Americans dominated the sport for years. This was never more evident than in the Olympics. From the first Olympics to the final game in 1972, the United States won an unprecedented 62 straight Olympic basketball games without a loss. The streak ended with one of the biggest controversies in Olympic competition.

Since that time, the Olympics have suffered from a U.S. boycott in 1980 and a Soviet-bloc boycott in 1984 as politics has come to play almost as big a role as sports competition. But much of the world was beginning to catch up to the United States in basketball, sending the equivalent of professionals to play against U.S. college players and other amateurs.

Finally, in 1992, the Olympic committee allowed the United States to send professional basketball players for the first time. The result was the Dream Team, made up of top NBA players and one college player. Not surprisingly, the Dream Team walked away with the competition, proving again that the best of the United States was head and shoulders above the rest.

Let's take a brief look back at all the men's Olympic basketball competitions, held every four years.

# 1936

## Berlin, Germany
## Head coach: Jim Needles

The United States won four straight games to take the gold medal. The games were held outdoors in a tennis stadium on clay and sand courts. The final game was played in a heavy rain that turned the court to mud, which kept the score down as the United States beat Canada, 19-8.

# 1940 and 1944

The Olympics were not held because of World War II.

 **1948**

**London, England**

**Head coach: Omar Browning**

The United States sent a powerful team of collegiate and AAU players, led by Kentucky stars Alex Groza, Ralph Beard, and Wah Wah Jones and Oklahhoma A&M's 6'10" center Bob Kurland. The team won eight straight games, including an easy 65-21 triumph over France in the gold medal contest.

 **1952**

**Helsinki, Finland**

**Head coach: Warren Womble**

Once again the United States breezed through eight games to capture the gold medal. This was a team that dominated underneath with the 6'10" Kurland returning, joined by 6'9" powerhouse Clyde Lovellette of Kansas. The United States twice whipped the team from the Soviet Union, 86-58 in the semifinal round and then 36-25 in the gold medal game.

 **1956**

**Melbourne, Australia**

**Head coach: Gerald Tucker**

This U.S. team featured Bill Russell, and that was more than enough to ensure continued superiority for the Americans. Joined by University of San Francisco teammate K. C. Jones, Russell led the U.S. squad to eight straight wins as the Americans outscored the opposition, 793-365. The gold medal game was a solid 89-55 victory over the Soviets.

**1960**

**Rome, Italy**

**Head coach: Pete Newell**

This was undoubtedly the most powerful U.S. Olympic team until the professional Dream Team in 1992. Listen to the roster of college players who cruised to Olympic gold: Oscar Robertson, Jerry West,

Jerry Lucas, Walt Bellamy, Terry Dischinger, Bob Boozer, Darrall Imhoff, Adrian Smith, and a couple of lesser knowns. But the nucleus reads like an intro into the Hall of Fame. Ten of the players on the Olympic team went on to NBA careers. The team was so powerful that John Havlicek, a future Hall of Famer, qualified only as an alternate.

The United States won each of its games by at least 24 points, averaging 102 a game. They gave up just 59.5. Lucas and Robertson led the way by averaging 17 points each. In the final, the United States topped Brazil, 90-63.

 **1964**                          **Tokyo, Japan**
                                       **Head coach: Hank Iba**

This was another outstanding squad of American college stars, led by Bill Bradley, Jeff Mullins, Walt Hazzard, Jim "Bad News" Barnes, Joe Caldwell, Larry Brown, and Luke Jackson. The team went unbeaten, winning nine games. In the gold medal game, an improving Soviet team lost by the score of 73-59.

 **1968**                    **Mexico City, Mexico**
                                       **Head coach: Hank Iba**

The surprise star of the U.S. squad was a 6'8" junior college player named Spencer Haywood. He dominated underneath and allowed Jo Jo White to do damage from the outside. Led by those two and Charlie Scott, the United States again swept nine straight games, in the gold medal game defeating a surprising Yugoslav team, 65-50.

 **1972**                    **Munich, West Germany**
                                       **Head coach: Hank Iba**

This was a talented U.S. team but not a great one. It did feature big men Tom Burleson, Tom McMillen, and Dwight Jones, as well as guards Doug Collins, Tom Henderson, and Kevin Joyce. The United States won its first eight games, running its Olympic streak to 62, then met the Soviets for the gold medal.

The Soviets had an outstanding team and kept the game close all the way. In fact, the Soviets led by five at the half and were up by eight with 6:07 remaining. Then the United States chipped away until, with six seconds left, they trailed by just a single point. The Soviets had the ball, but Collins intercepted a pass and was fouled.

He made both free throws to give the United States a 50-49 lead. The Soviets then inbounded with three seconds left. But two seconds later, the Brazilian ref noticed a disturbance at the scorer's table and called a timeout. The Soviet coach was claiming he had called a timeout before Collins's second foul shot.

His claim was disallowed, but then a British official ordered the game clock reset from one second to three seconds. That gave the Soviets a chance to make a long pass to Sasha Belov, who put in the winning hoop, giving the Soviets a 51-50 victory and handing the United States its first loss ever in Olympic competition.

The United States protested, claiming that the British official had no authority to order the clock set back from one second to three, and furthermore, that there was no reason to set the clock back. The protest was disallowed. In further protest, the U.S. team unanimously voted to refuse their silver medals.

 # 1976 Montreal, Canada<br>Head coach: Dean Smith

## 1976 — Montreal, Canada
### Head coach: Dean Smith

The United States regained the gold medal with another solid performance. Led by Adrian Dantley, Phil Ford, Walter Davis, Scott May, and Quinn Buckner, the Americans won all seven games. Their only close call was a 95-94 squeaker over Puerto Rico.

In the semifinals, a surprising Yugoslav team upset the Soviets, 89-84, depriving the United States of revenge. The United States won the gold medal game by a score of 95-74.

 # 1980 — Moscow, Soviet Union

The United States did not participate in the 1980 Games as a political protest against Soviet aggression in Afghanistan. The Yugoslav team won the gold medal.

 # 1984 Los Angeles, California
## Head coach: Bobby Knight

These games were tempered somewhat by a return boycott by a number of Soviet bloc countries. But the United States had a powerful team of collegians, led by Michael Jordan, Patrick Ewing, Alvin Robertson, Wayman Tisdale, Sam Perkins, and Chris Mullin. The only close game was a 78-67 victory over West Germany in the quarterfinals. In the gold medal game, the United States easily beat Spain, 96-65.

 # 1988 Seoul, South Korea
## Head coach: John Thompson

This looked like another loaded team, featuring big men like David Robinson, Danny Manning, J. R. Reid, and Charles Smith, plus fine players and future pro stars Stacey Augmon, Mitch Richmond, Willie Anderson, Dan Majerle, and Hersey Hawkins. Yet the team never came close to reaching its potential.

It was probably the biggest Olympic basketball disaster ever for the United States, which didn't make it to the gold medal game. They had to settle for bronze. The Soviet team took the gold, beating Yugoslavia in the gold medal game, 76-63.

 # 1992 Barcelona, Spain
## Head coach: Chuck Daly

Since the concept of the Olympics being strictly an amateur competition was long dead, it was finally ruled that NBA professionals could participate in the Olympics. The United States then proceeded to put together a squad of NBA elite players, plus one college star, Christian Laettner of Duke.

Listen to the rest of the team: Michael Jordan, Magic Johnson, Larry Bird, Charles Barkley, David Robinson, Patrick Ewing, Karl Malone, Clyde Drexler, Scottie Pippen, Chris Mullin, and John Stockton. Could any team in the world, professional or otherwise, really beat them? It's extremely doubtful, and a certainty that no Olympic team could come close.

The Dream Team swept eight games by an average of 43.7 points a game. The average score, rounded off, was 117-73. In addition, the stars were the most sought-after celebrities at the Games. Athletes from all over the world wanted a glimpse of Magic and Michael, the Mailman and the Admiral, Larry and Sir Charles. In the final, the United States won the gold with a 117-85 victory over a very good Croatian team. The feeling about the Dream Team can be summed up in the words of Brazilian star Oscar Schmidt after his team lost by 44 points and he saw five of his shots rejected. "I loved it," Schmidt said. "They [the Dream Teamers] are my idols. I will remember this game for the rest of my life."

 ## The Women

Women's basketball became an Olympic sport only in 1976. The U.S. women have done well but haven't dominated like the men. Perhaps that's because women's basketball didn't become a major sport in the United States until the 1970s, so the women didn't have the same head start the men had.

The United States has taken a pair of gold medals, a silver, and a bronze in four competitions (1976, 1984, 1988, and 1992—remember, there was a U.S. boycott in 1980). Many of the top collegiate stars such as Ann Meyers, Nancy Lieberman, Lusia Harris, Teresa Edwards, Lynette Woodard, Cheryl Miller, and Anne Donovan participated on the U.S. teams.

The Soviet Union and in 1992 the Unified Team (the former Soviet Union) has provided the biggest competition for the United States. The Soviet women won in 1976 and 1980, while the Unified Team took the gold in 1992. The U.S. women won gold in 1984 (when the Soviets boycotted) and in 1988.

If the United States continues to send NBA Dream Teams on the men's side, there should be no real competition for a long time. But with the women, it will always be a battle and an exciting competition.

# The Basketball Hall of Fame

## CHAPTER 21

*I*t's very fitting that the Naismith Memorial Basketball Hall of Fame is named after Dr. James Naismith, the founder of the game, and is located in Springfield, Massachusetts, where basketball began. It is the only Hall of Fame for the court game and includes players from both college and the professional ranks; men and women; players, coaches, referees, and contributors; as well as foreign players. In other words, anyone who has contributed to the game and helped it grow is eligible to be voted in.

The Hall was founded by the National Association of Basketball Coaches in 1949 and inducted its first members in 1959, yet it didn't open its doors to the public until February 1968. The first Hall was located on the campus of Springfield College, where the game was invented. In 17 years, an average of just over 37,000 people visited the Hall.

On June 30, 1985, a new, $11.4 million, three-story Hall of Fame opened off I-91 in Springfield. Since that time, attendance has averaged 135,639 visitors a year, with a 1993 high of 173,898 people passing through the front doors.

The present Hall of Fame is a virtual mixed bag of memorabilia, information, history, and fun. There are, of course, exhibits for all the  inductees. But visitors can do a lot more than just look at their former heroes. The Hall has 15 baskets where visitors can test their shooting skills in the popular Spalding Shoot-Out.

There is also a "How High Is Up" exhibit where visitors can test their vertical leap and jumping ability, as well as 20 different video monitors where guests can see some of the great moments in basketball history. The newest exhibit, which opened in June 1994, is called the Wilson Imagymnation Theater and allows visitors to participate in a series of graphically presented interactive games. Through the Wilson Theater, guests can actually compete against Hall of Famers like Julius Erving and Pistol Pete Maravich, as well as many current stars. The exhibit, using state-of-the-art interactive computer-fed video, is a great addition to the Hall.

As of 1995, there were 209 individuals and four teams enshrined at Springfield. Of the individuals, 44 are considered contributors, 103 were players, 50 were coaches, and 12 were referees. The four teams are the First Team (the one organized at Springfield by Naismith when he invented the game), the Original Celtics, the Buffalo Germans, and the New York Renaissance.

Only four players were elected when the first inductions were made in 1959. They were John Schommer, who led the University of Chicago to three straight Big Ten titles from 1907 to 1909; Charles Hyatt, who led the University of Pittsburgh to a pair of national championships and won three straight scoring titles from 1928 to 1930; Angelo "Hank" Luisetti, whose all-around skills and one-handed shooting helped revolutionize the game; and George Mikan, basketball's first superstar giant center, who starred at DePaul and for the Minneapolis Lakers.

Since that first year, all the great players have been elected to the Hall. Many of the players mentioned in earlier chapters of this book are also enshrined at Springfield. In 1995, the great Kareem Abdul-Jabbar was voted in, along with former players Vern Mikkelsen, Cheryl Miller, and Anne Donovan. Former Soviet coach Aleksandr Gomelsky and former Laker coach John Kundla also joined the Hall, as well as former NBA offical Earl Strom.

The list continues to grow.

# Hall of Fame Dream Teams

For the Class of 1994 Hall of Fame Yearbook, sportswriter Jack McCallum of *Sports Illustrated* was asked to select three teams of six Hall of Fame players each that he would like to coach. In choosing his first, second, and third teams, McCallum took into consideration success at both the college and pro level, plus the player's historical impact on the game. Remember, stars like Magic Johnson and Larry Bird, who are retired but not yet in the Hall, are not eligible for these teams.

McCallum's choices are on the next page. You should have read about these players earlier in this book.

## First Team

| Position | Player |
|----------|--------|
| Forward | Bob Pettit |
| Forward | Julius Erving |
| Center | Bill Russell |
| Guard | Oscar Robertson |
| Guard | Jerry West |
| Sixth man | John Havlicek |

## Second Team

| Position | Player |
|----------|--------|
| Forward | Joe Fulks |
| Forward | Elgin Baylor |
| Center | Wilt Chamberlain |
| Guard | Pete Maravich |
| Guard | Bob Cousy |
| Sixth man | Rick Barry |

## Third Team

| Position | Player |
|----------|--------|
| Forward | Jerry Lucas |
| Forward | Bill Bradley |
| Center | George Mikan |
| Guard | Calvin Murphy |
| Guard | Earl Monroe |
| Sixth man | Bill Walton |

You may not agree with all the choices, but that's what makes picking all-star and all-time teams fun. Everyone has an opinion. Look at these teams, however, and think about what has already been said about the players. All of these guys could play and each of these teams would win a lot of games in any league.

# The Art of the Game

## CHAPTER 22

T he game of basketball seems simple enough. Shoot the ball in the basket. Or, if you're tall enough and can leap high enough, just slam-dunk the ball into the basket. But getting that shot or getting close enough for a slam dunk is yet another story. It takes a number of great individual skills for a player to be able to mesh into his team and play the game smoothly and well.

He also has to play within a set of rules, which differ slightly from high school to college and then with the pros. Let's take a look at the basics of the game, the rules, and the skills that are necessary for every player to master if he wants to be the best he can be.

# The Court

The basic dimensions of the basketball court have not changed much over the years. The optimum length is 94 feet long and 50 feet wide. Some courts are slightly smaller, none larger. The free throw line is 19 feet from the end line and 15 feet from the backboard.

Two things have changed on the court since the beginning. The free throw lane used to be 6 feet wide. Now it is 12.

The other change has been the inclusion of the three-point line. The three-point field goal came to the college game in the 1986-1987 season, with the three-point line always placed at 19'9" from the center of the basket. The NBA adopted the three-point field goal prior to the 1979-1980 season, with the line 23'9" from the center of the hoop. It was changed to 22 feet prior to the start of the 1994-1995 season.

Despite periodic calls for a change, the basket has remained exactly 10 feet off the floor since the day James Naismith hung the first peach basket on the gymnasium balcony. In the early days, no one dunked. Today, almost all college and professional players can slam. Every now and then, someone has suggested raising the hoop to 11 or even 12 feet up to give the smaller men more of a role and eliminate some of the slamming and jamming. But the smaller men have the three-point rule, and the good ones survive very nicely. The hoop remains at 10 feet.

# The Game

The length of a basketball game changes as the players get older. High school games consist of four eight-minute quarters for a 32-minute game. College teams play two 20-minute halves for a 40-minute game. In the NBA, games consist of four 12-minute quarters for a total of 48 minutes. Tie games at the end of regulation must be decided by playing short overtime periods until there is a winner at the end of such a period. In high school, an overtime period is three minutes long, and in college and the pros it lasts five minutes. Teams play as many overtimes as necessary to decide a winner.

To speed up the games, a shot clock is used. In the NBA, teams have 24 seconds from the time they get possession of the ball to get a shot off. College men's teams have 35 seconds to shoot. Women's team have 30 seconds. These rules were put in to curtail stall tactics, which made for very boring games.

Basketball is supposed to be a sport of minimal contact. But the size and strength of the players today often make that impossible. Contact often results in a foul call by the referee and the awarding of one, two, or three foul shots. To limit excessive fouling, a high school or college player committing five fouls has *fouled out* of the game and cannot return. An NBA player fouls out after committing a sixth personal foul.

A team can lose the ball by committing a *violation*. Walking or traveling with the ball, a double dribble, kicking or losing the ball out of bounds, and palming or carrying the ball are examples of violations that cause a team to lose the ball.

*Technical fouls* can be called against a player or coach who argues a foul call or displays unsportsmanlike conduct. A technical foul gives the other team one or two free throws and then possession of the basketball.

Substitutes can enter the game at the end of a period, during timeouts, or during a stop in play for a foul or violation. Play cannot be stopped just to allow a substitute into the game.

Games are started with a *jump ball* or center jump. In the old days, there was a center jump after each basket. Today, there is only a center jump at the beginning of the game and beginning of an overtime period. (Teams alternate putting the ball in play at the start of the second, third, and fourth quarters.) Jump balls can also be called if two players reach a loose ball at the same time and neither clearly has possession. Also, there may be a jump ball if the officials cannot see which team touched the ball last before it went out of bounds.

# The Positions

There are three basic positions on a basketball team: *guards*, *forwards*, and a *center*. Most teams play with two guards, two forwards, and one center, though some players are capable of playing more than one position.

In recent years, the positions have become more defined. There is a *point guard* and a *shooting* or *off guard*. There is a *small forward* and a *power forward*. A center, or pivotman, remains a center.

Guards are usually smaller and quicker than the forwards and centers. But they can vary greatly in size. Muggsy Bogues of the Charlotte Hornets is a 5'3" point guard, while Magic Johnson played the same position at 6'9". So there are exceptions to every rule. Most guards are probably between 6'0" and 6'5".

While all players today must be able to handle the ball well, the point guard must be an exceptional ballhandler. He must be a skilled dribbler with both hands, must see the entire court, and must be able to throw any kind of pass as soon as a teammate is open. A top point guard will lead his team in assists. And the best ones can also score, are able to *bury the J* (which means hit the jump shot), and can drive, or take it to the hoop. Kevin Johnson of the Phoenix Suns is an example of a point guard who can do it all.

The shooting or off guard must also have multiple skills. He has got to be a good ballhandler and passer but should also be an outstanding shooter, with three-point range on his jump shot and the ability to go to the hoop. Michael Jordan is the greatest off guard ever, though he is so good he can play point guard and small forward as well. Joe Dumars of the Detroit Pistons, at just 6'3", is nevertheless one of the best shooting guards in the NBA.

The small forward can be anywhere from 6'6" to 6'10", depending on his all-around skills. In many cases, the small forward should be a solid scorer, capable of hitting the jumper from out front and from the baseline. He should also be able to go inside on offense and rebound well. Small forwards today must also handle the ball and pass well. Larry Bird of the Boston Celtics had all the skills the perfect small forward needs: ballhandling, passing, shooting and scoring, and rebounding. Bird was 6'9", but Julius Erving at 6'7" was another all-time great small forward.

A power forward must be big and strong, a tough defender and rebounder. Power forwards can be 6'8" and taller. They usually concentrate on defense and rebounding. Charles Oakley, the 6'9" power forward of the New York Knicks, is a perfect example of this kind of player. He can score but won't if the other players are hitting their shots. He concentrates on defense and rebounding and is a very important part of the team.

Karl Malone of the Utah Jazz is a power forward who is also one of the top scorers in the league. Malone is 6'9" and very strong, so he is also a good defender and rebounder. But because he is also a great scorer, he must work hard on both ends of the floor. Power forwards usually don't have to handle the ball as much as the small forwards, but in today's game, all players need all the skills they can get.

As has always been the case, a top center can be the key to a team's success. Look what Mikan, Russell, Chamberlain, Walton, Abdul-Jabbar, and Olajuwon have done for their teams. There are more than 25 NBA titles wrapped up in those six centers.

The center is usually the tallest player on his team. In the old days, he was often slow and lumbering. Today, a center should be able to run the floor, shoot from medium range and in close, and be a solid defender able to block shots and rebound. And the better passer he is, the more effective the entire team offense will be. So centers also have to have multiple skills.

Some have specialized offensive moves. Kareem Abdul-Jabbar had the unstoppable sky hook. Wilt Chamberlain shot a fallaway jumper and finger roll. Hakeem Olajuwon has lightning-quick spin moves underneath that enable him to get past his man for a layup or jam. David Robinson can run like a deer and hit the jumper. Patrick Ewing is a deadly medium-range jump shooter. All the great ones can block shots and rebound. That takes timing and practice. Much of both the offense and defense still revolves around the center.

# The Skills

## Dribbling

Bouncing the basketball, or dribbling, has been an important part of the game for many years. Every player on a team today, including the center, should be able to *put the ball on the floor*.

A basketball player cannot look at the ball as he dribbles. He must keep his eyes on the court, even when he changes hands quickly or puts the ball behind his back or between his legs. So dribbling must be second nature. The ball must almost feel as if it's an extension of the hands and fingers.

Good dribblers always keep the ball low, never bouncing it higher than their waist. Getting low, even bending at the waist and knees, can help give you more control in heavy traffic and make it more difficult for a defender to steal the ball. The fingers should also be spread with the ball controlled by the fingertips.

The forearm from the elbow to the fingertips should move in a kind of pumping action while bouncing the ball. Beginners should stand in one place and just practice the basic bounce with both hands. As the ball comes up off the floor, meet it with your hand, giving slightly as it hits. Then use your fingertips to push it back immediately toward the floor.

When you can bounce the ball in one place without looking at it, you've reached step two. Then you can begin dribbling while you move. First just walk slowly, bouncing the ball as you do and, as always, practicing with each hand. You can also begin dribbling as you walk backward, then side to side. Don't look. Just keep feeling the ball on your hand.

Other basic drills include bouncing the ball on your knees so that you get the feel of the ball on your hand. You can also practice with a blindfold so that you will resist the urge to look at the ball. Once you have mastered the basics, then you can begin to practice the advanced dribbling skills needed to play the game.

Of course, you first have to take the basics up to full speed. Instead of walking, begin to run slowly at first, then faster, until you can dribble up and down the court with either hand at full speed. You must also learn to change speed when you dribble, moving slowly, then accelerating to go past a defender. You do this by leaning forward slightly as you accelerate. This is called *leaning into the dribble*. Another thing to remember: When going full speed, it is necessary to let the ball bounce slightly higher than with a normal dribble. A good dribbler also has to be able to change hands in a flash. The simplest way to do this is to bounce the ball across the front of your body and receive it with the other hand. Just practice as you dribble—right to left, left to right, over and over again.

Sometimes a defender is too close for the dribbler to change hands in front of his body. That's when the behind-the-back dribble comes in handy. With this maneuver, you must bounce the ball behind your back and pick it up with the other hand. This is not something that can be done at full speed or you will simply run away from the ball. Bending at the knees helps, and you should always try to bounce the ball close behind your heels. The ball should come up just behind your opposite hip so you can reach back with your hand and get it.

Another trick is to turn your back on the defender while sliding one way, then suddenly change hands and go hard around him the other way.

All these ballhandling maneuvers take long hours of practice to master. You'll also learn to protect the ball with your body and to keep it in the right place by instinct. If you want to be a top player, then practice time is something you must do. There's no easy way to become a fine dribbler.

# Passing

The fastest way to move the ball on offense and get an open shot is by passing. That's why a slick passing team is usually more effective than a team with great dribblers who hold the ball too long. Passing keeps the defense from setting up and can often help neutralize even the toughest defender.

There are four basic passes in basketball: the *chest pass*, the *bounce pass*, the *overhead pass*, and the *baseball pass*. Each has a purpose and a good player will know which type of pass to throw in every situation. He must also be skilled at throwing all four.

The chest pass, also called the two-handed chest pass, is probably the most used pass in basketball. Strong wrists are a great help because that enables a player to snap the pass off quickly and with a lot of mustard on it.

To throw the chest pass, grip the ball with both hands, one on each side of the ball. Spread your fingers with the thumbs directly behind the ball so they are almost touching. Then hold the ball at chest level before you release it. The pass is made by taking a step toward the receiver. This gives the pass more power. As you step, push the ball toward the receiver, straightening your arms with a final snap of the wrists. Keep your elbows close to your body, palms out and fingers pointing toward your target.

The chest pass can be used for short- and medium-range passes. Stronger players also use it for longer distances.

The bounce pass is used when there is a chance the chest pass will be intercepted by a defender. The ball is bounced just once and should come up right into the hands of the receiver. The pass is made with the same basic technique as the chest pass, only the ball is released at about waist level.

Again, it can be a good idea to bend at the knees to get a better look at the passing lane. The ball should bounce about halfway between passer and receiver. That is the spot on the floor the passer should aim at, with his follow-through aimed at that spot. Some strong passers like to bounce the ball three-quarters of the way to the receiver. But they also put strong backspin on the ball, causing it to bounce high and to the target.

As a rule, a bounce pass is tougher for taller players to pick off, especially in heavy traffic. They just can't bend down quickly enough to grab the ball.

Overhead passes are also thrown with two hands. This type of pass is usually thrown over defenders, so it is released from up high. The ball is held with fingers spread and thumbs behind. As with the chest pass, the passer should take a step toward his receiver. The passing motion is much like the chest pass, but the straightening of the arms and snap of the wrists occur above the head.

It is the wrist snap that gives the pass its power. Don't bring the ball back behind your head for more power. If you do that, chances are the pass won't be as accurate.

The baseball pass is exactly what it sounds like. The basketball is thrown with one hand, much like a baseball. This pass is usually used to throw hard over a long distance, such as on a fast break when the rebounder has a teammate already breaking way down court, or on a long inbounds play.

Practice throwing the baseball pass from right behind your ear. If you bring your arm back farther, you may have trouble controlling the ball. The passer should step into the throw, let his elbow come through first, then snap the ball away with his wrist. The pass is more likely to be straight if the passer rolls his wrist inward as he throws, palm facing out.

Once you have mastered the basic passes, then you can make your passing game even better. You can learn to fake one way and throw the other way. You may also learn to pass with one hand right off the dribble to take a defender by surprise. And finally, you can begin practicing behind-the-back passes. A behind-the-back pass on a fast break is one of the most exciting plays in the game. But it takes a great ballhandler and passer to make this pass accurately. And that means hours of practice.

# Shooting

Most people who start playing basketball want to score a lot of points. After all, scoring is the object of the game. But as players like Magic Johnson and Larry Bird have proved, it is more important to play a complete game, to do everything necessary to win. And that means a lot more than just scoring. But when the chance to shoot the basketball is there, every player should know how to do it.

There are five basic shots in basketball: the *layup*, the *jump shot*, the *set* or *push shot*, the *hook*, and the *slam dunk*. The last isn't really a shot. Taller players who can jump well can simply slam the ball home. If you can do that, fine. But if not, don't worry about it. There are other ways to shoot and score.

The layup is the easiest shot to make. It is taken right under the basket. Unless someone blocks it, you should make a layup every time. But you still have to know the right way to shoot it.

A layup is taken with one hand. Whether approaching the basket from the right or left, the shooter puts the ball up against the backboard and banks it into the basket. If you approach the basket straight on, then you can simply push the ball over the front of the rim and in. But younger players and beginners should veer to the right or left and use the backboard.

A shooter driving in for a layup from the right side should jump off his left foot and shoot with his right hand. From the left side, it's just the opposite. All players should be able to shoot layups from either side and with either hand. This is important. Begin practicing by just standing under the

basket and banking the ball in. The ball should hit the backboard above and to the side of the basket. It should hit on the way up, glance just slightly off the backboard, then fall back through the hoop.

Soon you can practice taking two or three steps before shooting and finally as you dribble to the hoop. By the time you're finished, you should be able to make layups while going full speed to the basket. Concentrate on the shot and not on the defensive players around you unless one is standing directly in your path. You do not want to foul him by charging straight into him.

The jump shot, or J, has become the most popular shot in basketball. Top players can hit jumpers from anyplace on the floor. A jumper is shot the same way whether from 10 feet away or 25 feet out. The best way to practice is to begin shooting a jumper from a standing position. Later, you can begin shooting it off your dribble.

Rule number one is always to square your body so you are directly facing the basket. As you get ready to take the shot, grab the ball with both hands and bend at the knees. Your feet should be

shoulder-width apart, and when you jump you should come down on the same spot. The shot should always be taken at the top of the jump.

As the shooter jumps in the air, the shooting hand should be behind the ball with fingers spread wide. The nonshooting hand should be on the side of the ball to guide it. The shooter must keep his elbow under the ball and not out at an angle. The wrist should be cocked backward, almost as if the shooter were carrying a tray.

The shot is taken at the top of the jump by straightening the arm at the elbow, then snapping the wrist forward. The ball should roll off the middle and index fingers last and should have a backward spin. This will help the shooter develop a soft *touch* and sometimes give him a favorable roll. Follow through by making sure the wrist is all the way forward, and then hold your arm steady for a second after the ball is released.

This is the basic form that must be practiced over and over again. Concentrate on the basket up to when you release the shot. As you begin to get the knack, you can move farther and farther out. Then you can practice stopping your dribble and going up for the shot. Also practice taking a pass from a teammate and then going up with the J. And once you can do all that, you must learn to get the shot with a defender right in your face. Becoming a good jump shooter can take virtually years and years of practice. Every game you play gives you more chances to practice.

In many ways, the set shot is a part of basketball's old days. Players then took long, two-handed set shots. That shot is never seen any more. One-handed set shots stayed popular longer, but the jump shot has pretty much taken their place too. The set shot is still seen on the foul line. Most players take foul shots while standing on the floor.

The basics of the one-handed push are to place the feet shoulder-width apart. A right-handed shooter will have his right foot slightly in front of the left, but his body should be square to the hoop. The ball is held the same as a jump shot. Bend slightly at the knees, bring the ball up over your head, and release it with the same motion as the jumper.

With the set shot, the legs are also used. As you begin the shooting motion, straighten your legs. When you reach the follow-through, you should be up on your toes. If you care to take the one-handed push shot from farther out, your legs will help propel the ball to the hoop.

The hook shot is usually taken by a center and fairly close to the basket. Once in a while, a forward will also shoot the hook. It's a tough shot to stop because it is taken high over the head as the shooter turns sideways to the basket, so his body is between the ball and the defender.

The hook is probably the last shot you should try to develop. It is taken with a long, circular sweep of the arm. If you have a small hand, it's a difficult shot to control. A right-handed shooter taking a hook strides forward with his left foot and turns sideways to the basket. That's when he begins the upward sweep with his right arm.

He then rises up on the toes of his left foot and brings his right knee up. As he does this, he continues the upward arc of the arm. The ball is released at the highest point of the arc. It's done with a flick of the wrist with the ball rolling off his fingertips with a backward rotation. A left-handed shooter does it just the opposite way, releasing with his left hand.

# Rebounding

Rebounding, the battle under the boards, is a fight that goes on every game. The center and forwards are usually the best rebounders on a team. But every player should know the principles of rebounding so when they find themselves underneath, they'll have a chance to grab the ball.

A rebound occurs every time a shot is missed and bounces off the rim or backboard. A defensive rebound is when a defensive player grabs a missed shot from the offense and puts his team on offense. An offensive rebound is when a missed shot is grabbed by a member of the shooting team. An offensive rebound will often give the rebounder a short, easy shot at the hoop. Or, he will be fouled.

Position, timing, strength, and desire are the keys to good rebounding. Great rebounders fight for every loose ball. When going for the ball, a rebounder must jump as high as he can and extend his arms fully upward. He has to time his jump so he can grab the ball when he is at his highest point in the air.

Rebounders have to watch the ball carefully, judge how it will come off the rim, and then make a strong move to get the ball. That's where timing comes in. Good position, however, is just as important.

As soon as a shot goes up, a rebounder has to try to get to the spot where he thinks the ball will come down. He has to try to beat the other rebounders to the spot. But he cannot push opposing players out of the way. Once he is where he wants to be, he has to prevent others from getting in front of him. He can do this by getting low, spreading both his feet and arms, blocking the path to the basket. This is called *boxing out*.

Defensive players always try to box out opponents as soon as the shot goes up. Even the man guarding the shooter must turn and box him out so the shooter cannot follow his own shot for a possible offensive rebound and follow-up shot.

A rebound should be grabbed with both hands whenever possible. Hold the ball very tightly and with your elbows out. When you come down your opponents may try to slap the ball away and steal it. Another way to prevent this is to keep the ball up high as you pivot and look for a teammate. Good rebounders will also look to make a quick *outlet pass* to a teammate to start a fast break.

Remember, when that ball goes up, there may be five, six, or seven players from both teams looking for that rebound. So learning how to get to the ball first is very important. It's a combination of technique, instinct, and practice.

# Defense

Championship basketball teams almost always have one thing in common. Besides being able to put the ball in the basket, they also play great defense. Defense is just as important to an all-around player as offense.

Teams play one of two basic styles of defense. They are the *zone defense* and the *man-to-man defense*. In a zone, each player covers a specific area of the court. With the man-to-man, each player guards a specific opponent. In both styles of defense, players must work together, pick up for each other, and function as a team. Zone defenses are often used in high school and college ball but are illegal in the NBA.

The principles of playing defense are the same with both styles. First, there is the basic stance. Start with your feet at least shoulder-width apart, one foot a little bit in front of the other. Hands should be kept low and out to the side with fingers spread. Your weight should

be on the balls of your feet so you can move quickly in any direction.

Defenders should not lean forward. That's because they must often move back quickly and will lose that split second if they are leaning forward. So always keep your weight centered, maybe even slightly to the rear.

When your man has the ball, always play him tightly. Stay close, move your hands, and try to keep him from getting into the flow of his game. He should not be able to dribble past you time and again. It's important to keep him from going into the middle from where he can pass off or go to the hoop. Always stay between your man and the basket. And the farther away from the basket you keep him, the better. Use the quickness of your hands to slap the ball away on a dribble or to knock down or intercept a pass. But if you slap the hand or wrist of the man you're guarding, that's a foul.

Defenders have to work together. Sometimes that means talking to a teammate and telling him what is happening to his blind side or behind him. An offensive player will try to *pick off* a defender by running him into another offensive player. That will allow the man he is guarding to get free or even cause the defender to commit a foul by running hard into the *pick*.

Defensive players should take short, quick shuffle steps when moving side to side. They should not cross one foot over the other. That way, the defender is always in his basic stance and ready to change direction without his feet getting tangled.

There is a great deal to learn if you want to be a great basketball player. It takes hard work, practice, good coaching, and dedication. Only then will you finally master the full art of the game.

# Index

# B

Indianapolis Olympians, 40

Indiana, University of
NCAA winner, 151, 154, 162,
164, 166
NIT winner, 171
wins/losses, 222, 223

Inglis, Jack, 21

Iowa, University of, 7

Irish, Ned, 147

Irving, John, rebounding title
(college), 214

Issel, Dan, 28
career of, 87-88
total points scored, 118

# J

Jackson, Inman, 139-140, 142

Jackson, Jim, 28
college Player of the Year, 221

Jackson, Mark
assists leader (college), 216
Rookie of the Year, 127

Jackson, Phil, career of, 113

Jakubick, Joe, scoring champion
(college), 211

Jamerson, Dave, 186

Jennings, Karen, Wade Trophy
winner, 180

Jensen, Jan, top season scoring
of, 182

Johnson, Avery, 186
assists leader (college), 216

Johnson, Dennis, 26, 38
MVP, 61, 124

Johnson, Earvin "Magic," 14, 31,
65, 128, 229, 239
All-Time NCAA Team member,
169
career of, 88
MVP, 62, 64, 122, 123, 124

NBA draft, 131, 133
NCAA outstanding player, 163
playing center, first time, 43-44
retirement of, 66

Johnson, Gus, 39

Johnson, John, 36

Johnson, Kevin, career of, 99

Johnson, Larry
career of, 100
college Player of the Year, 221
NBA draft, 132, 133
Rookie of the Year, 127

Johnson, Marques, 32, 128
college Player of the Year, 220

Johnson, Vinnie, 64

Johnston, Neil, 29, 54

Jones, Bobby, 35

Jones, Dwight, 237

Jones, Erma, career scoring of, 182

Jones, K. C., 25, 57, 228, 236
career of, 111

Jones, Larry, 28

Jones, Popeye, rebounding title
(college), 215

Jones, Sam, 25, 57, 58

Jones, Wah Wah, 153, 236

Jones, Wally, 35

Jordan, James, 232

Jordan, Michael, 64, 229, 239
All-Time NCAA Team member,
169
average points per game, 120
career of, 100
college Player of the Year, 220
Defensive Player of the Year, 130
MVP, 65, 66, 122, 123, 124
performance after injury, 47
retirement of, 66, 100
Rookie of the Year, 127
total points scored, 119

Joyce, Kevin, 237
Jucker, Ed, Coach of the Year award, 208

# K

Kaftan, George, 153
Kansas, University of
    NCAA winner, 154, 166
    wins/losses, 222, 223
Kelly, Harry
    scoring champion (college), 210-211
    total points scored (college), 212
Kelly, Pam, Wade Trophy winner, 180
Kenon, Larry, 37, 137
Kentucky, University of, 188, 193
    NCAA winner, 153, 154, 156, 163
    NIT winner, 170, 171
    winning streak of, 225
    wins/losses, 222, 223
Kerr, Johnny, 35
Kidd, Jason, 28
    assists leader (college), 216
    Rookie of the Year, 127
    steals leader (college), 217
Kidd, Warren, rebounding title (college), 215
Kimball, Toby, rebounding title (college), 214
Kimble, Bo, scoring champion (college), 211
King, Bernard, 33, 34, 39, 128
King, Billy, Defensive Player of the Year (college), 221
Knight, Billy, 30
Knight, Bobby, 203, 205, 231, 239
    Coach of the Year award, 208, 209

Komives, Howard, scoring champion (college), 210
Kotz, John, 151
Krzyzewski, Mike, 204, 205, 233
    Coach of the Year award, 209
Kundla, John, 243
    career of, 111
Kurland, Bob, 152, 153, 236

# L

Laettner, Christian, 167, 190, 239
    college Player of the Year, 221
Laimbeer, Bill, 29, 64
Lamar, Dwight
    average points per game (college), 212
    scoring champion (college), 210
Lamar University, winning streak of, 225
Lambert, Jerome, rebounding title (college), 215
Lane, Jerome, rebounding title (college), 215
Lanier, Bob, 2, 29, 32, 128
    career of, 88-89
    NBA draft, 131, 133
Lapchick, Joe, 21
    career of, 111
    excitability of, 74-75
LaRusso, Rudy, 31
La Salle University, 193-194
    NCAA winner, 155
    NIT winner, 170
    wins/losses, 223
Lathen, Craig, assists leader (college), 216
Lavelli, Tony, scoring champion (college), 209
Lawrence, Janice, Wade Trophy winner, 180

rebounding title (college), 215
  Rookie of the Year, 127
Oregon State University, 144
  wins/losses, 222
Oregon, University of, NCAA winner,
  151
Orlando Magic, 67
  facts about, 34-35
  wins/losses, 117

# P

Parish, Robert, 26, 29, 62
  total points scored, 119
passing, 252-254
Paultz, Billy, 37
Paxson, Jim, 36
Pelkington, Bob, rebounding title
  (college), 214
Pellom, Sam, rebounding title
  (college), 214
Pelphrey, Karen, career scoring of,
  182
Penders, Tom, 204
Pennefather, Shelly, Wade Trophy
  winner, 180
Pennsylvania, University of,
  wins/losses, 222
Perkins, Sam, 28, 239
Perrot, Kim, top season scoring of,
  182
Person, Chuck, 30
  Rookie of the Year, 127
Petrie, Jeff, 36
  Rookie of the Year, 126
Petrovic, Drazen, 33
Pettit, Bob, 25, 54, 55, 136
  career of, 91
  Hall of Fame Team member, 244
  MVP, 121
  Rookie of the Year, 126

Phelan, James, 203, 206
Phelps, Digger, Coach of the Year
  award, 208
Philadelphia 76ers, 61, 62, 137
  facts about, 35
  NBA championships, 57, 63
  wins/losses, 116
  See also Syracuse Nationals
Philadelphia Warriors, 42-43, 48
  NBA championships, 52, 54
Philip, Andy, 29, 73
Phoenix Suns, 60, 66, 135
  facts about, 35-36
  wins/losses, 116
Pinckney, Ed, NCAA outstanding
  player, 165
Pippen, Scottie, 239
  career of, 103-104
Pitino, Rick, 205
Pittsburgh Ironmen, 40
Podoloff, Maurice, 121
Pollard, Jim, 31, 52
Pollard, LaTaunya, Wade Trophy
  winner, 180
Porter, Howard, 160
Porter, Kevin, 39, 60
Portland Trail Blazers, 65, 66
  facts about, 36
  NBA championship, 61
  wins/losses, 116
positions, 248-250
Price, Mark, 135
  career of, 104
Princeton University
  NIT winner, 171
  wins/losses, 222
Providence Steamrollers, 40
Providence, University of, NIT
  winner, 170, 171

# Photo Credits

**Inside Covers:** Brian Kobberger/Bill Smith Studio  **4:** © NBA Photos  **18:** Bettman Archive  **19:** UPI/Bettman News Photos  **20:** UPI/Bettman News Photos  **21:** UPI/Bettman News Photos  **25-39:** The NBA and member team logos reproduced in this publication are trademarks and copyrighted designs which are the exclusive property of NBA Properties, Inc., and the respective NBA member teams, are being used under license from NBA Properties, Inc., and may not be used without the written consent of NBA Properties, Inc.  **81:** Abdul-Jabbar: Photography Ink/Wen Roberts  **81:** Archibald: © NBA Photos  **82:** Baylor: Photography Ink/Wen Roberts  **83:** Bird: Photography Ink/Wen Roberts  **83:** Chamberlain: Photography Ink/Wen Roberts  **84:** Cousy: © NBA Photos  **85:** Frazier: © NBA Photos  **86:** Gervin: © NBA Photos  **87:** Hayes: Courtesy of Washington Bullets  **87:** Issel: Courtesy of Denver Nuggets  **88:** Johnson: Photography Ink/Wen Roberts  **88:** Lanier: Courtesy of Detroit Pistons  **90:** McHale: © NBA Photos  **91:** Pettit: © NBA Photos  **92:** Reed: Courtesy of New York Knickerbockers  **92:** Russell: © NBA Photos  **93:** Thomas: Courtesy of Detroit Pistons  **94:** West: Photography Ink/Wen Roberts  **97:** Barkley: Courtesy of Phoenix Suns  **98:** Dumars: Courtesy of Detroit Pistons  **98:** Ewing: Courtesy of New York Knickerbockers  **99:** Hardaway: © NBA Photos  **99:** Johnson: Courtesy of Phoenix Suns  **100:** Jordan: Courtesy of Chicago Bulls/Bill Smith  **101:** Malone: © NBA Photos  **102:** Miller: Courtesy of Indiana Pacers  **102:** Olajuwon: © NBA Photos  **103:** O'Neal: © NBA Photos  **104:** Pippen: Courtesy of Chicago Bulls/Bill Smith  **104:** Robinson: © NBA Photos  **105:** Sprewell: © NBA Photos  **106:** Stockton: © NBA Photos  **107:** Wilkins: © NBA Photos  **109:** Daly: Courtesy of Cleveland Cavaliers  **110:** Fitzsimmons: Courtesy of Phoenix Suns  **111:** Jones: Courtesy of Detroit Pistons  **112:** Brown: © NBA Photos  **113:** Jackson: Courtesy of Chicago Bulls/Bill Smith  **114:** Riley: Courtesy of New York Knickerbockers  **114:** Wilkens: © NBA Photos  **139:** Saperstein: Courtesy of Harlem Globetrotters  **140:** Jackson: Courtesy of Harlem Globetrotters  **141:** Tatum: Courtesy of Harlem Globetrotters  **141:** Haynes: Courtesy of Harlem Globetrotters  **142:** Neal: Courtesy of Harlem Globetrotters  **175:** Shank: Courtesy of Immaculata College  **175:** Meyers: Courtesy of University of California at Los Angeles  **176:** Lieberman: Courtesy of Old Dominion  **177:** Woodard: Courtesy of University of Kansas  **177:** Miller: Courtesy of University of Southern California  **178:** Lobo: Courtesy of University of Connecticut  **185:** Robinson: © NBA Photos